Christ
Is
Community

The Christologies
of
The New Testament

by

Jerome H. Neyrey, S.J.

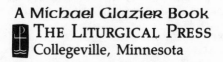
A Michael Glazier Book
THE LITURGICAL PRESS
Collegeville, Minnesota

ABOUT THE AUTHOR

Jerome H. Neyrey, S.J., is Associate Professor of New Testa-
at Weston School of Theology. He completed his theological
education at Regis College, Toronto; and his doctorate in New
Testament at Yale University. He is author of the commentary
on the Pastoral and Catholic Epistles in *The Collegeville New
Testament series*; his most recent book is *The Passion of St.
Luke*. His articles regularly appear in the *Catholic Biblical
Quarterly*, *Journal of Biblical Literature*, *Biblica*, and *Novum
Testamentum*.

A Michael Glazier Book
published by
THE LITURGICAL PRESS

2	3	4	5	6	7	8	9

Library of Congress Cataloging-in-Publication Data
Neyrey, Jerome, H., 1940—
    Christ is community : the christologies of the New Testament / by
Jerome H. Neyrey.
        p.   cm.
    Reprint. Originally published: Wilmington, Del. : M. Glazier,
1985. (Good news studies ; v. 13).
    "A Michael Glazier book."
    Includes bibliographical references and indexes.
    ISBN 0-8146-5465-7
    1. Jesus Christ—History of doctrines—Early church, ca. 30–600.
2. Bible. N.T.—Theology. I. Title. II. Series: Good news
studies ; v. 13.
BT198.N492 1990
232'.09'015—dc20
        90-41520
        CIP

TABLE OF CONTENTS

Chapter One

See p. 269

INTRODUCTION: THE PROJECT OF NEW TESTAMENT CHRISTOLOGY

The starting point of this book is the acknowledgement that in the New Testament there is diversity in the way Jesus is portrayed. Mark calls Jesus the "Son of Man"; Matthew names him "the Servant"; John calls him "Lord and God." Paul depicts him as the new or second Adam. Ephesians and Colossians designate Jesus as "the Head of the body which is the Church." It is a simple fact that the New Testament contains many and diverse images of Jesus.

This diversity may be viewed negatively and positively. For some, the diversity reflects the distortion of early church preaching about Jesus, the imposition on Jesus of categories foreign to him. Later and diverse Christological images and portraits are somehow suspect; they may be safely bypassed as we train our eyes on the central figure of our faith, the historical person of Jesus. This negative posture is balanced by another viewpoint which sees in this diversity a richness of Christian effort to confess Jesus adequately and to articulate his role and place in our lives in a relevant way. Far from distorting Jesus, the diverse portraits expand Jesus' meaning for the world and suggest a rather apt match between Jesus and the church, as the church tried to appropriate Jesus in its own experience.

Diverse people require diverse expressions of faith in Jesus.

Whence this diversity? What does it mean? It is the hypothesis of this study of New Testament Christology that the diversity in the portraits of Jesus may be explained in large measure in terms of the *experience* of the group which so described Jesus. "Experience" is a modern buzz word: we share our particular "experience" with others; we seek out "new experiences" to broaden us; learning for us is not real unless it is "experienced." But the reality behind this term is not new. We know that Palestinian Jews would experience Jesus differently from Greek pagans. Their languages are different, as are their cultures, religions, etc. Jew and Greek, then, experience Jesus and his message differently.

And this does not surprise us. For it makes a difference if one hears the message about Jesus in times of peace and plenty, after a devastating war, during a famine, or in conjunction with personal loss. How one hears and sees is conditioned, then, by one's experience. One's experience includes 1) *personal history* (whether I am young/old, male/female, slave/free), 2) *cultural location* (Jew/Greek/ USA), and 3) *national history* (1st or 20th century).

If there is diversity in the way things are received by hearers, then there is also diversity in the way things can be expressed by preachers. Paul echoes just this point when he described his missionary tactics as an adaptation of his preaching to the culture and experience of his hearers. We have his own explanation:

> I have made myself a slave to all,
> that I might win the more. To the Jews,
> I became as a Jew, in order to win Jews;
> to those under the law, I became as one
> under the law...To those outside the
> law, I became as one outside the law...
> that I might win those outside the law.
> To the weak I became weak, that I might
> win the weak. I have become all things

to all people, that I might by all means
save some (1 Cor 9:19-22).

It is the suggestion of this book that the diverse portraits
of Jesus in the New Testament are both shaped by and
articulated so as to match the experience of the group
being addressed. In a particular crisis, for example, the
author may choose certain aspects of the traditional
preaching about Jesus which can address that crisis
directly and offer a solution to it. The choice, then, is
governed by the experience of the audience. Or, the portrait of Jesus may be tailored to match the experience of a
given group, so that the group's story of Jesus adequately
reflects the lived experience of a Christian group.

Whether the scriptural author is attempting to persuade
people to take a new view of Jesus or whether he is
attempting to match the experience of the group with an
adequate understanding of Jesus, the author is responding
to the experience of his audience. He is taking into account
the vital fact that Jesus must be preached to and confessed
by *this* group, at *this* time in their lives, and in *these*
circumstances.

I.
Streams of New Testament Interpretation

The perspective and approach of this study of New Testament Christology is not radically new. It will help to
survey other recent approaches to New Testament Christology for comparison and contrast, to see how this present
perspective fits into our modern quest to articulate our
biblical faith.

One important, consistent stream of New Testament
Christology might accurately be called "the Quest for the
Historical Jesus" approach. In the 19th century, scholars
with a keen historical bent began to realize more and more
how the churches' reading of the gospel and confession of
faith in Jesus were not entirely in tune with historical

understandings of Jesus and the bible text. In a post-enlightenment era, the reading of the gospels and the churches' preaching were seen as culturally conditioned and as dogmatically controlled. Much that scholars learned through the study of languages, archeology and the discovery of ancient texts suggested that a fresh reading of the gospel was necessary, but *without* the filter of church dogma and piety. And so scholars came to realize how our confession of faith was conditioned by experience, but an experience which could often be confining and restricting. There emerged in this milieu a movement which sought to recover from the New Testament sources the historical person of Jesus without the overlay of church dogmatics or the overlay of accepted New Testament interpretation. Jesus without a filter! And so was born the Quest for the historical Jesus.

We can find numerous examples of the Christology which such a movement generated (Bousset, Perrin). Rather than go into great detail about that here, it seems better to discuss the focus, assumptions, benefits and liabilities of such an approach.

1. The focus is squarely on Jesus, not the church.

2. Inasmuch as this movement began as a reaction to church dogma and church structuring of the way Christians should see Jesus, it tended to take a negative position on the value of all church articulation of Jesus, regardless of whether that church was a New Testament church or the contemporary church. It was argued that Church preaching even at its best is a filter which comes between Jesus and the individual believer — a filter which can distort and impede access to Jesus. So the Quest for the historical Jesus tended to value only the authentic words and deeds of the historical Jesus and to devalue any later development of Christology.

3. It was assumed by those in the Quest that we could in fact recover Jesus' very words and learn accurately what he said of himself. This kernel of authentic material

would be intrinsically better than any secondary account about Jesus, just as we value autographs over biographies when we want accurate information about people. Not just in beverages do we seek "the real thing."

4. Both the process by which we try to recover the historical Jesus as well as the results of any of the processes tried are points of great and continuing debate in biblical circles. Some years ago, this debate over how we can/cannot recover the original Jesus led to an impasse. And since the Quest proved impossible by our present standards it quietly came to an end.

5. Implied in the Quest was an expectation that knowledge about Jesus was somehow timeless. Although scholars might criticize the churches for articulating the gospel about Jesus in timebound categories and historically conditioned dogmas, it was somehow assumed that a non-historical, timeless kernel of Jesus material could be recovered which would automatically suit *all* people, at *all* times, in *every* circumstance. It was assumed that Jesus could be reached directly, without a filter, and without any human mediation, be it the evangelist of the gospel or the church today. This is a highly debated issue.

6. If and when this kernel of Jesus material could be recovered, it would tend to be treated as the new, true "deposit of faith" which would be handed on as unobtrusively as possible. Congregations must conform to it; it should never be adapted to suit a congregation.

The Quest, then, was a complex and ambivalent project. It served to focus on Jesus, a most legitimate task. And it served to alert us to the possibility that even Christian churches could distort the image of Jesus and his message — an important but disturbing fact. Yet these legitimate points are not without qualification. For it is also legitimate to value the Church of God and to study how groups of Christians have attempted to articulate the message of

Jesus in a fresh way to new peoples in every age. For those of us who confess in our creed: "I believe...in the one, holy, catholic and apostolic Church," the Church is not automatically an obstacle to Jesus or a filter to be removed, but a legitimate mediation of Jesus to us. In fact, it may be that Jesus is always mediated to us through some form, be that of the apostolic preaching, the gospels, the sacraments, or the church. The Church is, after all, the sacrament of our encounter with Christ.

The whole canon of the New Testament scriptures, not just the historical Jesus kernel, is the Word of God for us. The whole canon is inspired by God's Spirit; and that same Spirit is abiding in the Church to assist it in faithfully handing on the gospel of Jesus. It is incorrect to devalue the New Testament scriptures in the way which characterized the Quest for the historical Jesus. A more positive assessment is due to post-Jesus transmitters of our gospel message. The Quest served us well, but it can serve to prejudice our appreciation of the New Testament canon as well as the legitimate role of Christ's Church in the ongoing proclamation of the gospel.

A second important stream of New Testament Christological study emerged almost parallel to the first stream. Even as the first stream focussed on the quest for the original Jesus, that very endeavor pointed to a vast amount of developmental data about how the original Jesus was interpreted and represented in later New Testament times. If the first stream sought a timeless Jesus, the second stream looked squarely at the history of Christological development in the early churches of the New Testament. (Although one can speak of the Church which Jesus founded [Mt 16:18], it is perhaps more accurate history to speak of the many, local churches which were founded on diverse continents, composed of diverse ethnic groups, speaking diverse languages and enjoying diverse cultures. We know that there was a focus of church unity among these local churches which was centered around the Apostles in Jerusalem [see Gal 2 and Acts 15]. But the reality of New Testament life was lived in local churches scattered around the Mediterranean basin.) If one could begin to peel away the layers of interpretation to get to the original Jesus, then those very layers of interpretation might form the object of legitimate inquiry. The focus of this second stream was squarely on the New Testament churches and their diverse and developing portraits of Jesus.

Diversity of Christological portraits was admitted, and rigorous efforts were made to map out the development of these confessions about Jesus from a strictly historical perspective. Already in the 19th century, F. C. Baur had proposed an historical perspective for assessing the development of New Testament thought. He was strongly influenced by Hegel and his dialectic of history: thesis, antithesis, and synthesis. Baur proposed that the New Testament writings could be studied under this rubric. Drawing on such key historical data as Gal 2 and Acts 15, Baur schematized the New Testament in this way: 1) there was a radical Jewish Christianity, represented by Peter (and Jerusalem), 2) which was opposed by Paul's more liberal and Hellenistic version, 3) which conflict was resolved in the compromise literature represented by Luke-Acts. Peter (*thesis*) vs Paul (*antithesis*) leads to Luke-Acts (*synthesis*). Baur's influence was enormous. Although his theory in large and small detail has been constantly subjected to valid and devastating criticism, it lurks everywhere in New Testament scholarly circles.

I call the reader's attention to Baur's suggestion that there is a straight-line, developmental trajectory in the New Testament. One begins on Jewish soil with a purely Jewish Christianity (read: "Judaizers" of Gal 1-2); Paul represents a shift to non-Jewish or Graeco-Roman soil and to a Hellenized Christianity. According to Baur's model the development of the New Testament writings, including its Christology, is thus represented and explained as a shift from Palestine to the Graeco-Roman world, from Jewish Christianity to Gentile Christianity.

Baur's suggestion has dominated New Testament scholarship, including the most recent decades of Christological studies. Refinements were made on Baur's historical model; it is too simplistic to speak of Jewish Christianity without qualification, for Judaism in the first century was itself very complex. Better to distinguish Palestinian Judaism (conservative, traditional) from Hellenistic Judaism of the great Mediterranean cities, such as Alexandria and Antioch (more liberal, syncretistic). If this is true of Judaism, then the Jewish Christianity of the early church might also be divided into two stages: early Jewish Christianity of Palestine and later Hellenistic Jewish Christianity. Thus Baur's model was stretched and made historically accurate to include three stages of Christological development:

> Palestinian Jewish Christianity
> Hellenistic Jewish Christianity
> Hellenistic Gentile Christianity

This model was applied extensively to the titles of Jesus in the gospels and in the Pauline writings. It was difficult to deal with "portraits" of Jesus, because these can tend to exist only in the eye of the beholder and not in the text. But one can be firm about titles, such as "Son of God," and "Lord."

To ascertain what these titles meant historically in their respective backgrounds, scholars had recourse to the abundant parallel literatures of Judaism and Graeco-Roman society. By comparison, one could suggest many things. For example, 1) whatever can be shown to depend on Aramaic or Jewish roots must be early. Certain titles which occur only in Jewish literature, must therefore be dated early, to Palestinian Jewish Christianity (e.g. "Maranatha," and "Son of Man"). 2) Conversely, certain titles are current only or especially in Greek circles, and so are dated late. "Lord" seemed to be more Hellenistic, hence later. It is noteworthy that this approach assumed that Christology *must develop* as it moves from one language to another and from one culture to another. The development of Christology, then, can be viewed rather positively from this perspective.

As we did with the quest for the historical Jesus, we can

also assess this second stream in terms of its focus, assumptions, benefits and liabilities.

1. The focus here is squarely on the apostolic churches of the New Testament. More specifically, the focus is on the titles of Jesus used in these churches and their preaching. This represents a severe reduction in data, for a lot more can be said about Jesus than the handful of titles which a given scholar deems to be important.

2. The attempt to be more rigorously historical is surely a gain, even if it challenges old ideas. Development did take place! And along these lines!

3. But the model of development is liable to severe criticism. No longer do New Testament scholars caricature Palestinian Judaism as so conservative and reactionary to things Greek. Since the return from the Exile in Babylon, Palestinian Judaism was constantly open to Greek influence. Jerusalem in the early second century was made into a thoroughly Greek city, with gymnasium for nude games, Greek proper names for citizens, and Greek education, etc. Nor is diaspora Judaism necessarily so liberal and adaptive. The Baur model has some truth to it, but it is fundamentally flawed and not reliable for a systematic and rigorous historical explanation.

4. Nor does the model allow for any assessment of development due to particular, local experiences. There is no way in this scheme of things to assess how an internal crisis in a Christian group might necessitate a new and special Christological word.

5. Implied often in the use of Baur's model is a value statement that what is Jewish in Christianity is limiting and of minimal value, but what is Greek is more ecumenical and universal, and so of greater value.

6. But the lasting value of this second stream is the permission, if not the method, to map out the history of the development of the Christologies of the New Testament.

At least some serious attention was given to the diversity of

Christology due to changing and different church experiences.

II.
Source, Form and Redaction Criticism

These streams of inquiry make more sense to us if we see them against the background of the developing methods of biblical scholarship. The prime question of the 19th century centered around the *sources* of the gospel, and scholars concerned themselves with developing methods and procedures for discovering these sources. If it could be shown who depended on whom, then the earliest source could be recovered; and this earliest source would then be the best bridge back to the historical Jesus. We take for granted today the "two-source theory" of the relationship of the synoptic gospels, but that "theory" is the fruit of a long inquiry which lasted many decades. As it led to the conclusion that Mark was the earliest gospel, Mark was seen for a while as the best source of information about the historical Jesus. *Source criticism*, since it is attempting to discover the earliest sources, puts a premium value on what is early. For Christology, this meant that for many generations there was a built-in bias toward the titles, images and self-descriptions of Jesus himself.

Wilhelm Bousset, in a most influential book, *Kyrios Christos*, had already moved beyond reductionistic source criticism to concern for the development of New Testament Christology. Rudolf Bultmann was standing within this new perspective when he attempted to explain how the gospel traditions about Jesus were shaped and expanded as they passed through the daily life of the early apostolic churches. The title to his major book entirely captures this interest: *The History of the Synoptic Tradition*. This perspective and the questions and methods it generated are called *form criticism*.

Along with other continental scholars, Bultmann could see the impasse which developed in the Quest for the his-

torical Jesus. As the Quest came to an end, he took the
position of an historical agnostic about what can be firmly
recovered about Jesus. And this agnosticism led him to
place greater value on the role and contribution of the
early churches in the growth and development of the Jesus
materials. Increasing attention was paid to the "experience" of these churches, which "experience" was called
the *Sitz im Leben* of the passage, i.e. the specific *life situation* or circumstances in which the gospel and other New
Testament passages were retained and developed. Preaching and liturgy were two of the most significant life situations which influenced the retention and development of
these materials. Thus the form and the function of early
church tradition became the legitimate object of biblical
inquiry.

Since the mid-fifties, a further development of form criticism has taken place. For decades scholars had noted that
the evangelists were themselves responsible for introducing
specific themes and titles into the gospels, for arranging the
events of the narrative in a specific sequence, and for taking specific editorial positions in writing the gospels. But
when the scholarly effort was focussed on the Quest for the
original Jesus, all this editorial activity of the evangelists
was viewed as so much varnish which clouded the original
canvas. Since it obscured the original and was clearly later
in time, it had no value for scholars, and so was peeled
away as useless like the outer layers of an onion or the husk
of a piece of fruit. But when form critics began paying
positive attention to this same material, a revolution took
place which restored this material to a position of interest
and value. Finally, continental scholars began paying
explicit attention to the specific contribution of the evangelist as a creative theologian who edited, adapted and
shaped the Jesus materials. The evangelist was no longer
described as a mere collector of old materials, but as a
theologian with a rich Christology and a dynamic view of
the church. No longer was the evangelist judged to have
created the gospel by the use of "scissors and paste," but he
was credited with freshness, creativity, integrity and re-

sponsibility. Finally the diversity of Christological materials could be properly and sympathetically investigated. This focus and the techniques by which it is pursued is called *redaction criticism*. By "redaction," scholars refer explicitly to the editorial activity of the evangelist.

The following diagram may help to summarize this information and explain the relationship of method and Christology:

BIBLICAL METHOD	AIM	VALUE	CHRISTOLOGY
source criticism	recovery of earliest authentic Jesus materials	1. early = best 2. later = bad	only authentic Jesus traditions
form criticism	history of the Jesus traditions in apostolic churches	1. the Quest is impossible; 2. early church is all we can safely know 3. this contribution is valuable	development of Jesus materials by life & preaching of the early churches
redaction criticism	theology of the evangelist	1. besides source & form criticism we can learn more 2. new value given to evangelist's contribution	full portrait of Jesus by the evangelist vis-à-vis his situation

We can readily see how the first stream discussed above meshes with source critical questions, assumptions and techniques. The second stream coincides with form and redaction criticism and their concerns, values and methods. Scholars now agree that a full exposition of a gospel or Christological passage must include concern for all three *Sitze im Leben,* that is, three life situations:

1. Jesus himself (30 AD)
2. the apostolic churches (30-65 AD)
3. the evangelists (70-100 AD).

The three situations, of course, correspond with the three types of gospel criticism which we outlined above.

III.

Vatican II and Biblical Criticism

This discussion of diverse approaches to the gospels and to New Testament Christology can be clarified by a further observation. The Vatican II Document on Revelation *(Dei Verbum)* was written in part to legitimate the valuable contributions made to our faith from modern bible scholarship. This modest document confirms the advances made in understanding the foundation documents of our faith, truly effecting an *aggiornamento* in the way Christians read and study the Scriptures. The Document on Revelation adopts an historical view of the New Testament writings. It speaks about the three life situations which were discussed above and validates the three-fold critical methods used in modern scholarship to study each life situation.

> First, there is an initial, pronounced emphasis on Jesus: For when the fullness of time arrived (Gal 4:4), the Word was made flesh and dwelt among us in the fullness of grace and truth (Jn 1:14). Christ established the kingdom of God on earth, manifested His Father and Himself by deeds and words, and completed His work by His death, resurrection, and glorious ascension and by the sending of the Holy Spirit (#17).

Clearly in this first paragraph there is a primacy given to the person of Jesus, which is the perennial basis of our gospel quest for the historical Jesus. This paragraph, then, refers to the first *Sitz im Leben*, the historical Jesus him-self; and the basic aims of "source criticism" as a study of the historical Jesus are validated.

In the next paragraph, the role of the early church is stressed as a locus for the development of New Testament Christology. The document speaks of this fluid, early period when the Apostles and subsequent apostolic preachers handed on the gospel in their preaching:

> The Church holds...that the four Gospels are of apos-tolic origin. For what the apostles preached in fulfilment of the commission of Christ, afterwards they themselves and apostolic men, under the inspiration of the divine Spirit, handed on to us in writing: the foundation of faith, namely, the fourfold Gospel, according to Mat-thew, Mark, Luke and John. (#18)

Yet this same document clearly admits that in this period, substantial development took place in the preaching of the church. For it continues:

> After the ascension of the Lord, the apostles handed on to their hearers what He (Jesus) had said and done. They did this with that *clearer understanding* which they enjoyed after they had been taught by the events of Christ's risen life and taught by the light of the Spirit of Truth (#19, emphasis added).

And so, the apostles saw "with clearer understanding" later on, and they expressed this *clearer understanding* of Jesus in new titles and names of Jesus and in new portraits of him. We admit, therefore, that there was a developmental period in church preaching after the ascension of the his-torical Jesus. This period is the second *Sitz im Leben*; its study is what is meant by "form criticism," a procedure which is endorsed in the church's official teachings about the Scriptures.

Finally in a third paragraph, the Document on Revela-tion takes up the final stage of New Testament development, the period of the final writing of the gospels and the final development of Christology in those writings. It offers a modest description of how the gospels came to be written:

> The sacred authors wrote the four Gospels, *selecting* some things from the many which had been handed on by word of mouth or in writing, *reducing* some of them to a synthesis, *explicating* some things in view of the situation of their churches, and preserving the form of proclamation but always in such fashion that they told us the honest truth about Jesus (#19, emphasis added).

On the one hand, the impression is given that the evangelists did not put down in any one gospel *all* that was known of Jesus. They "selected" and "reduced to a synthesis" — observations which are verified by careful comparison of the gospels. The suggested reasons for this are not caprice or idiosyncracy, but pastoral concerns for the needs of the churches being addressed. Alternately, it is admitted that the evangelist and other sacred writers might expand and edit the traditional material, not because they themselves had better information than their sources, but because of pastoral concerns "in view of the situation of their churches."

The document, moreover, suggests that the evangelists' "explication" of Jesus and his significance for their respective churches was done in dialogue with the authentic traditions of the early church. For they did their work "always in such fashion that they told the 'honest truth' about Jesus." That "honest truth" may be more than what Jesus actually said about himself, for the early preachers and the evangelists enjoyed "a clearer understanding after they had been instructed by the events of Christ's risen life and taught by the light of the Spirit of truth" (#19). That "honest truth" may be more than mere historical information about Jesus. And so in principle, the Document of Revelation admits that there was in fact development in New Testament Christology. And this perspective should not surprise us; for we now know more clearly that the purpose of the gospels was preaching, testimony and faith, and not simply the compilation of factual details. This third period is the third *Sitz im Leben;* its study is what is meant by "redaction criticism."

Vatican II, therefore, by speaking of these three *Sitze im Leben,* legitimates an historical understanding of the New Testament. In speaking of these three life situations, the Document indicates the validity of the claims that there is development in New Testament Christology; the Document even attempts to explain how and why the development took place. Finally, the document shows, not only the validity of studying the New Testament according to source, form, and redaction critical methods, but sees a positive value in the contributions to the church's faith which resulted in the development of New Testament faith in Jesus. Taking a fully modern stand on the nature of the Gospels, the Document:

   1) endorsed an historical model for studying the
      New Testament,
   2) agreed that development indeed took place,
   3) found comfort in the process.

It implied, moreover, that a full study of the gospels or of New Testament Christology must employ all three critical methods and view the text of the Scriptures according to all three *Sitze im Leben.*

IV.
The Perspective of This Book

What is the position and perspective of the study of New Testament Christology in this book? I fully respect the aims of source criticism and the need to be concerned with the original Jesus. Not to do so is to devalue Jesus' incarnation and his humanity. But this study will not be pursuing that line of inquiry. Rather, the focus here will be on the diversity of the portraits of Jesus in the gospels and other New Testament writings. The approach will be that of redaction criticism; and so I will give full respect to the creative and responsible job of the sacred authors for "explicating Jesus in view of the situation of their churches." This means that we will attend seriously to the third *Sitz im Leben,* the life situation of the individual evangelists and their respective churches.

In modern jargon, we call this respect for the "experience" of other people, for we know how experience shapes both how we tell a story as well as how we hear one. By "experience" I mean: a) the great events which jolt and shape a group (war, earthquake, death of a founding figure) and to which the group must respond, as well as b) the context of one's daily life (whether in the countryside or in a city, in a Jewish or Greek milieu, in a church of Jews only or of Jew-Gentile composition, at peace with or in tension with the synagogue). The axiom behind this study may be stated simply: the sacred authors had pastoral concern for their particular groups and "explicated" the gospel message so as to address those specific and particular situations.

I am not going to concentrate exclusively on the titles of Jesus, as has been the current practice in other studies of New Testament Christology. They are important; and I will deal with them, but only vis-à-vis the experience of the church which used this or that title. I am supplementing an analysis of the titles of Jesus with a study of the "portrait" of Jesus which emerges from the writings which we will read. A "portrait" is more than a name or title. It is a compilation of personal attitudes and positions attributed to someone. It includes study of the actions and behavior of the person portrayed. We are treated every Sunday to programs such as "Face the Nation and "Issues and Answers," in which we examine the actions of major political figures and ferret out their attitudes to issues. This is the stuff of which a "portrait" is made. It greatly supplements what we know about a person just from his or her title of government office. Without this knowledge of a person's opinions and attitudes, we hardly know anything about him or her. But this is not an attempt to write a biography about Jesus. Far from it. By focussing on the 3rd *Sitz im Leben,* and by taking the perspective of redaction criticism, I am trying to recover what the evangelist claims are the opinions and attitudes of Jesus. Each evangelist painted a different "portrait" of Jesus; I intend to respect that diversity and work with it. No! No biography here.

The cognitive model which is operative in this study is suggested by the noted theologian, B. J. F. Lonergan. He suggested that *all* dogmatic, theological, and biblical statements must be understood in a radically historical perspective. Every statement or formulation is embedded in the time, events, and culture of the group in which it arose. Lonergan suggested, moreover, that there has always been a development in Christian theology and always will be because the historical experience of Christian believers is always changing. His model for explaining and interpreting theological statements and their development may be summarized as:

experience — understanding — judgment.

One's *experience* is the horizon against which one hears and grapples with the meaning of the gospel. This hearing and grappling lead to *understanding* that message in the context of one's particular circumstances. And it issues in a *judgment,* an insight, a fresh confession, or a new formulation. This is the way the human mind works. And so we can see the philosophical basis for development of ideas, both ours and those of the first Christians.

One's experience changes — inevitably and necessarily. It was, after all, one of the early preachers of the gospel who said: "When I was a child, I spoke like a child, I thought like a child, I reasoned like a child; when I became mature, I gave up childish ways" (1 Cor 13:11). And so one must hear and grapple with the gospel message against the horizon of our ever-changing, new *experience* which will lead to new *understandings,* and issue in new formulations of *judgments.* The same is as true for our appropriation of Jesus as it was for the early church's.

This is the model I am suggesting for investigating the Christology of the gospels and other New Testament writings. I predicate that there are as many New Testament "experiences" as there were individual, local churches. Paul wrote in the 50s, to radically different churches, under totally different circumstances. One would expect Paul's Christology to reflect this difference. Each evangelist addressed a local church different from the other local churches both in time and in experience. As regards the gospels, proximity to the great war between Rome and the Jews and nearness to emerging Pharisaism should be expected to have strong impact on the early local churches. Finally, Ephesians and Colossians speak to still other local churches with their own particular sets of problems. No wonder there is diversity in the portraits of Jesus! The individual experiences of the individual churches were so diverse.

V.
Procedure and Method

In this book, we will first study the portraits of Jesus in each of the four gospels. This will be followed by an investigation of the portraits of Jesus in two of Paul's letters, 1 Cor 1:18-25 and Phil 2:6-11. Finally, the Christology of Ephesians and Colossians will be treated. These eight documents present a rich variety of portraits in diverse literary forms, which are addressed to a wide range of churches.

The variety of forms in which New Testament Christological data comes to us implies that a variety of procedures must be used to recover that material. For example, the portrait of Jesus in a gospel is diffused. Gospels, after all, are lengthy, narrative documents which present Jesus in a variety of situations, sometimes speaking and sometimes acting. Gospels provide a glimpse of Jesus addressing a variety of people (Pharisees, public sinners, Scribes, disciples, etc.), on a variety of topics (Sabbath observance, avoidance of scandal, discipleship, the end of the age, etc.), and in a variety of forms (parables, oracles, pronouncements). Although each evangelist has a focus in his presentation of Jesus, there is a notable lack of concentration in the gospels. This means that an adequate recovery of the portrait of Jesus in a gospel must canvas large amounts of material which contains very diverse titles, images and sayings of Jesus.

The opposite problem occurs in Paul's letters where there is usually a specific and highly condensed portrait of Jesus (e.g. Rom 5:12-21; 1 Thess 1:9-10; 1 Cor 1:18-25; 2 Cor 8:9 and 13:4; Gal 3:13-14). Paul's portraits of Jesus are of a confessional nature, in highly rhetorical form, and condensed in scope. Easier to isolate than the more diffused gospel materials, they require more careful study. As condensed formulae, every phrase and word in them is carefully chosen and serves a specific function in the context of the letter in which it appears. If the gospels are the large narrative canvases of Titian or Rubens, Paul's letters are like the Dutch miniatures of domestic scenes.

The portrait of Jesus in Ephesians and Colossians was chosen for study for two reasons. First, the image of Jesus in both letters is similar (Jesus = the "Head" of the body). Second, that common image, however, means different things in each letter and functions differently. This will require that we study the portrait of Jesus as the Church's "Head" in close connection with the situation of each church to see how it is functioning as an argument in response to the experience of each church. The variety of forms in which Christological portraits is found means that different procedures must be used to recover and assess those portraits.

PART ONE

THE GOSPELS: PASTORAL PORTRAITS OF JESUS

THE GOSPELS: PASTORAL PORTRAITS OF JESUS

Introduction

The aim of the next four chapters is to recover the diverse portraits of Jesus in the gospels and to assess them in the light of the particular experiences of the community which preserved and shaped them. But what procedure shall we follow to recover full and nuanced portraits of Jesus in the four gospels? The procedure must basically be descriptive, but what constitutes data for a "portrait" of Jesus? What focus shall we take?

Traditional New Testament Christologies have focussed on the titles ascribed to Jesus, his office, and position. But so much more goes into a "portrait" than name, rank and serial number. Biographies of great figures might give us a clue: it is important to know of a person being portrayed what opinions, ideas, and positions s/he held on a variety of topics, especially on the leading issues and agenda of the day. Television on Sunday mornings presents a variety of shows in which a prominent figure is interviewed. The interviewers and the audiences want to know not only what the Secretary of the Treasury thinks about the deficit, but also about the arms talks, acid rain, women's issues, trade with China, and the latest Washington scandal. We are interested in the fabric of the Secretary's viewpoint, its warp and woof; we are interested in the consistency of the Secretary's viewpoint and how s/he can hold several critical opinions in tension. "Face the Nation," "Meet the Press," and "Issue and Answers" all present a contemporary forum in which the viewing public gets a portrait of a public figure beyond his or her official title or role. And so I am suggesting that we supplement the traditional discussion of the titles ascribed to Jesus with a careful survey of the attitudes and opinions attributed to Jesus in each gospel on a careful range of topics: 1. mission and membership, 2. understanding the Old Testament, 3. eschatology, 4. ethics, and 5. group-self-understanding.

Why these five topics? They are not arbitrarily chosen; they touch on the basic issues of Jesus' day. Jesus is proclaiming a word of God to Israel and that word seems to be challenging the prevailing opinions of Israel's various parties and factions. Jesus' stance is considered normative for his followers. And so the opinions and attitudes attributed to Jesus are important for a full portrait. The early church needed to know 1) how Jesus differed from the parent religion, and 2) what his followers should think about these key issues as they take their place in the world. The five topics, therefore, all focus on various aspects of Jesus' word to Israel. And each topic individually contributes a special piece of information about Jesus as God's authorized covenant leader and prophet.

The five topics are comprehensive catchbasins for collecting and systematizing the positions of Jesus on major religious questions and issues of his day.

> 1. *Mission and Membership.* To whom was Jesus sent? Who is included in God's Covenant? These are all social issues of the greatest importance, especially in light of traditional Jewish separateness from sinners and Gentiles.
> 2. *Understanding the Old Testament.* The Scriptures are God's authoritative word, a clue to the way God sees

things and to how God's covenant people should act toward God and one another. How does Jesus understand and use these Scriptures? Is he said to have a distinctive hermeneutic, different from that of the Temple officials and the Pharisees? Does Jesus have a "canon within the canon," a special selection of Scriptural passages which legitimate his position and validates his authority?

3. *Eschatology.* How does Jesus situate himself and his mission in terms of God's overall plan of salvation? Is he just one more in a continuing line of prophets who reform the covenant? What is his relation to the issue of Israel's final, definitive redemption?

4. *Ethics.* Over against the synagogue with its Torah and the legal codes of the Old Testament, what are the chief virtues or actions which Jesus is said to enjoin on his followers? What behavior characterizes them? Conversely, what actions separate them from God and from the covenant-in-Jesus?

5. *Group Self-Understanding.* What did Jesus think he was doing vis-à-vis God's plan to gather a covenant people unto himself? How did Jesus describe his task to his followers? Are they the authentic Israel? or a totally new and distinct covenant which is discontinuous with Israel?

After this survey, we should try to indicate the specific "experiences" of the groups which recorded and shaped the portraits of Jesus which we are discovering. A sixth topic needs to be considered:

6. *Experience.* What were the dramatic, critical events which impinged on the groups and which needed to be squared with the traditional doctrine (e.g. the Roman-Jewish War, expulsion from the synagogue)? What were the influential events and situations in which the group shaped itself and found its own perspective stretched (e.g. the admission of Gentiles, the writing of Mark's gospel)? And what was the day-to-day situation of the

group (e.g. urban or rural; Syrian or Greek or Roman milieu)?

Whatever we can glean from the text of the gospels will be a significant contribution to the description of the "experiential" horizon against which each evangelist pastorally shaped his portrait of Jesus. One would expect to see a high degree of correlation between the experience of an individual gospel community and the way Jesus is portrayed in *this* set of circumstances, for *this* group of people.

Only after this is done shall we take up a seventh topic, the specific and distinctive *Christology* of gospel. At this point we are ready to investigate the titles attributed to Jesus. Even here, it will be important to assess the function of the distinctive titles and offices ascribed to Jesus vis-à-vis the experience of the respective gospel groups. For Jesus was not decked out with honorific titles and medals for their own sake. Such titles are presumed to be clues to and reflections of the functional position of Jesus vis-à-vis the group which so named him. This is not to deny that traditional confessions of Jesus from the early church appear in the gospels. But one should also assess what was chosen and highlighted by each evangelist, especially in light of the pastoral posture of the evangelists to describe Jesus in ways relevant to the needs and situations of their respective groups. In each gospel, there are distinctive ways of naming Jesus and distinctive functions attributed to him. These redactional materials should be studied, especially in concert with the other aspects of the portrait of Jesus. This procedure is rather limited to a literary form such as the gospel, for the Pauline epistles do not present so diffused a portrait of Jesus who comments on topics from the creation to the end of the world.

Chapter Two

THE CHRISTOLOGICAL PORTRAIT OF MARK'S GOSPEL

Why do we start out study of the gospels with Mark? It is generally admitted that Mark's gospel is the first full narrative of Jesus' career, starting from the baptism and ending with his Passion and Resurrection. In saying that Mark is the first full, written gospel, we do not deny that Mark was preceded by years of oral traditions about Jesus. For there is evidence that before Mark was written, miscellaneous miracle stories of Jesus were already collected and edited (Mk 4:35-8:26); likewise a collection was made of parables attributed to Jesus (Mk 4:1-34). But Mark appears to be the first person to write a continuous narrative of Jesus' career, which includes all those earlier pieces of information about Jesus, and to give the narrative his own distinctive, editorial perspective.

When we begin our study of the portrait of Jesus in Mark's gospel, we bring forward our five topical catchbasins. We hope to recover the attitudes and positions attributed to Jesus on these five crucial issues.

MEMBERSHIP AND MISSION

When Jesus begins his career in Mk 1:14-15, he is portrayed as a missionary, "preaching the gospel of God." And his first act is to call four co-missionaries to himself, who will be "fishers of men" (1:17). Mark, then, immediately portrays Jesus in a missionary mode, a mode which will dominate all of Jesus' actions in chs 1-8.

If mission is Jesus' first and favorite activity, we are warranted in asking about the people to whom Jesus went on mission. He was obviously calling them to membership in God's covenant group. And it would matter whether Jesus thought that covenant membership, was restricted to ethnic Israelites, for that would affect Mark's presentation of Jesus. And so, mission and membership are related issues.

The fact of the matter is that Jesus immediately turns his attention to people on the margins of Israel's covenant, those who were unclean or sick. Jesus expels a demon (1:21-28), suggesting that full membership in God's covenant is offered to those possessed. He healed the sick (1:29-31), and dispossessed others of their demons (1:32-34, 39); he healed a leper (1:40-45) and forgave sins (2:1-12). Jesus' initial mission, then, embraced people marginal to the covenant. When cured or forgiven, such folk are part of God's inclusive kingdom (in this line, see 5:1-20, 21-43).

Jesus then sits at a table with public sinners, again extending membership in the covenant to outsiders. He calls Levi, a tax collector, to labor with him (2:13-14) and eats at his table with other public sinners (2:15-17). He justified this with the remark that "Those who are well have no need of a physician, but those who are sick. I came not to call the righteous, but sinners" (2:18). This attitude was in sharp contrast to that of Jewish groups such as the Pharisees or the Qumran covenanters, who avoided all such unclean folk and so restricted covenant membership to the few, the pure. According to Mark, Jesus' policy is decidedly inclusive.

When we attempt to track Jesus' geographical journeying and to see to whom he preached and whom he healed, we confirm this sense of inclusive membership in God's covenant. In what is surely a passage dealing with mission (3:7-19), it is stated that Jesus attracted and accepted people "from Galilee, Judea, Jerusalem, Idumea and from across the Jordan" — presumably Jews — as well as "from Tyre and Sidon" (3:7-8) — clearly non-Jews. This brief summary statement by Mark of Jesus' inclusive mission is filled out by Jesus' extensive travels in chs 4-8. He is constantly crossing the Lake of Galilee from Jewish territory to Gentile lands (see 4:35; 5:1-2, 21). And he offers God's covenant blessing to Gentile sick. We are told that Jesus went up to "the region of Tyre and Sidon" (7:24),where he healed the Syrophoenician woman's child. From there he went on an extended tour of gentile territory, going east and then south through the ten Hellenistic cities called the Decapolis: "From the region of Tyre, he went through Sidon to the Sea of Galilee, through the region of the Decapolis" (7:31). Finally Jesus goes north to Caesarea Philippi, an important center of Graeco-Roman civilization in the area. It is in this gentile environment that Jesus is acclaimed "the Christ" by Peter (8:27).

Mark, then, depicts Jesus as extending his preaching mission to Jews and Gentiles alike, to upright covenant Jews and to marginal folk as well. This can be seen in parabolic form in the prodigal behavior of the sower who casts seed even in the most unlikely places — the path, rocky ground, and thorns (4:3-9); no soil or terrain is *a priori* excluded as a fitting place for God's word. And this inclusive strategy is confirmed when Jesus remarks later that "the gospel must be preached to all nations" (13:10).

And so Jesus' basic activity is missionary. And his mission is to call a wide variety of people to membership in God's covenant group.

UNDERSTANDING OF THE OLD TESTAMENT

Relative to the other gospels, Mark does not contain many references to or citations from the Scriptures. Yet what he records is of great importance for a full portrait of

Jesus. On at least seven occasions Jesus cites a passage from the Old Testament and comments on its meaning. What is of interest here is the way these Old Testament passages function in Jesus' discourse in a distinctively polemical fashion.

Mark	*Polemical Passages*
4:12	Isa 6:9-10
7:6-7	Isa 29:13 LXX
7:9-11	Deut 20:12
10:4-8	Deut 24:1-3 vs Gen 1—2
11:17	Isa 56:7 & Jer 7:11
12:19	Gen 38:8; Deut 25:5
12:26	Ex 3:2-16
12:36	Ps 110

Jesus uses the citations from the Old Testament to criticize Jewish custom and practice, implying that some Jews are putting themselves outside of God's covenant. 1. Jesus cites Isaiah's prediction (Isa 6:9-10) to comment on Jews of the covenant who do not believe in Jesus as God's designated covenant leader (Mk 4:12). 2. Jesus quotes again from Isaiah (Isa 29:13) to criticize Jews who substituted human precepts for God's holy doctrine (Mk 7:6-7). 3. Jesus contrasts the prescription of God to "Honor your father and mother" (Ex 20:12) with the view of certain Jews that would seemingly permit people to supercede that command (Mk 7:9-13). 4. In Mk 10:4-8, Jesus criticizes as "hard of heart" those who seek permission for divorce; he cites God's original plans for human marriage (Gen 1-2) over against the concession of Moses which allows for divorce (Deut 24:1-3). There is, then, a stream of Old Testament material which Jesus used which is a) polemical, b) against so-called covenant members, c) accusing them of violating the basic covenant relationship with God. According to these citations of Jesus, such corruption was not only part of Israel's past, but was predicted by the prophets of the present generation as well. If the bulk of Israel finds itself outside of God's covenant-in-Jesus, then the fault lies with Israel, not God. Israel has constantly

distanced itself from God's covenant. As Jesus cites these
Scriptures and formulates a criticism of Israel, he functions
as a prophet judging God's covenant people. Implied in
this posture is the claim to be able to reform the covenant
people and to teach authoritatively.

There is no question for Mark about the continued
validity of the Old Testament as Scripture and Word of
God for the true covenant people. The Old Testament is
eternally valid as God's word for covenant members. But
Jesus does act distinctively to prune away from the Old
Testament materials which distort God's original covenant
laws for the chosen people. We saw above how Jesus
pruned Moses' divorce concession from a valid reading of
the Old Testament by appeal to God's original intentions
for marriage as found in Gen 1-2 (10:4-8). Jesus also criticizes the plethora of purity rules which crept into the understanding of what it means to be a law-abiding covenant
member. The Pharisees, for example, attempted to protect
the core law by making a fence around it and defending
that outer fence through purity concerns (7:1-5). They
effectively added to the Old Testament laws, so that a body
of 613 distinctive laws could be codified and observed. This
extension, however, served to limit authentic membership
in the covenant to a select few; and for this reason we find
Jesus attacking such accretions to Israel's basic covenant
law (7:1-13). In this vein, we find Jesus repeatedly affirming the essential, even minimal, covenant law of God, the
Ten Commandments. To inherit life, one must keep the
commandments, not the Pharisees' 613 commandments,
but God's basic covenant commandments.

You know the commandments:

> Do not kill,
> Do not commit adultery,
> Do not steal,
> Do not bear false witness,
> Do not defraud,
> Honor your father and mother (10:19).

These commandments, which are found clearly in the Old Testament, are permanently valid and should not be set aside in favor of man-made regulations (see 7:9-13). And it is violation of just these basic covenant laws which puts one outside the covenant, not the breaking of the Pharisaic purity laws (7:21-23).

Jesus, moreover, provides a hermeneutical principle which renders many of the laws in the Old Testament obsolete. Jesus himself stopped the carrying of vessels through the temple, vessels with sacrificial materials (11:16). He thus ended, even temporarily, the cultic life of Israel. He declared the temple a "house of prayer for all nations" (11:17), thus reinforcing a negative attitude to the sacrificial cult. And when asked about the "first commandment," Jesus proclaimed love of God and love of neighbor as first (12:29-31). This core law was then acclaimed as worth "more than all whole burnt offering and sacrifices" (12:33). Jesus himself, therefore, proclaims an interpretation of the Old Testament law which renders obsolete cultic and sacrifical prescriptions in that same Old Testament.

What is implied in this action of Jesus? Since worship of God through temple sacrifice was a distinguishing factor of Jewish piety, Jesus was acting in a most bold and authoritative manner. The function of his affirmation of the "first commandment" (12:29-31), and his negation of purity rules and cultic laws fits in with a continued opening of God's covenant to non-Jews and with a continued attack on practices through which Jews separated themselves from Gentiles. Jesus is clearly not attacking the Old Testament law *per se* or law in general; he is most definitely upholding the lasting validity of God's covenant law. But he is refusing to endorse those aspects of that law which served as distinguishing boundaries between Jews and Gentiles. The reformed and essential covenant law is the law for all God's people, Jews and Gentiles.

There is a third usage of the Old Testament by Jesus in Mark's gospel. The Scriptures are still valid, but basically as prophecies of Jesus and his new covenant community. By emphasizing the prophetic function of the Scriptures,

Mark stresses the continuing validity of the Bible for the church, but restricts its meaning and validity for non-believing Jews. The following list summarizes the Old Testament texts which Mark considers prophetic:

> *Prophetic texts in Mark*
> 1:2-3 . . . . Isa 40:3; Mal 3:1
> 7:6-7 . . . . Isa 29:13 LXX
> 11:17 . . . . Isa 56:7
> 12:1 . . . . Isa 5:1-2
> 12:26 . . . . Ex 3:2-16
> 12:36 . . . . Ps 110:1
> 13:14 . . . . Dan 9:27
> 14:27 . . . . Zech 13:7
> 15:24 . . . . Ps 22:18
> 15:29 . . . . Ps 22:7
> 15:34 . . . . Ps 22:1

Through a prophetic interpretation, God's actions and oracles in the Scriptures are seen as true and valid, but primarily in terms of the new covenant-in-Jesus.

Jesus, therefore, does not abolish the Old Testament. He sees a core within it which is permanently valid for covenant members for all times. In it he finds a warrant for critiquing the sins and excesses of his day. Yet Jesus basically considers the Old Testament as a prophecy of himself and his covenant people.

ESCHATOLOGY

Jesus' eschatological teaching comes to us in two basic streams, which correspond to the two halves of the gospel. In the first half of the gospel (chs 1—8), we are told of the kingdom of God and of Jesus' activity in proclaiming it, speaking parables about it, and inaugurating it. In the second half of the gospel (chs 8-16), we are told of a future vindication of Jesus and of his coming to vindicate his covenant people.

In chs 1-8, one correctly gets the sense of a present

inbreaking of God's promised kingdom. Jesus heralds its imminance (1:14-15); he speaks of it as a small seed which grows into a large shrub (4:30-32). He reveals to his followers "the secrets of the kingdom of God" (4:11). In many ways Mark sees Jesus as inaugurating God's kingdom. This can be seen especially in his portrayal of Jesus as God's champion in combat with Satan and Satan's kingdom (chs 1-3). Jesus binds Satan and despoils his possessions, i.e., he liberates the possessed, sinners, and others from Satan's power. His exorcisms point to the end of the kingdom of sin and death and the beginning of the new kingdom of God in a new covenant people. Jesus' miracles and exorcisms, then, are signs of God's power in Jesus to inaugurate the kingdom. This new kingdom, moreover, includes the new covenant group which Jesus gathers around himself; and so, we see Jesus as the King of the kingdom of God. Chs 1-8, then, tell the story of God's kingdom already inaugurated in Jesus. The eschatological view here underscores the presence of God's power and kingdom *already* available in Jesus. This explains how Jesus' group understands the importance and value of belonging to Jesus' group: they are *already* part of God's kingdom.

In chs 8-16, however, Mark tells another story. It should not be seen as contradicting the viewpoint in the first half of the gospel, but rather as supplementing it because it speaks to a different experience and offers different answers to a different set of questions. Although one may be told that Jesus has already inaugurated God's kingdom, one's experience of alienation and hostility in the world may challenge that. Even Jesus, who heralded God's kingdom, was himself confronted with massive hostility and was crucified. How could he claim that the kingdom was *already* inaugurated? A new eschatological perspective was needed.

It is commonly pointed out that the gospel is divided into two halves: a) miracles and preaching (chs 1-8) and b) predictions and narrative of the passion (chs 8-16). As we saw, chs 1-8 tell of God's kingdom already inaugurated. But from 8:31 on, we are repeatedly told of Jesus' coming death, a new fact of life which in some way challenges the perspective of chs 1-8. The disturbing facts are not ignored; on the contrary they are brought forward for special consideration. The fact of rejection and death calls for a new eschatological word from Jesus. One of the ways that this new fact of rejection and death is dealt with is through Jesus' repeated prediction of his passion. And so, chs 8-16 are full of Jesus' repeated predictions of his passion, which set the stage for a new eschatological word. But it is important to speak not only of "passion predictions" in the last eight chapters, for Jesus' predictions are much richer than that. They are predictions of rejection (passion) and vindication (resurrection).

Rejection	*Vindication*
A. The Son of Man must suffer many things and be rejected and be killed...	...and after three days rise again (8:31).
B. The Son of Man will be delivered into the hands of men and they will kill him...	...after three days he will rise (9:31).
C. The Son of Man will be delivered to the chief priests and scribes and they will condemn him to death, and deliver him to gentiles, and they shall mock him, and spit upon him, and scourge him and kill him...	...and after three days he will rise (10:33-34).
D. The stone which the builders rejected...	...has become the head of the corner; this is the Lord's doing and it is marvelous in our eyes (12:10-11).

E. You will all fall away; for it   ...but after I am raised up, I
    is written, 'I will strike the   will go before you into Gali-
    shepherd, and the sheep will   lee (14:29-30).
    be scattered"...

Even as the disturbing news of Jesus' death is given, it is being dealt with in the context of a new eschatological word. For Jesus' vindication and resurrection will erase the doubts cast on his great work of inaugurating God's kingdom. By raising Jesus from the dead, God will confirm that Jesus has inaugurated the kingdom and is its King and Lord. Jesus' vindication, then, becomes an important eschatological word which confirms Jesus' earlier eschatological word about God's kingdom.

Just as Jesus faced rejection and death, his followers may begin to wonder whether God's kingdom is real for them if they too face rejection and hostility. Told that they belong to the kingdom which is already inaugurated, they do not experience the reality of that when faced with negative experiences. A further eschatological word is needed to deal with the church's negative experience. This word comes from Jesus himself during his trial.

In his trial, Jesus is rejected by the Jewish elders. They seek "false witnesses" against him (14:55-59); and they reject his own statements when he speaks (14:62-64). Yet in the midst of this rejection Jesus predicts his vindication: "You will see the Son of Man seated at the right hand of Power and coming with the clouds of heaven" (14:62). This prediction, of course, speaks of Jesus' own resurrection. When Jesus spoke of "sitting at the right hand of the Power," he was referring to his immediate vindication in the resurrection (see 12:36/Ps 110). But the vindication of Jesus is also the vindication of Jesus' covenant followers. So, when Jesus says that the world will see him "coming on the clouds of heaven," Jesus was referring to that future moment when he would definitively answer the problem of his followers' rejection and death. He will come back in glory to prove to the enemies of his followers that he is the leader of God's kingdom and that his followers are truly members of God's kingdom. On that future day, God will finally complete his grand plan of salvation and confirm Jesus as the kingdom's leader with a demonstrable gift of great power and dominion, power such as was given to the Son of Man in Daniel 7. The kingdom may be already inaugurated in Jesus' ministry, but the final confirmation is still a radically future event. Nevertheless, it is a sure thing, for Jesus has predicted it.

Jesus, therefore, tells us two, complementary eschatological words. 1. Jesus inaugurates God's kingdom; in him Satan's rule is ended; salvation is already available in him; he gathers around himself the new and definitive covenant people of God. 2. Faced with rejection and death, Jesus tells a second eschatological word, his resurrection. For in his resurrection he is vindicated as the inaugurator of God's kingdom. And just as Jesus' resurrection provides proof that he is truly the inaugurator of God's kingdom, so his definitive return in glory will confirm his covenant followers as genuine members of God's true kingdom. For in that final moment, all objections to God's plan and to God's Christ will be silenced (see 8:38). Two stories are told, which are complementary: one about the present and one about the future.

ETHICS

What basic values does Jesus enjoin on his followers? What special virtues does Jesus prescribe? what vices proscribe? As we saw in the Markan interpretation of the Old Testament, Jesus indicates that the "Law of Love" is the basic covenant law for his followers. Inasmuch as Jews of Jesus' time were expanding the sense of legal observances for orthodox Jewish living, Jesus' focus on a core covenant law is striking. We see Jesus' position worked out in several important scenes in the gospel. In a formal discussion of the law, Jesus answered the Scribe's question about the fundamental covenant law: "You shall love the Lord your God with all your heart, with all your soul, and with all

your strength...You shall love your neighbor as yourself"
(12:30-31). This discussion should be seen in combination
with another incident where Jesus is formally questioned
about behavior for a genuine covenant member. When
asked "What must I do to inherit eternal life?" (10:17),
Jesus responded:

> You know the commandments!
> Do not kill,
> Do not steal,
> Do not defraud,
> Honor your father and mother (10:19).

The Ten Commandments, then, would seem to be the
embodiment of the "Law of Love." Jesus clearly and suc-
cinctly proclaims a core covenant law for his followers.

In still a third place, Jesus proclaims a list of vices (7:21-
23) which separate one from God and God's covenant people. The list is important for it seems to have been shaped
on the Ten Commandments, as the following diagram
shows:

10:19	*7:21-23*
Do not kill	murder
Do not commit adultery	fornication, adultery, licentiousness
Do not steal......................	theft
Do not bear false witness	envy, slander
Do not defraud	coveting
Honor your father and mother	(see 7:9-13)

Jesus retains, then, the basic covenant law from the Scriptures as the moral code of his followers.

Beside enjoining a basic covenant law, Jesus prescribes
for his followers a premier virtue to be practiced: faith,
viz., acceptance of him as God's authorized covenant
leader. This is not surprising for acceptance of Jesus as
Christ and covenant leader is precisely what distinguishes
Christian from Jew and what constitutes membership in

Jesus' group. The radical importance of faith is brought out in many ways in Jesus' actions and remarks. For example, Jesus lavished praise for the soil which received the seed, "the word" (4:14-20). The word-seed was offered prodigally to soil on the path, among rocks, and near thorns; but the word was not received. The good soil received it and brought forth a rich harvest. The healed demoniac, although not permitted to follow Jesus in his very company, nevertheless proved to be a follower by "proclaiming Jesus in the Decapolis" (5:20). It is not enough to acclaim Jesus as just another prophet; the crowds identified him "with John the Baptist...Elijah ...one of the prophets" (8:28). True faith is the confession of Jesus as "the Christ," God's covenant leader (8:29). Full and accurate confession of faith in Jesus, then, is the chief virtue prescribed for the true members of God's covenant people.

Alternately, the worst vice is rejection of Jesus, of which the gospel is full. Pharisees and others constantly criticize Jesus (2:7, 16, 24); his own reject him at Nazareth (6:1-6). Some go so far as to proclaim Jesus as a sinner, as a person possessed by Satan (3:22). This rejection is identified as the eternal sin: "'Whoever blasphemes against the Holy Spirit never has forgiveness, but is guilty of an eternal sin' — for they had said 'He has an unclean spirit' " (3:29-30).

Jesus, then, clearly teaches his followers a basic covenant morality. He names faith in him as the premier virtue and rejection as the worst vice. Belief or rejection, moreover, constitute membership in God's covenant.

GROUP SELF—UNDERSTANDING

In the gospel of Mark, Jesus gives his followers both a sense of continuity with Israel as well as discontinuity with it. In all probability, Mark's Christians would claim to be the authentic covenant people of God, and so see themselves in continuity with the basic thrust of Israel's Scriptures and history.

1. To be sure, the Scriptures were the Christian Bible as well. In them they found God's law and prophecies of God's Christ. There is no question of its validity for them.

2. The great parable in 12:1-12 speaks of a vineyard, the traditional image of God's covenant people (see Isa 5:1-2). This image serves as a cipher for Mark's Christians, for they would surely see Jesus as the "Beloved Son" sent to that vineyard (12:6), a son whom they themselves acknowledge, even if others reject him. They would surely see in the words "He will give the vineyard to others" (12:9) and "he has become the head of the corner" (12:10) allusions to their own claims to be God's vineyard and God's dwelling.

3. Jesus' blood is poured out as "blood of the covenant" (14:24), extending covenant ideology now to them.

4. Jesus' titles (Son of God, King, Christ, and Prophet) are all covenant leadership titles, indicating that true covenant membership is now found only in Jesus.

Jesus' followers in Mark, then, would basically understand themselves in terms of Jewish covenant ideology and images, and thus see themselves in continuity with Israel's past.

Yet in many significant ways, Jesus proclaims a strong strain of discontinuity with Israel.

1. Jesus emphasizes the radical nature of the discontinuity when he tells the Jews who object to his practices that new cloth is not put on an old garment, nor is new wine put in old skins (2:21-22). The term "new," which is used here, does not mean simply "new-in-time" (i.e., the latest), but "new-in-kind" (i.e., qualitatively different). The latest can be easily replaced with a newer model, but what is "new-in-kind" is lasting.

2. The differences between Israel-as-covenant and Church-as-covenant may be found in Jesus' attitudes to

basic Jewish customs such as a) fasting (2:18-20), b) Sabbath observance (2:23-3:6), c) purity concerns (1:40-45; 7:14-23), d) ritual washings (7:1-4), e) divorce (10:1-8), and f) temple (11:16-17). On all of these important issues, Christians break continuity with the Jews.

3. According to 7:19, Jesus abrogated the formidable Jewish dietary customs for his new covenant members. The dietary customs separated Jews from non-Jews (see Acts 10:28; 11:3), but now also separate Christians from Jews.

4. We saw earlier that Christians will read the Old Testament differently than Jews; for them, it is now a prophetic document. As Jesus now interprets it, it is voided of accretions and cultic observances.

Yet Jesus would basically affirm that God has not abandoned his covenant people. God is faithful! Since the Old Testament is fundamentally valid, God is still in the process of choosing a covenant people. In this sense one can say that, discontinuity aside, Jesus' followers in Mark's group would consider themselves as the true Israel, the authentic covenant people, now gathered and led by Jesus.

The self-understanding of the group is most evident in Jesus' handling of the temple theme in Mark. Jesus predicts the destruction of the old temple: "Do you see these great buildings? There will not be left here one stone upon another" (13:2). Earlier he had stopped the cultic practices in the temple (11:16) and declared that the temple is not a house of sacrifice but "a house of prayer" for all the people (11:17). He affirmed that covenant love was worth more than "all whole burnt offerings and sacrifices" (12:33), thus relativizing their importance. One senses in all of this an end of the old covenant, especially since the temple was a symbol of the old Israel, its piety, and covenant.

It is replaced, moreover, by a new temple in Jesus. The stone rejected has become "the head of the corner" (12:10). The sense of a new temple in Jesus is best explained in the passion narrative where witnesses ironically attest that Jesus predicted "In three days I will build another (temple),

not made with hands" (14:58). That remark is repeated at
the cross: "Aha! You would destroy the temple and build it
in three days!" (15:29). And so, at the climax of the story,
we are told of Jesus' predictions of the end of the old
temple and the foundation of a new one. When Jesus dies
the old temple is radically affected: "The curtain of the
temple was torn in two, from top to bottom" (15:38), sym-
bolizing the end of the old temple and the covenant linked
with it. If we are correct in linking Jesus' death with the
destruction of the old temple, then his resurrection
assuredly must be the building of a new temple, "not made
by human hands." That new temple, with Jesus as "head of
the corner," includes all who acclaim Jesus as God's covenant leader. For, as Jesus said about God's true temple:
"My house is a house of prayer for all the nations" (11:17).
This new temple, then, is new and radically different; it
indicates a new meeting of God and God's new covenant
people. Since the temple is the focal symbol of God's presence with the covenant people, a radical change of temples
indicates a radical change of covenant peoples.

The greatest problem faced by Jesus' followers in Mark
was an explanation for what happened to the old, empirical Israel and its temple, the symbolic locus of Jewish covenant faith. If we are correct in assuming that Mark's gospel
was written after the Roman conquest of Judea and the
destruction of the temple, then the need for an answer was
all the more urgent. Mark clearly indicates who belongs
and does not belong to God's covenant people. Those who
reject Jesus clearly do *not* belong to the covenant, among
whom are numbered:

1) those who reject Jesus' praxis (2:14-18,24; 3:2; 7:1-23),
2) those who call Jesus possessed of Satan (3:22-30),
3) those who reject Jesus in his homeland (6:1-6),
4) those who reject God's prophets and kill them (12:2-9),
5) those who put Jesus to death.

We saw above that this massive and persistent rejection

was prophesied by Isaiah. But it proved that in rejecting Jesus, the rejectors rejected God and put themselves outside of God's covenant. The destruction of Jerusalem and the ruin of the old temple only confirmed that Israel had broken faith with God and suffered the consequences of that rupture. The fault, then, lay not with God but with the former covenant people. They rejected the messengers which God repeatedly sent to the vineyard (12:2-8), and so they are severed from that vine and covenant (12:9).

Jesus, then, gives his followers both a sense of continuity with God's plans to gather a covenant people and a sense of discontinuity with Israel which rejected that plan. This is most clearly seen in Jesus' remarks on the vineyard and the temple. Jesus' followers in Mark's group would see themselves as belonging to the new temple and as heirs of the vineyard.

EXPERIENCE

From the foregoing investigation we can know a number of facts about Mark's group. 1. It is an inclusive group, containing Jews and Gentiles, saints and sinners, noble as well as marginal people. 2. It now sees itself as distinct from Israel and increasingly different from it. 3. Yet it calls itself the covenant people of God (14:24) and sees itself as belonging to God's kingdom.

But what can we know about the specific historical situation of this group? What events, great or small, shaped its experience? First, Mark seems to have been written after the Roman-Jewish war of 70 AD. Mark 13 contains hints of this war: "When you hear of war and rumors of war, do not be alarmed" (13:7) and "When you see the desolating sacrilege set up where it ought not to be..." (13:14-16). Jesus then tells his followers two things: a) avoid the conflict completely: "Let those who are in Judea flee to the mountains" (13:14), and b) do not be disturbed by it: "Take heed, I have told you all things beforehand" (13:23). Although Christians did not participate in the Roman-Jewish war, they were affected by it. The destruction of

Israel's most focal symbol, the Temple, was interpreted by them as the termination of God's special relationship with the Jews and as the confirmation of the new beginning made in Jesus. The war, then, was an important watershed in the self-understanding of the Markan group.

Alongside the cryptic remarks about the war, Jesus predicted that his followers would be made the object of bitter, judicial processes (13:9-13). These processes should be distinguished from the war, for they point to different social experiences for the Markan group. Christians might expect to be "delivered to councils"; they might even receive "disturbing-the-peace" sentences, such as beatings (13:9; see Acts 16:22). But this is only briefly mentioned and not at all highlighted. It seems that Jesus' followers in Mark's group were not formally persecuted or excommunicated, as was the case with John's Christians. We are to understand Jesus' remarks in terms of the crises caused by conversion to Jesus' group. Faith in Jesus might split families in two and cause a believer to leave "house or brothers or sisters or mother or father or children or lands for my sake and for the gospel" (10:29). Following Jesus might be described as a crisis which causes the believer to "deny himself and take up his cross and follow me" (8:34) and to "lose his life for my sake" (8:35). Jesus' followers, then, would be viewed as radical people who break all family and ethnic and national ties — dangerous actions indeed. And so they would occasion hostility from their neighbors which would lead to judicial inquiries and even chastisement for "disturbing the peace." It is important to keep this material in mind as we discover more about the experience of Jesus' followers in Mark's group.

Throughout the Markan narrative, the reader is told of constant tension between Jesus and the Jewish leaders. The following chart lists the major controversies in Mark between Jesus and his followers and the Jews, controversies in which Jesus takes a stand radically different from that of his critics.

A. *Jesus and His Adversaries:*

B. *The Disciples and Their Adversaries:*

Although these controversies are found throughout the Markan narrative, they are concentrated in three places, Mk 2-3, 7, and 11-12. The controversies occur over important issues, the very issues which Jews see as distinguishing them as the chosen covenant people. To be a Jew in Jesus' day, one would practice certain customs which both identified one as belonging to the Jewish covenant group and distinguished one from non-members. The specific, distinguishing customs were: a) circumcision, b) dietary rules, and c) Sabbath observance. The key controversies in Mark touch on these basic customs. Although there is no formal mention of circumcision in Mark's gospel, its very absence is a clue; for, it is belief in Jesus which constitutes membership in the covenant, not circumcision. Yet Mark records controversies over dietary rules (#s 4, 11, 12, 14) and Sabbath observance (#s 2, 13). And so, in differing from the synagogue on these key issues, Jesus and his followers were distinguishing themselves from the Jewish covenant.

The controversies, moreover, all deal with differences between Jesus and the synagogue.

> 1. Jesus did not link forgiveness of sin with Temple sacrifices, but claimed God's own authority to forgive sins (# 1). After all, he was to "baptize with the Holy Spirit."
> 2. Moses allowed divorce for the synagogue; Jesus criticizes this concession (# 6).
> 3. The Pharisees objected to paying taxes to pagans; Jesus disagreed (# 8).
> 4. The synagogue interpreted the Scriptures as Torah, expanding it scope to 613 precise laws; Jesus restricted it.
> 5. Jewish religious practice was focused on the temple and it sacrifices; Jesus proclaimed an end to the temple and its practices.

On point after point, the controversies serve to distinguish Jesus and his followers from the Jewish synagogue. They function, then, as important clues to the history of the Markan group, for they point to the major experience of that group. It was a group in the process of separating itself from the synagogue.

Although Mark reflects a relatively stable and untroubled Christian group vis-à-vis the Roman-Jewish war, he indicates that the followers of Jesus for whom he writes were engaged in a long and painful process of separating themselves from the synagogue. The controversies are the window on that process. As Jesus' followers realized that they were different from the synagogue, that difference was made real and symbolic in the controversies between Jesus and the Jews. Christian self-identity kept defining on every level and in numerous ways how Jesus and his followers differed from the Jews. And so we may say that the prime experience of the Markan group was its growing self-awareness as the authentic covenant and its necessary differentiation from the synagogue.

This prime experience is the horizon against which Mark

edited his narrative. It is the *Sitz im Leben*, or live situation, of the group for whom he edited the story of Jesus. And it gives coherence and clarity to the five catchbasin topics discussed immediately above. *Membership* in God's covenant people is not restricted to orthodox Jews only, as the synagogue asserts. Rather membership in the new, authentic covenant is open to all. What a difference! The *Old Testament* is not interpreted as a code of 613 laws, as the synagogue asserts. Rather it teaches a core covenant law, the Ten Commandments, and it enjoys a prophetic interpretation as well. A significant difference! As regards *Eschatology*, there is a sense of realized eschatology in belonging to Jesus' covenant group, a sense which distinguishes his followers from the synagogue. They are *not* in God's kingdom. Even the future aspects of eschatology distinguish Jews and Christians; for what the Jews reject, God vindicates. *Ethics* also distinguish Jews and Christians. Since the prime virtue is belief in Jesus, this immediately separates synagogue and church. The *Group Identity* of the Christian group differs from that of the synagogue; for Jesus' followers are the new, authentic covenant group and they find God in a new Temple. The Jews, however, are cut off from the vineyard; their old temple is destroyed. On every level, Christians differ from Jews. This is not surprising, if one recalls that the primary experience of Jesus' followers in Mark's group is differentiation from the synagogue.

The portrait of Jesus which was sketched according to the five catchbasin topics conveys an image of Jesus as the new covenant leader. Jesus proclaims a teaching which is distinctively different from what was held by members of synagogue and temple alike. His opinions and attitudes not only point to a reform of old customs, but also to the inbreaking of God's kingdom which calls for a radical conversion of heart and mind. After all, the first words from Jesus' mouth were: "Repent and believe in the gospel" (1:15). On every issue, Jesus' teaching indicates that God's kingdom and covenant differ from prevailing Jewish ideas. Hence, the pervasive controversies.

But this pervasive confrontation makes sense when seen in the light of the experience of Mark's group. For all of his controversies, Jesus and his original followers remained in the synagogue and continued to frequent the temple. The split with synagogue and temple came much later. It is the experience of Mark and his fellow Christians which tells of the process of separation from the synagogue about the year 70. In all probability, the split with the synagogue has already taken place, and the Markan community is in the process of understanding itself as different from the synagogue which does not believe in Jesus. This is the situation in light of which Mark edits his gospel; this is the experience which shaped Mark's special portrait of Jesus.

EXISTENTIAL CHRISTOLOGY

We turn now to more traditional studies of Christology by reflecting on the names and titles given to Jesus in the gospel story. But inasmuch as our focus is on the evangelist's community and his experience, we are not so much interested in dredging up the Jewish background of these names and titles so much as understanding them in terms of the experience of the community for whom the gospel was written. Our attention is on the third *Sitz im Leben*, the life situation of the followers of Jesus for whom Mark wrote. The names and titles no doubt have a long history, but we are interested in how these function for this later group of followers. And so, when we investigate the names and titles of Jesus, these should be seen against the horizon of the experience of the group which so named Jesus.

If the determining experience of Mark's Christian group is its separation and distinction from the old covenant group, we would expect this experience to color the way this group would name Jesus. First and foremost, Jesus is proclaimed as the authentic covenant leader, the authentic ruler of the Markan group. All of his titles refer to this:

  1. *Son of God* (1:10-11; 9:7) is the title God gives him in the great theophanies of the baptism and the transfig-

uration. It does not mean that Jesus is divine, for "Son of God" is the name given to God's chosen people (Ex 4:22; Deut 14:1; Hos 2:1), but especially to Israel's rulers (2 Sam 7:14; Ps 2:7 and 89:27). It may refer to the king of the covenant people or to their judge (see Ps 82:6). The dominant idea underlying this title in Mark was of divine election for a leadership role vis-à-vis God's people.

2. *The Christ* (8:29), of course, refers to God's anointed ruler, such as a consecrated king (e.g., Saul in 1 Sam 10:1 or David in 1 Sam 16:13). It helps to remember that "Christ" is derived from "chrism" or oil used for anointing. The consecrated ruler might also be a priest, such as we find at Qumran.

3. *Prophets* had leadership roles for God's covenant people; so when Jesus is acclaimed as "prophet," either as rejected prophet (6:4) or as prophet like the prophets of old (6:16; 8:27-28), he is cast in the role of a leader of God's covenant people.

4. Finally, Jesus is acclaimed the *King of the Jews* (15:2, 9, 18, 26), that is, authentic ruler of God's covenant people.

All of the major titles in Mark continually point to Jesus in his capacity as authorized and consecrated leader of God's covenant people.

As leader of God's covenant people, Jesus has "authority." This authority is ascribed to him by God in the baptism and the transfiguration; and it is both recognized by the people (1:21-28) and disputed by his critics (11:27-33). But for Mark's group, Jesus has authority. This authority extends to many of Jesus' actions.

1. He can clarify and enjoin a basic covenant law for God's people (12:30-31). He can determine how the Sabbath will be kept (2:23-28) and what diet may be eaten (7:19).

2. He can render new and authoritative interpreta-

tions of the sacred books of God's covenant people (10:1-10; 7:7-9).

3. He has the ultimate responsibility to admit or exclude humankind from God's covenant and God's presence. This is negatively expressed in 8:38 where exclusion is mentioned: "Whoever is ashamed of me and of my words in this adulterous and sinful generation, of him will the Son of Man be ashamed when he comes in the glory of his Father with the holy angels." It is more positively expressed in 13:26-27 when that same Son of Man will "come in the clouds with great power and glory and will send out the angels and gather his elect from the four winds."

4. This same leader can loose humankind of its sins (2:10) and bind others who are guilty of an eternal sin (3:28-30).

The authority of Jesus as covenant leader is radical, fundamental, and sweeping.

The portrayal of Jesus as God's authorized and consecrated covenant leader is given flesh when it is seen in conjunction with other aspects of Jesus. To make this clear, we recall how under the catchbasin of *Eschatology*, we noted that Jesus tells us two different eschatological words. The first half of the gospel describes Jesus in terms of his missionary activity; he goes about preaching "The Kingdom of God is at hand" (1:15). His preaching is itself an act of leadership vis-à-vis God's covenant people, for he preaches God's authentic word. His preaching, moreover, determines the shape of the covenant people, for he preaches an inclusive covenant open to all people: saints and sinners as well as Jews and Gentiles. The kingdom which Jesus preaches, moreover, is made tangible in Jesus' miracles.

It is often claimed by some Markan scholars that interest in miracles betrays a defective Christology — a misplaced emphasis on glory rather than on the cross. Some critics have claimed that Mark wrote his gospel precisely to correct the traditional and excessively optimistic view of Jesus conveyed by his miracles; Mark is said to have written the second half of the gospel, which is about Jesus' rejection and death, as a corrective to the miraculous first half of the gospel. These perspectives often reflect the scholars' own uneasiness with miracles rather than Mark's. Since the evangelist exercised great independence and editorial creativity in adding to, deleting, and changing traditonal materials, it seems strange to hear of claims that Mark disapproved of miracles when he seems to spend one half of the gospel carefully articulating their meaning and significance. No, Mark sees great importance and significance in Jesus' miracles.

The important question to ask is not "Did the miracles happen?" but "What do they mean?" "How do they function?" and "What Christology is implied by them?" Inasmuch as the miracles all occur in the first half of the gospel, the half which presents Jesus as the missionary of God's kingdom, the miracles should be seen as related to Jesus' role as authorized leader of God's covenant people. In this context, we can see that the miracles of Jesus function in Mark's gospel as his credentials. The crowds who call him a "prophet" are correct in their conclusion, because all of Jesus' miracles find a parallel in the careers of Israel's classical prophets. This is what genuine prophets do! The following chart is intended to show how Jesus' miracles in Mark resemble those of the prophets; the crowds who see Jesus' miracles are quite correct in evaluating them as evidence that Jesus is God's prophet to the covenant community.

Jesus' Miracles		*Prophetic Miracles*
1.	Food Multiplied ....1.	Ex 16: 1 Kg 17:8-16;
	6:34-44; 8:1-10	2 Kg 4:1-7
2.	Dead Raised ....2.	1 Kg 17:17-24; 2 Kg 4:18-37
	5:35-43	
3.	Lepers Cleansed ....3.	2 Kg 5:1ff
	1:40-45	
4.	Sea Miracles ....4.	Ex 15; 2 Kg 2:6-8 & 12-14
	4:35-42 & 6:45-52	

5. Blind Given Sight ....5.   Isa 29:18; 35:5
    8:22-26
6. Deaf/dumb Healed ......6.   Isa 29:18; 35:5
    7:31-37
7. Lame Healed............7.   Isa 35:6
    2:1-12

One familiar with the Jewish Scriptures would never conclude that Jesus was "divine" because he worked miracles.
All of the prophets performed miracles, and monotheistic
Jews would never call Jeremiah "God" or Elijah "Lord."
But hearing of Jesus' miraculous deeds would lead a Bible-
trained mind to say: here is a prophet, like Elijah or one of
the old prophets (6:13-14; 8:27-28).

   The miracles, moreover, are examples of covenant blessings on God's covenant people. Feeding the hungry, healing the sick, cleansing lepers and raising the dead are
samples of God's covenant care for his chosen ones. Miracles are signs, likewise, of the advent of the kingdom or
reign of God when the results of sin and death will be swept
away.

   The fact that many miracles are done for pagans is significant, for it indicates that they, too, are invited by God
into a covenant relationship. The healing of Gentiles (7:24-
30), of outcast Israelites (1:40-45), and of polluted Jews
(5:24-34) indicates the extension of God's covenant concern to those who previously would have been judged to be
on the margins of or outside the boundary of the covenant.
This replicates what we have seen about Jesus' inclusive
mission to saints and sinners, Jews and Gentiles alike.

   Jesus' miracles, then, serve as his credentials as covenant
leader. They are symbols of the saving blessings of God's
kingdom, now made visible and available in Jesus. They
are, moreover, indicative of the inclusive character of
God's covenant people. The miracles confirm Mark's basic
presentation of Jesus as herald, covenant leader, and ruler
of God's inclusive kingdom.

   Jesus, however, tells us a second eschatological word
which covers the agenda of the second half of the gospel.

Mission to Israel is replaced by hostility from it; miracles yield to suffering and death; titles denoting a covenant leader (Son of God, Christ) take second place to titles telling the story of the rejected leader. Chs 8-16 tell the tale of a rejected covenant ruler. We noted above how Jesus was engaged in controversies with various leaders of the synagogue and temple. The following list merely highlights the various groups who opposed Jesus' every word and deed.

> *Rejection by:*
> A. Pharisees: 2:16, 24; 7:1-5
> B. Chief Priests and Elders: 8:31; 10:33; 11:28; 14:1, 10, 43, 53-65; 15:10
> C. Scribes: 2:6-7; 8:31; 10:33; 11:28; 14:1, 43, 53-65
> D. Sadducees: 12:18-27

Only in 6:1-6 and 15:6-13 is Jesus ever rejected by crowds, but these two stories are probably only reinforcing the official reaction to Jesus by the leaders of the old covenant.

In light of this persistent rejection of Jesus, Mark introduced a new title for Jesus. "Son of Man," the dominant title of Jesus in the second half of the gospel, most basically refers to Jesus in two ways: a) as the rejected one, b) whom God vindicated. The background of this comes from Dan 7, where the martyrs, who were rejected and slain on earth, are vindicated by God in heaven. This information helps to explain why this new title occurs primarily in predictions of Jesus' rejection and vindication:

> 8:31 The *Son of Man* must be rejected...
> 9:31 The *Son of Man* must be delivered...
> 10:33 The *Son of Man* must be delivered...

The same title is used in Jesus' response to the Sanhedrin's rejection of Jesus as God's covenant leader, as God's "Christ, the Son of the Blessed." As this self-identity is rejected, Jesus speaks of the vindication of the rejected one: "You will see the *Son of Man* seated at the right hand of the Power" (14:62). Mark, then, does not ignore this bitter and negative aspect of Jesus' career: he was the stone rejected (12:10), the despised and crucified one. But Jesus is also the one whom God vindicated and raised up (14:62/Dan 7:13-14).

Returning to the conflicts and controversies between Jesus and his adversaries, we find this also adequately reflected in Mark's portrait of Jesus. Mark is not merely interested in recalling *that* there was tension and friction, but in showing how Jesus triumphed over such negative experiences. In the title "Son of Man" Mark finds a symbolic way of telescoping the story of Jesus' rejection and vindication. We recall that "Son of Man" was the name given in Dan 7 to persecuted and martyred Jews who were rescued by God. Rejected on earth by men, they were vindicated by God in heaven. "Son of Man," then, is a code word in Mark for an orthodox person who is rejected and vindicated. When people object to Jesus' forgiveness of sins, Jesus uses "Son of Man" to describe his present state of rejection by the Jews: "That you may know that the *Son of Man* has authority on earth to forgive sins..." (2:10); when Pharisees object to Jesus' different Sabbath observance, he uses this title in reference to himself in this rejected situation: "The *Son of Man* is Lord even of the Sabbath" (2:28). The linkage of "Son of Man" and rejection helps to explain why this title is dominant in the controversy passages of the gospel and especially in the materials dealing with Jesus' suffering and death. Mark does not ignore this bitter and negative aspect of Jesus' career: he proclaims Jesus as the stone rejected by the builders (12:10), the despised and crucified one. But even as he is the "Son of Man," rejected by men, he is also the Son of Man whom God vindicates. The rejected one, moreover, becomes the judge of those who rejected him.

Although Jesus is never formally called a "judge" in Mark's gospel, he exercises the authority of a judge. Jesus makes judicial pronouncements and takes on a formal judicial role. 1. Jesus can declare sins forgiven (2:10; 3:28) and sins retained (3:29). 2. Jesus judges who is inside God's kingdom and who is outside. Those who say that "He (Jesus) has an unclean spirit" (3:29-30) are declared permanently outside God's presence. Those who are "ashamed of me and my words" are likewise declared outsiders (8:38). Alternately, the Son of Man will bring inside God's kingdom those who accept him as God's covenant ruler. For, when he returns at the parousia, he will send out his angels "to gather his elect from the four winds" (13:27). Judge is but another aspect of leadership of God's covenant people. But in Mark's account, it is ironical, for the judged one ultimately becomes the judge; and those who judge Jesus find themselves judged in turn. The saying is true: "With the judgment you pronounce you will be judged" (Mt 7:2).

Yet Jesus' judicial role is perceived as a role which he will exercise in the distant future, when the final judgment comes. In this regard, it is important to note the surprising absence of polemical condemnations and woes spoken by Jesus against present enemies or against present sinners. For example, 1. one finds in Mark no "woes" against the Pharisees *et al.* as hypocrites and false teachers, such as we find in the Q tradition (Mt 23; Lk 11:39-51). 2. There is in Mark no scrutiny of members of the group, pointing out their sins and demanding immediate repentance or excommunication, such as we find in Mt 5:21-22 and 18:15-18. 3. Mark's Jesus makes no demand for perfection or total purity, such as is found in Mt 5:48 or 5:27-30. 4. There is no prophetic judgment by Jesus against Jerusalem for killing the prophets and rejecting those sent to it, as is found in the Q tradition (Mt 23:37-39 and Lk 13:34-35; yet see Mk 12:9). This assessment of Jesus' judicial role coheres with the earlier observation that Jesus is portrayed basically as an inclusive figure who calls all to God's kingdom, sinner and saint alike. Like the Prodigal Sower in 4:3-9, Jesus sows the word of the kingdom everywhere, even on hard ground, on rocks, and among thorns. One would not expect such a Jesus to be a fiery prophet who judged sinners and condemned them in the present to eternal exclusion.

We have seen how Jesus' titles as Son of God and Christ

identify him as covenant leader. These titles reflect also the missionary aspect of Jesus as herald of God kingdom and as gatherer of the inclusive covenant people. The miracles of Jesus, moreover, enflesh this aspect of Jesus and replicate his role as covenant leader. These aspects of the portrait of Jesus in Mark's gospel reflect the experience of a group which is now full of new Gentile members. This portrait serves as the foundation stone for Gentile membership in the covenant community and for the non-Jewish character of that new group.

But Mark's community has more than one experience which shapes its portrait of Jesus. Alongside a missionary experience which brought saints and sinners, Jews and Gentiles into the inclusive covenant, Jesus' followers in Mark's group had a decidedly negative experience as well, viz., separation from the synagogue and hostility from it. And so a new portrait of Jesus was crafted to reflect this new experience. A new title was brought forward, "Son of Man," which would encode the experience of controversy and friction with the parent covenant community. Son of God functions exclusively in the story of the rejection of the covenant leader and his constant controversies with the leaders of synagogue and temple.

The gospel claims, moreover, that with Jesus as the cornerstone, a new holy temple will be built. Not like the old, material temple, made by human hands (14:58)! Not like the old temple with its inadequate cultic sacrifices (11:16; 12:33)! The new temple will be made by God. It will be a different kind of temple, "a house of prayer of all nations" (11:17). This new temple is linked in Mark with Jesus and the covenant-in-Jesus. And so, holiness and purity can only be found by proximity to Jesus and by being joined to him and his covenant people.

Mark, then, deems it very important that a reader or hearer of his narrative begin the story by knowing of Jesus' radical holiness. But the story of Jesus' holiness effects the picture which Mark also presents of the covenant-in-Jesus. Jesus by no means abolishes all purity boundaries; as Son of Man, he will finally separate believers from unbelievers, insiders from outsiders (8:38; 13:27). But he lowers the height of the wall made by Jewish purity boundaries and he makes more gates in the wall. Unclean gentiles, sinners, polluted people, and marginal folk are all offered God's full covenant blessings. In Jesus' basic actions, the radical Jewish sense of purity and therefore of membership in the covenant was lowered. The height of the Jewish purity walls, maintained by strict dietary customs, Sabbath observance and washing rites, was lowered. According to Jesus, purity is found in the keeping of the basic covenant laws (7:21-23; 10:19). Sins must still be forgiven, and they are (2:10); God's commandments must still be obeyed, and they are (10:19). Christians must still worship in God's true temple, and they do (12:10; 14:58). No, purity is still a prime value for Mark's group, but the height of the wall is lowered and more gates are made through it for the stream of gentile converts who are joining God's covenant people.

Mark's story about Jesus' purity and his new strategy for purity rules has direct bearing on the issues discussed in the first half of this chapter. Purity rules function as boundaries; they separate Jew from Gentile and saint from sinner. By making doors through the high purity wall, Jesus is indicating that Gentiles are welcome in the covenant and that sinners and unclean folk are welcome to find purity in Jesus' touch and his word of forgiveness. And so, the mission of the Markan church is widespread and the membership of the group is inclusive in character. By lowering the height of the Jewish purity wall, Jesus is re-interpreting the Old Testament Scriptures, abolishing rules and customs which functioned basically to separate Jew from Gentile: food laws, Sabbath observance, etc. Thus with lowered walls, Gentiles find it easier to be accepted in the covenant group. Holiness no longer resides in washings but in keeping the Ten Commandments and in faith in God's Covenant Leader. If the Markan group sees itself as the authentic Israel and if God's blessings are found only in that group, then it matters greatly that Jesus proclaims a *new* time and a *new* place of salvation wherein gentiles and unclean folk have access to God and God's blessings. The Markan use of the language of purity, then, is specific cultural language of the first century which conveys in those coded terms what we tried to explain in terms more recognizable to our specific culture.

Chapter Three

THE CHRISTOLOGIES IN MATTHEW'S GOSPEL

The starting point for investigating the portraits of Jesus in the Gospel of Matthew is the awareness that this gospel as we now read it reflects the faith of a community with a long and changing history. This gospel is the final product of an evangelist whom we call "Matthew," who wrote in the 80s. Yet it mirrors more than Matthew's perspective, for it contains layers of tradition which come from earlier periods and expresses the viewpoints of other preachers than the final redactor, Matthew.

When we ask further about the sources of this gospel, we begin to ask about its history. We can quickly determine that this gospel contains at least these sources:

a) an early tradition called "Q" (Q = *Quelle* or "source"), which basically contains sayings and parables attributed to Jesus;

b) the Gospel of Mark, which tells of miracle stories and a passion narrative;

c) materials called "M," some of which are distinctive to the final editor of the gospel.

This source analysis correlates with the many *Sitze im Leben* which we noted in the introduction. The Q source seems to have developed in the apostolic period of the early church (30-60 AD). Mark's gospel is dated around 70 AD, and the final redactor of Matthew represents still later New Testament churches and their perspective (80-85 AD). The text of Matthew's gospel, then, is like an archeological excavation site, containing many layers of materials which come from different periods of history.

Working from a source-critical perspective, which is a radically historical perspective, we quickly become aware that the viewpoint of the Q source is quite different from that of Mark or the final editor of the Matthean gospel. It is important to admit this striking diversity from the beginning of our study of the gospel text. Given the diversity of sources, we should expect to find different traditions which reflect different experiences, different histories, and different points of view. This suggests that the different sources might also reflect different portraits of Jesus. Failure to recognize this at the outset leads one to a homogenized view of Matthew's text which ignores differences in source, time, experience and perspective. Just as we allow for an individual to develop mentally, physically, and intellectually through many stages of growth and experience, so we should allow for a New Testament community to develop and to have different viewpoints at different periods of time, in light of different experiences. The portrait of Jesus was by no means static for forty years.

The task now is to find a useful procedure for assessing the differences in the sources. We identified three sources above (Q, Mk, M), but the issue is more complicated than that neat trajectory would suggest. For example, we know that Matthew's gospel incorporated Mark's text. But it is unclear whether this happened at the time of Matthew's own final redaction of the gospel, or earlier. Moreover, the materials unique to M are not all late material, reflecting the perspective of the final redactor. Some of them may be earlier, contemporary with the Q source materials. But how to determine this?

As we shall shortly see, the perspectives of the Q source and Mark's gospel are quite strikingly different. I propose to compare and contrast these two sources in Matthew's gospel. And special M materials (without parallels in Q or Mk) can be conveniently sorted out on the basis of whether they share the perspective of Q or Mark; and so M materials can be tentatively identified as early or late on the basis of this principle of coherence. Although there are many sources in Matthew's gospel, we will risk oversimplifying the issue by comparing and contrasting earlier with later materials, Q with Markan perspectives.

To recover the different perspectives of the earlier and later sources, I propose to examine them in terms of five basic categories noted in the introduction, for they can serve as covenient catchbasins for collecting the attitudes and viewpoints of the respective sources. Jesus is credited with informing and instructing his followers on these issues, so a full sketch of the portrait of Jesus in these sources can and must include the ideas and ideals attributed to Jesus. In this way, we hope to recover a full portrait of Jesus which includes the sayings and actions attributed to Jesus as well as a list of titles. In recovering Jesus' alleged attitudes and positions on key issues, we can see a portrait of Jesus vis-à-vis the dynamic experience of the Christian group which so remembered and so shaped its preaching about Jesus. As the Vatican Council urged us to do, we should see the gospels as explications of Jesus in view of the situations of the respective churches and the respective periods of their development.

I.
The Portrait of Jesus in the Q Source

Let us begin with an investigation of the portrait of Jesus in the early sources contained in Matthew's gospel. We are trying to recover what the Christian group who wrote and preserved these sources attributed to Jesus and what portrait of Jesus is reflected in these attributions. We turn to the Q source and also to special M materials which closely resemble its perspective.

MEMBERSHIP AND MISSION

One of the key questions for both Christians and Jews in the first century was "who's in God's covenant community?" In the early stage of the Matthean community's history, the answer to this was surprisingly restricted: Jews only and only pious Jews. According to Jesus' own mission instruction in Mt 10, he charged the apostles whom he sent out to preach: "Go nowhere among the Gentiles, and enter no town of the Samaritans, but go rather to the lost sheep of the house of Israel" (10:5-6). This sums up the sense of mission and membership in the early stages of this community's history: exclusive membership for Jews only. In the later sources, there is a revoking of this narrow sense of who should receive God's covenant blessings (e.g. story of Jesus' dealing with the Canaanite woman, 15:21-28). But that revocation only proves the point, viz. how clearly the early group understood its earlier, restricted sense of mission. In that later dialogue with the Canaanite woman, Jesus repeated his earlier assertion that the mission is restricted. He clearly states that he understands it to be God's will that *he also* avoid Gentiles: "I was sent only to the lost sheep of the house of Israel" (15:24). Jesus himself, then, is credited with enjoining a restricted mission on this community.

As regards membership, a restricted mission also implies restricted membership. The mission may be to Jews only, but not all Jews are truly members of the covenant. Although we are accustomed to hear that Jesus called tax collectors to be his disciples and ate with sinners, we seldom reflect that this aspect of Jesus is known to us through Mark's gospel, a later source. It is *not* the perspective of the earlier sources, which record a more restricted sense of mission and membership in the Christian covenant community. In the Q source, for example, Jesus speaks disparagingly of tax collectors, sinners, and Gentiles. Jesus remarks how they act on a quid-pro-quo basis with their neighbors, which Jesus criticizes: "If you love those who love you, what reward have you? Do not even the tax collectors do the same?" (5:46//Lk 6:33). Christians are told not to pray like the Gentiles: "Do not heap up empty phrases as the Gentiles do" (6:7). When an unrepenting member is expelled from the group, Jesus tells the community to distance itself from the separated one as one does from tax collectors and Gentiles: "Let him be to you as a Gentile and a tax collector" (18:17). Despite what we read in Mark and later traditions, Jesus is said to authorize a rather restricted mission and to restrict membership in the covenant to Jews only and only reformed Jews.

OLD TESTAMENT

There is no doubt that this reformed covenant community considers the Hebrew scriptures as still valid for itself. Unlike later Christian groups which will begin to interpret these scriptures as writings which are prophetic of Jesus, this early group accepts them fundamentally as *halakah,* as legal instructions on holy behavior which befits God's holy people. The lasting validity of these scriptures is emphatically affirmed: "Do not think that I have come to abolish the law and the prophets; I have come not to abolish them but to fulfil them" (5:17).

We noted earlier that Jesus described his followers as the authentic and reformed core of Israel. As such, he intensified for them the correct observance of the Law as prescribed in the Scripture. For example, control of anger is as important as avoiding murder; avoidance of lust in the heart is as necessary as correct sexual behavior. And so, according to Jesus' commands, they maintained covenant laws such as "You shall not kill" and "You shall not commit adultery" (5:21, 27). But precisely as a reform group, Jesus also commanded that they put a hedge around these laws in the control of anger and lust in the heart (5:22, 28), as assurance of keeping the core of the law perfectly. Jesus' reformed, authentic Jewish covenant community has no doubts about the Old Testament as a legal document. It has even built a protective hedge about it.

ESCHATOLOGY

Pervading this reformed covenant community is an intense sense of prophetic judgment. John the Baptizer, the evident hero and saint of this group, preached an imminent judgment when good and evil will be separated; the wheat will be gathered into the barn and the chaff burned (3:12//Lk 3:17). "Even now the ax is laid to the root of the trees" (3:10//Lk 3:9).

Jesus' sense of imminent judgment is reflected in his words to the unbelieving Pharisees and to "this wicked and adulterous generation." They will be judged by the people of Nineveh and by the Queen of the South who heeded the prophet's words and accepted the wisdom of God's king (12:41-42//Lk 11:29-32). Jesus himself pronounces "woe" on the cities of Galilee for not heeding the words of God's prophet: "Woe to you Chorazin! woe to you Bethsaida ...and you Capernaum, will you be exalted to heaven? You shall be brought down to Hades" (11:20-23//Lk 10:13-15).

Besides the cities of Galilee, Jesus singles out Jerusalem for judgment. Her sin is the constant rejection of God's prophets and their murder. "I send you prophets and wise men and scribes, some of whom you will kill and crucify and some you will scourge in your synagogues and persecute from town to town" (23:34). Indeed God's prophets have always been maltreated by those to whom they were sent (5:12//Lk 6:22-23). Nevertheless, Jesus would gather Jerusalem's children together as a hen gathers her brood under her wing, "And you would not" (23:37//Lk 13:34). Hence, judgment is pronounced on the sinful city: "Behold, your house is forsaken and desolate" (23:28//Lk 13:35).

Jesus' sense of soon and sure judgment serves many important functions in the early Matthean community. 1. It serves to reinforce the sense of identity of the reformed covenant group by distinguishing the perfect from sinners, the wheat from the chaff (3:11//Lk 3:17) and the wheat from the tares (13:24-30). The perfect are those "within": within the barn, within the marriage feast. They are the ones who have "entered" the kingdom of God (5:20; 7:21; 8:11-12). The wicked are those who are "outside," those who are burned in unquenchable fire.   2. Judgment language replicates the boundaries which Jesus commanded this perfect group to erect to guard its perfect inside. Judgment language is itself a boundary which puts non-members "outside" and under judgment.   3. Judgment language supports the group's sense of perfection by encouraging a regular prophetic posture which identifies sin and calls down judgment upon it (see 5:21-22; 18:15-18). Thus judgment language strengthens group boundaries and confirms the covenant community in its sense of being God's holy and elect group. All the others face perdition. This judgment language, moreover, is attributed to Jesus, the leader of this reformed covenant group.

ETHICS

Although it is clear that Jesus reaffirms for his covenant community the Hebrew scriptures as its *halakah,* one can ask: a) is there a particular virtue valued by Jesus or a vice abhorred by him, and b) is there any behavior particularly prescribed or proscribed by him? As regards a virtue which Jesus valued, it must be said to be an acute sense of sinlessness or perfection. Jesus tells them quite clearly; "Be ye perfect as your heavenly Father is perfect" (5:48). In the Antitheses in 5:21-47, Jesus teaches this perfection as the radical avoidance of sin by his insistence that his followers put a protective hedge around the Law. Perfection extends not only to external keeping of a law, but also to internal attitudes: not only is murder proscribed, so is anger (5:21-22), not only adultery, but also lust (5:27-28), not only false witnessing, but also oath taking (5:33-37).

The same sense of perfection can be picked up in the dualistic view of human beings attributed to Jesus: they are either all good or all bad. For example, if one organ of the body is not perfect, the *whole* body is seen as corrupt: "If your eye is not sound, your *whole* body will be full of darkness" (6:23). And that darkness is total and terrible.

According to this perfectionistic perspective, one cannot have two masters (6:24) or two treasures (6:19-21). So, a radical choice must be made either for good or for evil; there is no allowance for compromise or ambiguity. This radical sense of dualism recurs when Jesus tells his followers to be perfectly good or else they are evil: "Either make the tree good and its fruit good or make the tree bad and its fruit bad" (12:33).

In keeping with this sense of radical perfection, Jesus indicates that the prescribed behavior for his followers is avoidance of evil, correction of it, or separation from it. One avoids sin by intensifying the law, but especially by building boundaries between the holy group and all others, so that one knows unmistakably where good and evil lie. Besides building boundaries, one maintains them; and so when evil occurs within the group or when an unworthy person enters the perfect group, that group reacts to correct the errant member. If a member is angry with a brother, he is taken immediately before the group's council (5:21); if someone insults a fellow member or calls him "you fool," he is forthwith liable to judgment (5:22). We noted earlier the elaborate corrective process in 18:15-18 for dealing with sinners in the group.

It follows, then, that sin is intolerable within this reform group. And so Jesus enjoins exclusion and amputation as the proper responses to sin. He commands that offending eyes, hands, and feet be necessarily cut off (5:29-30; 18:6-9). Offending members are excluded (18:18) and treated like "outsiders." Perfection (the total avoidance of evil) is the prime value; and boundary building (to wall off sin) and maintenance of those boundaries are the chief actions prescribed by Jesus for this group to keep its perfection.

Conversely, the premier vice which Jesus censures in this group is hypocrisy. All covenant members are expected to keep the prescriptions of the law but Jesus especially fears people who externally seem to keep them but within are corrupt, viz. hypocritical. So hypocritical piety is censured:

a) Beware of practicing your piety before people in order to be seen by them (6:1).
b) When you give alms, sound no trumpet before you as the hypocrites do (6:2).
c) When you pray, you must not be like the hypocrites (6:5).
d) When you fast, do not look dismal, like the hypocrites (6:16).

An external show of piety without the correct internal attitude is a terrible sin. Yet, according to Jesus, hypocrisy is a widespread phenomenon. It is found in outsiders (6:1-18) as well as in members of the group. Jesus warns his followers of false prophets who come to it "in sheep's clothing, but inwardly are ravenous wolves" (7:15). Pharisees in particular are branded as hypocrites by Jesus. While they seem to keep the law externally, they are unclean in heart and attitude: "You cleanse the outside of the cup and the plate, but inside you are full of extortion and wickedness" (23:25). Their sin is "to appear outwardly righteous, but within to be full of hypocrisy and wickedness"(23:28).

Hypocrisy is the premier vice, but it is closely followed by the sin of scandal, viz., leading a holy and innocent person into sin. Jesus proclaims a terrible curse on those who cause scandal: "It would be better for him to have a great millstone tied around his neck and to be drowned in the depth of the sea" (18:6). That is why Jesus censured the Pharisees so severely for corrupting their converts. He accuses them of making of their proselytes "twice as much a child of gehenna as yourselves" (23:15) for teaching only external observance without corresponding internal attitudes. They make hypocrites of their converts under the guise of making them holy.

The premier virtue is perfection, which manifests itself in keeping the law as perfectly as possible and distancing oneself as far as possible from those who do *not* so observe it. A characteristic action of Jesus and his followers, then, is the prophetic identification of sin, followed by judgment passed on unrepentant sinners. For example, Jesus regularly identifies sin:

> *Identification of Sin:*
> a) hypocrisy (6:1-16)
> b) blasphemy (12:31-32)
> c) scandal (18:5-6)
> d) hypocrisy (23:13-36).

And Jesus regularly pronounces judgment on sin and sinners:

> *Judgment on Sin:*
> a) Woe to you Chorazin...Bethsaida...Capernaum (11:20-24).
> b) Whoever speaks against the Holy Spirit will not be forgiven (12:32).
> c) It would be better for a great millstone to be fastened around his neck (18:6).
> d) Woe to you, Scribes and Pharisees...(23:13, 16, 23, 25, 27, 29).
> e) Jerusalem, Jerusalem, killing the prophets...(23:37-39).

The characteristic virtues and vices which Jesus is said to enjoin on his followers correlate with Jesus' mission instructions and with the self-understanding of his followers. Membership is clearly restricted to the few, reformed followers of Jesus. They, moreover, see their perfection as characterizing them as the few worthy members of God's covenant. Their perfection in keeping the Law also means that they avoid anyone not perfect, especially people who falsely claim perfection. Pure in heart and action, Jesus' reformed followers are constantly sensitized to spot and shun people who are not as they are, especially hypocrites. These few, reformed covenant members necessarily prize the virtues described above: they distance themselves from sin, hypocrites, and scandal; they build hedges, not only around the Law, but around themselves as well. There is a strong correlation, then, between the sense of membership which Jesus proclaims and the self-understanding of his followers and their characteristic virtues and vices.

GROUP SELF—UNDERSTANDING

Related to this sense of exclusive membership is the self-understanding of Jesus' group as the only authentic reform movement in Judaism. Preaching only to Jews, Jesus' followers obviously perceive themselves still as Jews, as members of God's covenant with Israel. But they see themselves as the authentic members of that covenant, as the reformed core group which is the true Israel. This may be grasped by the terms which this group records Jesus using to distinguish them from other Jewish groups. Followers of Jesus are the "few who enter through the narrow gate," as opposed to the many who travel the wide and easy way to destruction (7:13-14//Lk 13:23-24). Jesus' followers are the sheep among wolves (10:16//Lk 10:3), the wheat growing in a field of tares (13:24-30), the obedient sons who do their father's bidding, as opposed to those who promised obedience and did not comply (21:28-32). They are the wheat which is stored in barns, as opposed to the chaff which is burned (3:12//Lk 3:17). The elite sense of this reformed group is expressed when it is exhorted to be "the salt of the earth" (5:13//Lk 14:34-35) and "the light of the world" (5:14//Lk 11:33).

According to the Q source, Jesus described his followers as the only authentic reform movement within Judaism. He made exclusive claims on their behalf which distinguished them from other reform groups. For example, reform groups like the Pharisees not only kept the Law of Moses, but guarded it by building a hedge around it, so as to ensure perfect observance of the inner core of the Law by vigilance of the extended and related issues. Jesus enjoined his reformed community to build its own hedge about the law, and he made claims that his way of observing the Law was the only perfect, total observance of it. In the "Antitheses" in the Sermon on the Mount, Jesus proclaimed the perfect keeping of the Law, which a) builds a hedge about the Law, and b) which distinguishes his teaching from all others. The form of the proclamation clearly signals all this: "You have heard it said of old...but I say to you." In substance, the perfect keeping of the Law must entail an extended keeping of the legal minimum. It is not enough to avoid murder or adultery: what is required is also an attitude which avoids anger (leading to murder) and lust (leading to adultery). Reform Christians, too, put a hedge around the Law. Their hedge, moreover, is better than that of the Pharisees.

The antithetical formulation ("It was said of old...but I say to you," 5:21, 27, 33, 38, 43) makes exclusive claims on Jesus' behalf, claims which distinguish Christians from their reform rivals, the Pharisees. This is brought out in Jesus' remark: "Unless your righteousness exceed that of the Scribes and the Pharisees, you will not enter the kingdom of God" (5:20). In keeping with this, we recall how in the Q source Jesus was constantly critical of reform Pharisees and other religious figures. In one extended passage alone, Jesus criticizes them for a host of things:

  a) they preach but do not practice (23:3),
  b) they burden others but do not help lift the burdens (23:4//Lk 11:46),
  c) they love the externals of the Law (23:5),
  d) they shut the kingdom against men (23:13//Lk 11:52),
  e) they fuss over the agricultural rules, but neglect the essence of the law (23:23//Lk 11:42),
  f) they are hypocrites: externally reformed but internally corrupt (23:25-28//Lk 11:39-41).

Jesus' constant criticism of his archrivals supports his own claim that his covenant group is the only authentic reform group. And its criticism serves constantly to distinguish his group from that of his rivals.

Jesus' reformed group, then, has a keen sense of perfection which distinguished it from Jewish non-members. Jesus requires that their fasting, prayer, and almsgiving be perfect as well as different from that of even the pious of Israel (6:1-18). They must distance themselves, moreover, from all unreformed folk, if not distancing themselves from others through their constant criticism of them. This extends even to their own membership. If there is an imperfect member, this imperfection or sin threatens to contaminate the whole reformed group and so must be separated from the perfect, holy covenant group. And so, Jesus demands that a contaminating eye be plucked out, a gangrenous foot amputated, and a polluted hand severed (5:29-30; 18:8-9). According to Jesus, sinners within the group should be immediately confronted and required to repent of their sin and so to be perfect again (5:21-22). Jesus himself is credited with establishing a procedure for this group to correct deviant members (18:15-18), a process which will lead either to reform or to expulsion.

According to Jesus' teaching, then, his followers consider themselves as the authentic Israel, the reformed core of true Jews of the covenant. Since it is a saintly, reformed group, it distances itself from other so-called reform groups and weak covenant members, as well as public sinners and Gentiles. There is no ambiguity about its self-understanding: they are the authentic, reformed elite. It is Jesus who tells his followers to think of themselves in this way.

EXPERIENCE

This stage of the Matthean community should be described as a reform movement in first-century Judaism. Alongside other reform movements, the Matthean community was claiming to have the special word of a unique prophet, Jesus, as the foundation of a new and purified way of thinking and living as a God's covenant people. This claim was not unchallenged, for there were other reform movements, such as the Pharisees. The Christian claims, however, were radical: they asserted that Jesus alone had taught the only correct way to be a Jew and that other proposed ways were wrong. These claims are fully reflected in the Christian demands for perfection and for radical purity of heart as well as hands. Christians made strong demands even on members of the group to be perfect or to face the judgment of the group. And part of the posture of this reform group was to identify sin and failures to be perfect wherever they existed. This led to an aggressive public posture which was judgmental and critical, both of group members and rivals alike. The experience of this community, then, may be characterized as critical, aggressive, perfection-oriented, and judgmental. The claims and standards of this group were strong and high. Such a posture was bound to produce a constant distancing of the group from its neighbors. And it is not surprising that its neighbors would, in turn, be critical of its claims and posture. Intense and prolonged friction was bound to exist as a result of the claims and postures of this group. It is not surprising, then, that Jesus utters a special beatitude to those who are rejected:

> Blessed are you when men revile you, and persecute you and utter all kinds of evil against you falsely on my account. Rejoice and be glad...for so men persecuted the prophets before you (5:11-12//Lk 6:22-23).

In modern jargon, we would call this group a "sect," a group which is defining itself against its neighbors and claiming to be the only elite group in its neighborhood.

We do not know much about the historical experience of this group. We know that it is an exclusively Jewish group, on Jewish soil (10:5). It is probably a group or series of groups living in Jewish villages, centered around the synagogue rather than the temple. There is no mention in the Q source of Temple, cult, priests or elite figures who presided over the chief religious center of Israel's faith in Jerusalem. Rather this early Matthean community is in competition with non-elite, would-be reformers, such as the Pharisees. The synagogue, not the Temple, is the arena; the issue is not cult but the purity of daily lives. Jesus' followers were engaged in a mighty process of self-definition. They are claiming to be the few worthy ones, the perfect keepers of covenant law, the authentic members of the reformed Israel. These claims define them, but imply an inevitable distancing of them from sinners, tax collectors, Gentiles, and even from fellow Jews. Self-definition means the erection of boundaries and the building of hedges around oneself. This is the primary experience of this early group.

CHRISTOLOGY

Christology is often equated among New Testament scholars with the titles of Jesus. The title of Jesus which occurs most frequently in this source of tradition in Matthew's gospel is the "Son of Man." And perhaps the clearest sense of its meaning is found in 11:19, where we are told about the rejection of God's prophets, John and Jesus. John displayed the more traditional prophetic behavior "neither eating or drinking" and they called him possessed (11:18//Lk 7:33). Alternately, the "Son of Man" came "eating and drinking" and they rejected him (11:19//Lk 7:34). The basic meaning, then, of "Son of Man" is *the rejected one.* Yet the rejected Son of Man is vindicated by God, just as Jonah was rescued from the whale by God (12:40//Lk 11:30). This Son of Man, moreover, is ironically transformed by God into the judge of those who rejected him: the Judged One becomes the Judge. And so it is as the vindicated Son of Man and Judge that Jesus is described in 24:27, 37-39 and 44//Lk 17:24, 26-30; 12:40. This title is appropriate to Jesus in these circumstances because it identifies his rejection in a proper apologetic way and links him to the rest of God's prophets. In fact, rejection becomes a touchstone of truth, proving that Jesus' word was distinctively different from the word of his rival and like the word of the prophets.

But titles alone do not tell half the story of Jesus in this stratum of the Matthean community's history. When we recall all that is attributed to Jesus in the Q source we have been studying, we get a much fuller portrait of Jesus. Jesus is perceived as proclaiming a radically reformed Torah, estab-

lishing his followers as the true Israel, the authentic covenant people. He is said to enjoin perfection and to build an
elaborate series of boundaries which distinguish the holy
covenant people from other less pious Jews and which
separate them from sinners and Gentiles. Jesus is perceived
as restricting membership in God's covenant people to Jews,
and especially to pious and perfect Jews. These actions
suggest a portrait of Jesus as a holy figure who reforms
God's sinful people and teaches an authentic Torah which
requires perfection of heart as well as hand.

Or we might more adequately say that according to these
early traditions, Jesus is the consummate prophet. He does
what prophets basically do: he identifies sin in the covenant
people, corrects it by a reform of covenant law; or failing
that, he proclaims God's imminent judgment on unrepentant sinners. These actions are just what we saw attributed
to Jesus in the description of his ministry according to the
categories used to recover the perspectives of the community just cited.

The reforming prophet was bound to be transformed into
the rejected Son of Man. For the claims of the reforming
prophet were a constant source of friction and judgment in
the Jewish village where Matthew's early community
resided. And rejection was in some sense a validation of the
reforming prophet; for a prophet should preach *not* peace
but war, *not* blessings but woes.

The portrait of Jesus implicit in the Q tradition seems
somewhat harsh and even distrubing at times. And this is so!
But we can also see how it corresponds adequately to the
experience and history of the early Jewish-Christian communities for whom it was an adequate view of Jesus. These
groups were basically Jewish-Christian groups, in intense
conflict with other Jewish groups and they distinguished
themselves as the only authentic and reformed covenant
people. This experience and self-understanding was con-
tributory to the shaping of the portrait of Jesus, the covenant leader, as an authentic and typical prophet, just like the
classical prophets who came to reform Israel. Like them, he

engaged in reforming actions; like them, he was rejected by all but the few righteous covenant members. There is, then, a basic congruence between the portrait of Jesus as reforming prophet and the exclusive and perfectionistic view of the covenant community reflected in the Q tradition.

II.
The Portrait of Jesus According to the Evangelist

We postulated that the Q tradition represents a relatively early tradition which was espoused and developed in an early Matthean community. And we noted that this early community can be distinguished from the later group for whom the evangelist edited the final draft of the gospel as we now have it. In the interval between these two versions, the Matthean community changed and changed radically. It did not continue to see itself as the exclusive and reformed Jewish covenant people; nor did it continue to preach Jesus as the prophet of this reform. Changes took place both in the community and in the world in which the community lived. For example, the larger Christian church to which the Matthean community belonged did not continue to shun and exclude Gentiles from membership, a move which had far-reaching implications for the sense of self-identity of all Christian groups. Second, the Roman-Jewish war climaxed with the destruction of the temple, which helped to crystallize a critical interpretation of Judaism from a Christian point of view. Finally, the Gospel of Mark was written which told of Jesus' directives about a radically different kind of covenant community. And Mark's gospel told a different Jesus story and proclaimed a different portrait of Jesus than the one found in the Q tradition.

These events impinged on the Matthean community and became part of its own experience and its own reflection and self-understanding. The internal changes within the Matthean community are more difficult to document, but we can clearly see the *effects* of these many changes, just as a photograph can show the vapor trails of nuclear particles when they collide. In practically every area, the later Matthean community took a different stand from the earlier group on topics such as membership, self-understanding, ethics, eschatology, etc. These changes were presumably well underway before the final redaction of the gospel as we now have it; for the strict early group had already sufficiently changed to be able to accept the Markan gospel without a wrenching crisis. The changes were already so substantial and pervasive that a figure in the mid 80s, whom we call Matthew the Evangelist, produced a redaction of the earlier traditions and of the Gospel of Mark which reflected the latest Matthean group's new view of itself as a covenant community and its different understanding of Jesus. We turn now to this later version of the gospel tradition in the Matthean community.

MISSION AND MEMBERSHIP

The later Matthean covenant community did *not* have a restricted sense of membership. In this later stratum, Jesus repeated to the Canaanite woman the earlier directive concerning restrictive membership: "I was sent only to the lost sheep of the house of Israel" (15:24). But by granting her the cure of her daughter, Jesus indicated that the former exclusive sense of membership was changed. She and her daughter are now included in the scope of God's blessings. This story and several others (see 21:41; 27:54) which speak of salvation extended to non-Jews, came to this community through Mark's gospel. Such ideas seemed to have been readily acceptable to the later Matthean group by that time. Not only were these stories incorporated from Mark by the evangelist, but Matthew also added materials on his own which favored inclusion of the Gentiles. For example, whereas Mk 1:14 noted that Jesus came to Galilee to start preaching, Mt 4:12-16 dilates on this by stressing that it is to the Galilean territory of Zebulun and Naphtali that Jesus came, thus fulfilling Isa 9:1-2 where Galilee is described as "gentile territory":

The Land of Zebulun and land of Naphtali,
toward the sea, across the Jordan,
Galilee of the Gentiles (4:15).

The insistence that Jesus himself preached to Gentiles is emphasized in the note of the evangelist that Jesus' fame spread "through all of Syria" and that great crowds "from Galilee and the Decapolis" followed him (4:25-26). According to Matthew, from the very beginning of Jesus' mission, he was *not* restricting God's word only to Jews.

The clearest examples of the new and welcome attitude to Gentiles come from the most significant places in the gospel text, viz., from its beginning and its end. In Mt 2:1-12, pagan Magi are summoned by God through the star and through dreams to come and worship Jesus. And in Mt 28:16-20, Jesus commissions the apostles to make "disciples of all nations." There is no doubt that this later Matthean community had a very inclusive view of mission and membership.

In keeping with this new sense of mission, one can see a welcome offered not only to Gentiles but also to unclean and marginal Jews. The earlier Matthean group, which was a perfect, reformed covenant group, excluded all contact with sinners and the like. But in the later community, Jesus exercises a dramatic ministry to sinners.

1. Jesus calls a tax collector, a public sinner, to be an intimate apostle (9:9).

2. Jesus tells the church "to leave the ninety-nine on the hillside and go in search of the one that went astray" (18:10-13), a posture incompatible with the early group's avoidance of all sin and uncleanness.

3. Jesus proclaims a doctrine of mercy and forgiveness to sinners. For example, he adds a gloss to the Our Father, which emphasizes just this issue: "If you forgive men their trespasses, your heavenly Father will also forgive you; but if you do not...neither will your heavenly Father forgive you" (6:14-15).

4. Jesus actually forgives sins; he says to the paralytic: "Take heart; your sins are forgiven" (9:2). By healing the paralytic, he proves that "the Son of Man has authority on earth to forgive sins" (9:6), and authority which is also "given to men" (9:8). Jesus refused Peter's request for a limit to the number of times a group member must forgive an errant sister or brother: "I do not say to you seven times but seventy times seven" (18:22). The subsequent parable about mercy (18:23-35) only confirms this teaching.

5. In the parable about guests invited to the king's feast, Matthew's version states that when the invited guests refused to come, the king sent the messengers out to gather "all whom they could find, *both good and bad*" (22:10).

There is no doubt that the membership of the later Matthean community has changed. No longer just Jews, now Gentiles, too. No longer just the perfect and reformed, now sinners, too.

Inclusive membership extends to classes of people who were marginal to the reform group's sense of perfection. People who were physically defective were also classified as unholy (see Lev 21:18-20). As physically imperfect, they could not attain perfection according to Jewish standards. Yet in the later Matthean group, Jesus conducts a ministry among these very people, signaling God's full acceptance of them as covenant members.

1. Lepers are cleansed (8:1-4).
2. The lame are healed (9:1-8).
3. The blind are given sight (20:29-34).
4. A menstruating woman, the archetype of uncleanness in Israel, is made whole (9:20-26).
5. The dumb are made to speak and hear (9:32-33).

According to the perspective of the later evangelist, Jesus authorized and practiced a truly inclusive mission; he formally revoked the exclusive sense of membership of the earlier period. Now the Christian covenant community consciously accepted Jew and Gentile, perfect and sinner, whole and sick, good and bad.

OLD TESTAMENT

One of the major differences between the early and later communities is the understanding and use of the Hebrew scriptures. As was the case with the earlier Matthean group, there is no question but that the Old Testament scriptures are still valid as God's word. The difference between the views of the early and later groups lies in the new sense that the Hebrew scriptures are now a basically prophetic document which prophecy is fulfilled in Jesus and the new covenant people. How often in the later edition of Matthew do we find the formula: "This was to fulfil what was written in the scriptures..." (1:22; 2:5; 3:3; etc.). This formula introduces a citation from the scriptures which is seen as directly related to Jesus' actions as prophecy is to fulfilment. The following diagram lists many of the major passages from the scriptures which Matthew sees as directly fulfilled by Jesus:

Matthew	*Old Testament*
1. 1:23	Isa 7:14
2. 2:6	Micah 5:2
3. 2:18	Jer 31:15
4. 3:3	Isa 40:2
5. 4:15-15	Isa 9:1-2
6. 8:17	Isa 53:4
7. 9:13	Hos 6:6
8. 11:10	Mal 3:1
9. 12:7	Hos 6:6
10. 12:18-21	Isa 42:1-4
11. 13:14-15	Isa 6:9-10
12. 13:35	Ps 78:2
13. 15:7-9	Isa 29:13
14. 21:4-5	Isa 62:1; Zech 9:9
15. 21:16	Ps 8:2
16. 21:42	Ps 118:22-23

17. 22:43-44 . . . . Ps 110:1
18. 26:31 . . . . Zech 13:7
19. 27:9 . . . . Zech 11:12-13

This perspective might be expected of Old Testament prophetic materials (Isaiah, Jeremiah, Hosea), but Jesus is said to indicate that even the legal books of the Old Testament are "prophetic" as well: "All the prophets *and the law prophesied* until John" (11:13).

Complementing this fundamentally prophetic understanding of the Scriptures is a different sense of the validity even of the legal prescriptions of the Bible. Whereas the earlier group built a hedge around the Law so as to keep all the laws as perfectly as possible, the later group tended to focus on the permanent validity of the essential covenant law, the Ten Commandments. They are the divine ordinances which one must keep to enter life:

> You shall not kill.
> You shall not commit adultery.
> You shall not steal.
> You shall not bear false witness.
> Honor your father and you mother (19:18-19).

This same sense of the essential covenant law is reflected in the distinctive Matthean list of vices found in 15:19-20. It is argued there that being "clean" before God is interpreted by some as focused in the extended rites such as the washing of hands, part of the hedge around the law (15:1-2). But Christians are told that only failure to keep the basic covenant code will render one "unclean" before God. It helps to grasp the structure of the list of vices catalogued by the evangelist in 15:19 by comparing them with the Ten Commandments.

Exodus 20:12-17   *Matthew 15:19*
Honor your father and mother
You shall not kill . . . . murder
You shall not commit adultery . . . . fornication

You shall not commit covet.......theft
You shall not bear false witness ...false witness, slander

Of course, Jesus objects to the Pharisees' disregard of "Honor your father and mother" (15:4-6), which, because it is being violated, belongs in consideration with the vice list in 15:19. No, the evangelist's community has a very clear covenant law, the basic law for all of God's people. It does not espouse "lawlessness." But it has a much more restricted sense of the correct covenant law than did the earlier Matthean group (cf. Antitheses, 5:21-48).

There is a fundamental hermeneutical principle articulated in this later stage of Matthew's community which points to what the evangelist saw as the core or essence of the covenant law: "love of neighbor." This summary, overriding law is found in Lev 19:18; but it becomes the distinctive hallmark of the evangelist's group, distinguishing it from the Pharisees and their insistence on the perfect keeping of all the laws equally. "Love of neighbor" summarizes the covenant law (19:18); it is the greatest commandment (22:39). In response to Pharisaic claims that certain Old Testament laws are normative for all righteous people, such as Sabbath observance, Jesus is credited with citing a passage from Hosea, which reflects the essential impulse of God's law: "If you had known what this means, *I desire mercy, not sacrifice*" (12:7/Hos 6:6). This same text of Hosea is used to justify Jesus' table fellowship with sinners and tax collectors (9:13). Jesus not only proclaimed covenant love as the fundamental law of the later Matthean covenant, he also gave an example of it in the feeding of the hungry on that Sabbath. Covenant love, then, is the fundamental law of Jesus for the Matthean covenant community; it is summarized in the Leviticus injunction to "Love your neighbor as yourself." As Jesus remarked, "Whatever you wish that men would do to you, do so to them; for this is the law and the prophets" (7:12).

The scriptures, then, are still valid for the later Matthean community. But they are basically interpreted by Jesus as a document prophetic of Jesus and his followers. Yet this later community is not "lawless," even if it ceased to see the legal sections of the Old Testament as still binding on it; for Jesus regards as permanently valid the essential covenant law: a) the Ten Commandments, and b) the Christian expression of them in the "Law of Love."

ESCHATOLOGY

One can detect in the later edition of Matthew notable changes in the attitudes about eschatology. There is still a strong sense of judgment but the scenario for judgment is quite different. Whereas Jesus enjoined on the earlier group the practice of internal judgment and correction of imperfect members, in the later stratum of the gospel tradition Jesus is said to command a sense of tolerance and forgiveness of wayward members. This shift led to the realization that all judgment should be left in God's or Jesus' hands. Judgment will indeed come, and sinners will most assuredly be held to account (see 22:11-14); but judgment is the prerogative of the Lord of the Covenant, not of the prophets of the group. It is the Lord Jesus who will execute judgment when he sends out his holy angels to do his judgment (13:30, 49-50; 24:30-31).

Even as all judgment is put in the hands of the Covenant Lord, the imminence of his judgment is less urgently affirmed in the later stratum. There is evidence of a sense of delay in the scenario of the earlier Christian tradition about the coming judgment of the Son of Man. We hear of a steward who boasts that "my master is delayed" (24:48) and so begins to live riotously in light of that delay. The sense of delay is heightened in the parable of the Ten Maidens who wait and even "sleep," awaiting the long-delayed coming of the Bridegroom (25:5).

And so, the Jesus of the later Matthean tradition teaches an eschatological doctrine which is considerably different from that attributed to Jesus in the earlier stratum:

a) all judgment is left to Jesus, not to the church's prophets or leaders,

b) judgment is neither imminent or immediately desired, for a great period of evangelization is begun, and time is needed to bring all into the kingdom, "both good and bad" (22:10),

c) as forgiveness and mercy are preached, judgment is downplayed and there is even a sense of the delay of judgment.

ETHICS

Unlike the earlier group, the later Matthean community no longer considered perfect observance of all the Old Testament laws as its chief virtue. Nor in its sense of perfection did it distance itself from non-reformed people, sinners and tax collectors alike. Its premier value is covenant love, which is expressed as forgiveness, mercy and charity. For example, Jesus is said to append a gloss to the Our Father which dilated on the part of the prayer which prays for forgiveness. Prayer for God's forgiveness (6:12) would be vacuous if it were not accompanied by a personal exercise of the same forgiveness toward others, "For if you forgive men their trespasses, your heavenly father will also forgive you; but if you do not forgive men, neither will your heavenly father forgive your trespasses" (6:14-15). In striking contrast to the earlier group's horror at the presence of scandal and sin within the covenant group (18:6-9, 15-18), is the positive advice from Jesus on forgiveness (18:21-35). How many times should we forgive offending members? Is there a limit? "Seventy times seven," Jesus says, indicating a radically more tolerant attitude to sinners within the group (18:22).

Whereas the chief virtue of the earlier group was avoidance of sin, the building of boundaries to protect the holy group from outsiders, and judgment on sin, in the later group Jesus sees sinners as invited to God's covenant table (22:9-10; 9:10-13). And so, a greater toleration is urged by

Jesus. This is exemplified in the parable of the lost sheep. The Christian group is now told by Jesus to act like shepherds and to go in search for "the one sheep that went astray" (18:12). This is a new command by Jesus which supercedes his earlier injunction to be "perfect as your heavenly father is perfect" (5:48). Now the will of God is clear: "It is not the will of my heavenly Father that one of these little ones should perish" (18:14). In short, the motto of the later community may be summed up in Jesus' word: "do unto others as you would have them do unto you: this is the law and the prophets" (7:12).

If the premier virtue which Jesus urges is mercy, tolerance and forgiveness, then the vice he most condemns is a judgmental attitude to sinners, foreigners and unclean people. Numerous crises arise in the later strata of the gospel in which Jesus sides with sinners, and in which merciful action provokes controversy and criticism. For example, Jesus ate with tax collectors and sinners, an action unthinkable for those whose chief value was perfection and the avoidance of all things sinful and unclean. Jesus justified his action by claiming the role of a doctor: "Those who are well have no need of a physician, but those who are sick" (9:12//Mk 2:17). The encounter concludes with a reproach for those of the perfection standard: "Go and learn what this means: 'I desire mercy, not sacrifice'" (9:13/Hos 6:6). What is pleasing to God is not the perfect avoidance of uncleanness, but compassion and forgiveness. In a similar situation, Jesus defends his disciples' eating grain on the Sabbath, "for they were hungry." When reproached for this lapse from perfection, Jesus criticized those who criticized him: "If only you had known what this means: 'I desire mercy, and not sacrifice,' you would not have condemned the guiltless" (12:7). When Jesus criticizes or judges, he does so on the basis of a *lack* of mercy or compassion. For example, Jesus criticizes the Pharisees, not for their keeping of the law, but for omitting "justice, mercy, and faith" (23:23). Even community members will be judged before the throne of the Son of Man on whether they have shown covenant love to needy community members, giving water to the thirsty, clothing to the naked, and food to the hungry (25:31ff). Lack of mercy (18:23-35), lack of forgiveness (9:12-13), and lack of covenant love (25:41-45; 15:4-5) are all heavily censured by Jesus in the later Matthean group.

GROUP SELF-UNDERSTANDING

Even at this later time, Matthew's community still considered itself within the orbit of God's plan to gather a covenant people to himself. No longer does this group define itself as the authentic, reformed covenant people because of its perfect keeping of the Law of Moses. Rather, it takes its identity from a different sense of covenant found in the Scriptures. It comes to see itself as the fulfilment of the "covenants of promise" (Eph 2:12) made to Abraham and David. New Testament critics generally make a distinction between two types of covenant in the Hebrew scriptures: 1) a *covenant of promise* made to Abraham (Gen 15) and David (2 Sam 7), based on God's free and unconditional election, and 2) a *covenant of obedience* made to Moses (Ex 20), based on the observance of the covenant law. With its insistence on the perfect keeping of Moses' law, the early Matthean community saw itself in line with the covenant with Moses. The later community, however, defined itself in terms of the covenants made with Abraham and David. In the genealogy of Matthew, for example, there is no mention of Moses; but Jesus' descent is traced to the founders of the covenants of promise: "The book of the genealogy of Jesus Christ, the Son of David, the Son of Abraham" (1:1, 17).

The shift in covenant models also shows up in the sense of a newness proclaimed by Jesus in this later stratum of the gospel text. Jesus declares obsolete old practices, so appropriate to the old covenant. Fasting, for example, is no longer in force "because the bridegroom is with them" (9:15; contrast with 6:16-18). According to Jesus, new cloth is not used to patch old clothes, nor is new wine put in old skins (9:16-17). Thus Jesus proclaims a radical sense of newness as part of the self-understanding of his covenant community.

The distinctive sense of newness is clearly brought out in two pivotal passages, 16:17-19 and 28:16-20. In response to Simon Peter's confession (16:16), Jesus acclaims him as the foundation stone of "my church," that is, my distinctive, new covenant people. And at the end of the gospel, the Risen Jesus commissions the apostles to make disciples of all nations, "teaching them to observe all that I have commanded you" (28:20). These are not the words of one who is merely reforming the old covenant, but of one who is establishing a new and different covenant people for God. For, as we shall shortly see, Jesus' new teaching will be distinctively different from the practices of the old covenant community. Sabbath observance will be different (12:1-8); marriage will be indissoluble (19:1-19); sins will be forgiven (18:21-35); Christian purity rites will replace Jewish washing rituals (28:19 15:1-20).

This sense of a new and different covenant is confirmed for this group by Jesus' negative judgment on the old covenant. In the vineyard parable, the community is told of the old covenant's rejection of God's most special messenger, God's Son; that rejection resulted in the old covenant's rejection by God: "Therefore I tell you, the kingdom of God will be taken away from you and given to a nation producing the fruits of it" (21:43). In this same parable one hears of the retributive destruction of the city of those who rejected God's messengers, "He will put those wretches to a miserable death" (21:41), even as he lets the vineyard to other tenants. In the very next episode in Matthew, a second parable is told which repeats this basic message. The invited guests reject wave after wave of invitations to the king's banquet, and so they are rejected and requited; "The king was angry and sent his troops and destroyed those murderers and burned their city" (22:7). They are replaced by a fresh batch of invitees, "both the good and the bad," who are gathered from the thoroughfares (22:9-10). The old covenant people are reproached and requited for continually rejecting God's prophets (23:32-36). And so the way is open for Jesus to gather a new covenant people to God.

This later Matthean community, then, understood itself as a new and different covenant people. This group's most

precious ritual, the Eucharist, celebrates the formation of a
"new covenant" in the blood of Jesus. Not like the old
covenant made with the blood of animals, the new covenant
bonds God and Jesus' covenant group in his own blood. In
fact, bonding with God can only be had in the blood of
Jesus.

We can now begin to summarize the extensive and sharp
contrasts in the teaching attributed to Jesus in the earlier
and later strata of the Matthean community.

Early Matthean Group   *Later Matthean Group*

1.
MEMBERSHIP AND MISSION

a) Jews only . . . . a) Jews and Gentiles

b) the few, worthy ones . . . . b) good and bad, clean and
unclean, saints and sinners

2.
OLD TESTAMENT

a) OT as legal document . . . . a) OT as prophetic document

b) hedged about by tradition . . . . . . b) rejection of custom/
and customs   tradition

c) all of OT laws in force . . . . c) essential Law of Love
in force

3.
ESCHATOLOGY

a) imminent & sure judgment . . . . . a) future, even distant
judgment

b) prophetic judgment of . . . . b) all judgment put in Jesus'
the church and by the church   hands, not those of the
church

4.
ETHICS

a) virtue: perfection & separation . . a) virtue: mercy &
from sin, evil and uncleanness   forgiveness

b) vice: hypocrisy and scandal . . . . b) vice: lack of charity

5.
GROUP SELF-UNDERSTANDING

a) reformed, authentic .... a) new covenant group
   covenant group
b) based on Mosaic model........ b) based on promises to
   of covenant   Abraham and David

Any portrait of Jesus in Matthew's gospel must include the teaching attributed to him. And the preceding sketch of the different attitudes and instructions of Jesus on key topics indicates the extent of the difference in the two portraits of Jesus contained in the one text of Matthew.

EXPERIENCE

We must next ask a very difficult question. What was the experience of the later stratum of Matthew's community which formed the context for the change in the portrait of Jesus? What events and circumstances impinged on it? While it is difficult to be overly precise about the exact details of the new situation of Matthew, some key factors can be noted.

First: *the Fall of Jerusalem*. In the Jewish-Roman war of 70 AD, the holy city and its Temple were sacked and destroyed. Clearly the destruction of the locus of God's worship, the profanation of the place where God dwelt, and the ruin of the visible center of Israel's religion was bound to send profound shock waves through Jewish and Christian groups. The Fall of Jerusalem was an event of such importance that it begged for an explanation. Two related explanations were given in the course of early Christian history. a) In the earlier Q source, Jerusalem's destruction was predicted by Jesus; it was expected as an act of God's judgment on Israel for the rejection of God's messengers: "Jerusalem, Jerusalem, killing the prophets and stoning those sent to you... Behold your house is forsaken and desolate" (23:37-38//Lk 13:34-35). This prophetic judgment of Jesus is reflected also in the parable of the Marriage Feast where the guests first invited to the feast "seized the messengers, treated them shamefully, and killed them" (22:6). In response to this evil deed, the king acted in judgment: "He sent his troops and destroyed those murderers and burned their city" (22:7). In the earlier traditions, then, Jesus himself heralded the fall of Jerusalem as a coming, prophetic judgment which is being called down upon a sinful Israel. b) A second explanation appears later via the Markan Parable of the Vineyard. The tenants of the vineyard reject the messengers sent to them, including the Son of the owner of the vineyard (Mt 21:37-39//Mk 12:3-8). In turn the owner of the vineyard "will put those wretches to death and let out the vineyard to other tenants who will give him the fruits in their seasons" (Mt 21:41//Mk 12:9). Thus the fall of Jerusalem is expanded in scope, coming as retribution for Israel which proved unfaithful to its covenant Lord and so was judged; a new covenant people was sought by God to replace them, which echoes the missionary expansion of the church.

Whereas in the early explanation, Jesus is basically said to pronounce a future judgment on those who reject God's prophets, in the later explanation Jesus is said to suggest that a new covenant people is formed in the aftermath of the judgment of Israel. In the forming of a new covenant people, one hears a note of self-legitimation by the later Matthean group: *we* are the authentic Israel; *we* are the replacement of the old, sinful covenant people; *we* are now God's elect. The fall of Jerusalem was an occasion for further self-definition.

Second: *Mission*, especially to the Gentiles. Perhaps the most formative influence for the later Matthean group is the radical opening of the church to the Gentiles. This process was well under way in Paul's time (50s-60s) and is celebrated in Mark's gospel. By the time of the last edition of Matthew, the pluralistic composition of the Christian covenant community was an established fact. As we noted earlier, the change in membership from a reformed, Torah-based group of Jewish saints to a covenant of "good and bad" (22:10) Jews and Gentiles was a most radical shift.

The later Matthean group, moreover, was intensely missionary, considerably more so than the early group. The scope of the mission was wider: not just Jews but Gentiles too, not just to Israel but to the ends of the earth. The impact of this opening of the church must have been like the American experience when the non-propertied classes were enfranchised and when women were given the right to vote. Many more people were involved who thought and acted differently than the more elite class which first comprised the group.

Third: *Self-Definition*. The early Matthean group was in constant friction with the synagogue. As a reform group, it heralded its program as better than that of its rivals, the Pharisees. Accentuating its good points and attacking its rivals' weaknesses, the Christian group began the process of self-definition. Scholars suggest that in the later years, the Matthean group clearly separated itself from the synagogue and became independent and free-standing. This process seems to be largely over by the time of the later Matthean group. But we still read of great friction between Jew and Christian, between Pharisees and Jesus. The tension between the synagogue and the Christian covenant group must be expected to continue for centuries to come (e.g. Justin Martyr and Trypho the Jew). The Jewish renaissance which arose after the fall of Jerusalem would surely grow increasingly critical of all Jews who did not share its program, Christian Jews included. And the Christian group would surely continue to define itself vis-à-vis the old covenant people, especially after the destruction of Jerusalem. The critical difference between the way the earlier Christian group defined itself and the way the later Matthean group did the same, lies in the conviction of the later group that it is a "new" covenant. The War of 70 proved to be the event that ended the chances of the old Israel; it is now replaced by a new covenant group which is founded on the covenant blood of Jesus (26:26) and which accepts Jesus' teaching as its Torah.

Fourth: *Mark's Gospel*. The earlier Matthean group was shaped around the Q tradition, with its particular perspectives and its distinctive portrait of Jesus. Many years later the next generation of this group found a new and different way of thinking and talking about Jesus through the Gospel of Mark. A new story about Jesus was shaped by Mark and the community for which he wrote, a story which the later community found acceptable and useful. The advent of this new gospel in Matthew's later community surely had a great impact on it. For it gave the later Matthean community fresh ways of understanding itself and its covenant Lord. The new Jesus story stressed a) miracles, especially healings of Israel's unclean and marginal folk, b) forgiveness of sins not judgment, c) inclusion of Gentiles, d) replacement of cultic laws by the law of love, and other new perspectives. Although it must be presupposed that Matthew's later group was aleady open to many of these new ideas, the appearance of a new literary form, the gospel, and the new story of Jesus which it told, gave permission to the Matthean group to revise its portrait of Jesus. And so the later Matthean group found in the Markan gospel a charter for its own development, a legitimation for it and a further impetus to its own growth. The gospel of Mark served as a powerful catalyst to the Matthean church, a new way of seeing its own change and development legitimated in the new Jesus story.

CHRISTOLOGY

Even if one is restricted to the titles of Jesus, the later Matthean group would differ from the earlier one which acclaimed Jesus as prophet and Son of Man. Pre-eminent in the later community are the acclamations of Jesus as covenant leader such as Christ, Son of David, Lord, and Son of God. All of these titles speak of Jesus' commissioned role vis-à-vis God's covenant people. It is not enough to investigate the Jewish background of these titles, as inconclusive as that may prove at some times. Rather, the contextual meaning and function of these titles is of prime importance for an evaluation of the portrait of Jesus in this later community.

1. *Christ* . In acclaiming Jesus as "Christ," the evangelist has basically followed the traditions found in Mark's narra-

tive. Peter confesses that Jesus is not merely a prophet but is "Christ, the Son of God" (16:16). The Sanhedrin questions Jesus: "If you are the Christ, the Son of God..." (26:63); Barabbas is contrasted with Jesus, "who is called Christ" (27:17, 22). To these instances, the evangelist has added the designation of Jesus as Christ in the genealogy (1:16, 17); "the Christ" is sought by the Magi (2:4). Essentially this title designates Jesus as God's anointed one, a holy figure who is established as leader of God's covenant people. One of the key places where Jesus is called Christ is the response of Jesus to the Baptizer's disciples who were sent to Jesus after hearing of "the deeds of the Christ" (11:2). Jesus' acts of righteousness and salvation for God's covenant people are the functional expression of what it means to be "anointed" for service and leadership of God's people. "Christ," moreover, is a title appropriate for a Gentile audience as well, inasmuch as the Magi come in search of God's "Anointed One" (2:4).

2. *Son of David*. More important to this evangelist is the acclamation of Jesus as Son of David, that is, the legitimate ruler of God's people. Great attention is paid to Jesus' genealogical place in David's line, both in the formal genealogy (1:1, 17) and through Joseph, whom the angel from heaven addresses as "Joseph, son of David" (1:20). The crowds welcoming Jesus into the royal city confess him as "Son of David" (21:9, 15). These references all serve to validate Jesus as the fulfilment of the ancient promises to David that a son of his line would be the Shepherd of God's covenant people.

The naming of Jesus as "Son of David" also serves a second function, viz., to stress Jesus as the fulfilment of the covenant promises to David. Hence the Davidic model of covenant is quietly being asserted as the way Jesus' followers are to view themselves. Not Moses' covenant, but the covenant with Abraham and David is the proper way of describing Jesus vis-à-vis God's saving plans. This serves to distinguish Jesus' followers from the synagogue.

Calling Jesus "Son of David" means also that one sees Jesus fulfilling the role of David, which was that of Shepherd of God's people. But what's a Davidic Shepherd to do? Jesus is repeatedly called " Son of David" in healing contexts, which has led one scholar to speak of a "therapeutic Son of David." Two blind men beg a share of God's covenant blessings as they approach Jesus for this favor: "Have mercy on us, Son of David" (9:22; see also 20:30-31). When the blind and dumb demoniac was cured, the crowds are led to inquire about Jesus, "Can this be the Son of David?" (12:23), the one who mediates God's unconditional covenant blessings to the people. Even pagans are portrayed as asking for a share of those blessings in acclaiming Jesus as Son of David, as did the Canaanite woman, "Have mercy on me, O Lord, Son of David" (15:22). The honorific title clearly has important functions in this version of the gospel; it is frequently linked with healings, thus underscoring Jesus' therapeutic role vis-à-vis God's people. Inasmuch as it is used by pagan as well, it suggests that the people for whom Jesus is covenant leader includes Jews and pagans alike. And "Son of David" serves to distinguish Jesus' followers from the synagogue who would celebrate the covenant made with Moses.

3. *Son of God* . When we consider the meaning of "Son of God" as used of Jesus, we are retracing much of the ground we have already covered. For "Son of God" denotes a figure who is divinely commissioned, even a covenant leader. Hence at his baptism and again at the transfiguration, Jesus is acclaimed as "My beloved son" (3:17; 17:5), that is, as the one who is directly authorized by God to preach the coming kingdom and to lead God's people. In Matthew, "Son of God" is basically equivalent in function to "Christ." In Matthew's version of Peter's confession, Jesus is "Christ, the Son of the living God" (16:16); the High Priest asks Jesus if he is "the Christ, the Son of God" (26:63). Like "Christ" and "Son of David," "Son of God" reflects Jesus' commissioned role as leader of God's people. In this vein, then, the references to him as King of Israel are but further indications of the church's sense of Jesus as ruler of God's covenant people (see 2:2; 21:5; 25:34; 27:11, 29, 37, 42).

4. *Lord* . In many places Jesus is called "Lord" *(kyrios)*.

Although this may be a polite honorific title which means "Sir," there is a much richer level of meaning attached to it. If we start with the climactic scence in 28:16-20, we see that, although Jesus is not formally called "Lord" here, he is invested with maximum authority vis-à-vis God's people, which is the content of the title. We follow the recurrence of the term "all/every" (in Greek, *pas*) in this passage, for it holds the key to understanding Jesus' unique position: a) "*all* power in heaven and earth" is given to him (28:18); b) the apostles are to make disciples "of *all* nations" (28:19); c) Jesus' converts are to observe "*all* that I have commanded you" (28:20a); and d) Jesus is with them "*all* days, even to the close of the age" (28:20b). He is Lord of all people, ruling for all time, authoritative teacher of all, because God has given him all authority: he is Lord of the covenant people.

From this exalted perspective, we re-evaluate the way Matthew's later covenant community looks to Jesus for power, healing and teaching. He is the "Lord" who makes a leper clean (8:2); who heals a sick servant (8:6) and cured a possessed son (17:15). As "Lord," then, he dispenses God's healing to the covenant people. He is also the "Lord" who saves his disciples in a storm (8:25) and who reaches out to Peter as he sinks into the sea (14:30). As "Lord," he will come to judge the world (24:42). These diverse aspects all speak of Jesus' Lordship in relation to a covenant people, viz., his authority and leadership of the covenant group.

And so the diverse titles in this stratum of the gospel all point in the same direction to Jesus as the honorable, official and definitive covenant leader. He is not a peasant, but the royal leader, the Son of David. He is not a sinful apostate, but the one whom God himself has anointed, "the Christ." He is no upstart pretender, but the fulfilment of God's ancient promise to David (see 1:22-23; Isa 7:14). He is not ruler for Jews only, but Shepherd of Jews and Gentiles alike. As one whose blood formed a covenant bond between God and his followers, he is mediator of that covenant (26:28). As God's anointed one, he established a covenant people on a rock, Simon Peter (16:17). But he is the unique and supreme Lord of God's covenant people, replacing scribe, priest and Pharisee; for he possesses all authority, for all time, calling all people into this covenant relationship with God.

5. *Miracles*. As important as the titles are, it is imperative that we observe what Jesus does and says to gain a full and adequate portrait of him in this community's preaching. One of the striking differences between the early and later traditions in Matthew's gospel is the new importance of Jesus' healing miracles. In the Q tradition, there is only a terse summary of healings (11:2-5) and only one narrative which alludes to a miracle (8:5-13//Lk 7:1-10) — not much interest in miracles at all. Evidently miracles were of minor importance in that earlier telling of the Jesus story. But in the evangelist's portrayal of Jesus, miracles assume a pivotal position. The evangelist basically incorporated Mark's miracle stories into his own narrative. But he gave them a significance which they did not have for Mark. They are "the deeds of the Christ" (11:2), his covenant blessings on the covenant people. They are not restricted to Jews only; but as covenant membership is extended to Gentiles, so are God's miracles (4:24-25; 15:20-28). They are performed on people who, according to the perfection-oriented standards of the early community, were unclean and separated from the holy or perfect group. For example, lepers (8:7), menstruating women (9:20-21) and dead bodies (9:25) are touched and cured by Jesus.

The miracles, moreover, are given special interpretation by the evangelist. For he has added numerous interpretive comments to them. First, after Jesus "healed all who were sick," Matthew interprets this as the fulfilment of Isaiah's prophecy, "He took our infirmities and bore our diseases" (8:17/Isa 53:4). Again, Jesus styled himself as the physician who was sent to those in need, not to the healthy or the perfect (9:12-13). In a third instance, Jesus showed compassion on the crowds, "healing every disease and every infirmity;" for the crowds were helpless and harrassed, like sheep without a shepherd (9:36). Finally, Jesus is the

Servant of Isaiah 42, who does not "break the bruised reed or quench the smoldering wick" (12:19/Isa 42:3). The miracles, then, speak of the compassion of the covenant leader and of his concern with the normal daily lives of a needy, even unclean people. As David and other kings shepherded God's people, feeding, protecting, and teaching them, so David's true son is the source of God's covenant blessings to this new people. The miracles are the perfect illustration of this leadership.

6. *Savior*. Support for this is found in the heralding of Jesus as the one who would "save" his people from their sins (1:21). His name means "savior"; he pours out his blood in forgiveness for the errant neighbor (6:14-15; 18:21-35). Linked with this is the proclamation of mercy as God's prime command. The strict keeping of the Sabbath yields to the demands of the needy (12:1-3); strict table separation from sinners is moderated in consideration of their being led to conversion (9:10-14). It is Jesus who establishes the principle, "I desire mercy, not sacrifice" (9:13; 12:7). Thus Jesus' healing miracles of unclean folk and his forgiveness of sins are two sides of the same coin. Jesus is Israel's Savior.

In the earlier stratum, Jesus was primarily a prophet who proclaimed a reformed Torah with a firm hedge about it, who identified sin, who called for correction or judgment, and who preached exclusively to the few, worthy Jews. In the later community, Jesus' mission is one of touching and healing what is unclean, sick or sinful — not avoidance of such. He proclaims a new Torah whose focus is on mercy, forgiveness and love — not on a perfect keeping of the Old Testament law. He is King to Gentiles, Physician to sinners, and Shepherd to the sick and unclean; for his covenant is radically more inclusive than the earlier Matthean group. And so Jesus is not merely a prophetic reformer of the old covenant, but the anointed Lord whom God authorizes to gather a new covenant people.

Conclusion

Although the contours of the new portrait of Jesus by the evangelist and final redactor of the gospel are clear, one must ask how so different a portrait could emerge and exist side-by-side with the earlier portrait in the same document. It is not merely a question of different sources, as though Mark and Matthew had better or newer sources of information about Jesus than the Q source. The difference in portraits lies less in sources than in the changing history and experience of the two communities which articulated the story of Jesus in such different ways. For the more sectarian early community, Jesus was perceived as a prophetic figure whose banner was holiness, reform, perfection, and separation from evil. This is a preaching about Jesus commensurate with the experience of an exclusively Jewish community in tension with other Jewish communities also claiming to be reform movements. For the later community, Jesus was preached as the leader who opened the covenant to all people, Jews and Gentiles, saints and sinners. His banner was appropriately toleration, forgiveness, and mercy. The Christian covenant group which told this story of Jesus had moved beyond competition with Jewish synagogues, for it understood itself as a new covenant, both more inclusive than Israel and less obsessed with perfection. It was a group based on the "covenant of promise" (see Eph 2:12), not a covenant of law. Abraham and David are its patron saints, not Moses. The later portrait of Jesus as covenant Lord, as David's successor, as Christ and Shepherd, is coherent with the new experience and self-understanding of the later Matthean community.

As we pointed out in the first chapter, the new portrait of Jesus may be understood from a practical, pastoral point of view. We recall the hints offered by Vatican II about the formation of the gospels. The sacred authors *selected* some of the many things handed on about Jesus, *reduced* them to a synthesis, and *explicated* some things in view of the situation of their churches (*Dei Verbum*, #19). The story of Jesus was articulated in view of the different circumstances and the different experiences in which the believing community found itself.

Chapter Four

THE CHRISTOLOGY OF LUKE-ACTS

Turning to the Third Gospel, we must remember to adjust the lenses of our glasses, for Luke's gospel will tell us a story of Jesus quite different from that of Mark and Matthew. To understand Luke's distinctiveness, it is helpful to remember some basic facts about Luke and his gospel.

First, Luke has written two volumes, the Gospel and Acts. This means that he has a large historical perspective which does not end with Jesus' resurrection, but extends over the history of the early church. And in retelling the story of the early church, Luke is quite aware of radical changes which took place in regard to the membership of the Christian covenant community and in regard to the way members would act. It took a heavenly vision to convince Peter that God's covenant included both Jews and Gentiles (Acts 10-11); Peter and others initially protested that this went against the way they formerly understood covenant membership. And so, there is consciousness of a major change. Second, at a solemn convention of the early church, it was discussed whether new converts were to be circumcized and made to keep the traditional law of the Mosaic covenant. The group decided against those distinguishing Jewish customs. Again, there is consciousness of a major change. This suggests that we view Luke as a writer who surveyed the growth of the early church, especially with an eye to its development and adaptation. Change is no stranger to Luke.

Second, Luke and the community for whom he writes know of earlier traditions about Jesus, both the Q document and the gospel of Mark. This is an assured result of modern biblical scholarship. And this means that Luke knows two quite different portraits of Jesus which these sources present. Again, Luke is no stranger to diversity. This suggests that, inasmuch as Luke knows diverse sources, his distinctiveness may be credited to a conscious editorial activity on his part. He did not mindlessly reproduce his sources, but edited them and even went beyond their perspective.

Third, Luke writes late in the first century, after the Roman-Jewish war and after the writing of the gospel of Mark. He reflects the state of the Christian groups well after the missionary thrust to the Gentiles was begun. As Acts shows, Luke knows the broad sweep of the history of the early Christians. This surely implies that he is sensitive to the current historical issues of his own day.

Fourth, Luke is rightly called an historian. He is author not only of the preaching about Jesus, which is the Third Gospel, but also of the Acts of the Apostles, an account of the faith and growth of the covenant-in-Jesus. Luke, then, paints a large canvas. His claim to be called an historian does not mean that he has better facts about Jesus than did Mark or Matthew. Luke, for example, was not the private secretary of Mary, the Mother of Jesus. We know that he was careful about the data, as all historians are; for he tells us about his awareness of previous accounts and his concern "to follow all things closely":

> Inasmuch as many have undertaken to compile a narrative of the things which have been accomplished among us, just as they were delivered to us by those who from the

beginning were eyewitnesses and ministers of the word...(Lk 1:12).

But an historian in antiquity was no mere collector of facts and anecdotes; rather an ancient historian is best described as one who strove to see patterns in history and to express in a philosophical or religious way how the miscellaneous events and pieces of information fit together in a coherent way. Luke expresses this in the prologue to his gospel when he says: "It seemed good to me also, having followed all things accurately for some time past, to write an *orderly account*...that you may know the *truth* concerning the things of which you have been informed" (1:3-4). *Orderly account* and *truth* are Luke's way of saying that he sees things fitting into a pattern. With the history of God's deeds in the Old Testament as the dominant pattern, Luke interpreted the facts of Jesus' career and the emergence of the covenant-in-Jesus in terms of the prophecies of these in the sacred writings of Judaism. It is an accepted fact of scholarship that Luke thoroughly knows a host of literary forms used in the Scriptures and reuses them in his own account. He constantly remarks that Jesus and his followers fulfil the prophecies of Scripture. Luke the historian, then, consciously shapes his account to highlight the patterns of salvation history which he finds in the Scriptures.

Fifth, Luke write two volumes: a gospel about Jesus and the Acts of his apostles. Any full study of the gospel must include a careful study of Acts, for Luke's sense of pattern and "history" can only be grasped when the full story of Jesus and his followers is seen *in toto*. It may be that what is only hinted at in the gospel is fully developed in Acts; small editorial changes in the gospel account are the source of great shadows cast in Acts. Acts, then, serves to clarify and confirm the sense of Luke's editorial activity in the gospel, and so we will refer to Acts extensively in trying to understand the patterns of Luke's perspective in the gospel. Knowing this important information about the author of the Third Gospel, we are in a better position now to read his gospel and recover his portrait of Jesus.

MISSION AND MEMBERSHIP

Like Mark and the last editor of Matthew, Luke describes an inclusive Christian covenant community open to Jews and Gentiles alike. The clearest evidence of this is found in the commands of the risen Jesus to his disciples in both Luke and Acts. On Easter evening, Jesus instructs the apostles that "repentance and forgiveness of sins should be preached in his name *to all nations"* (24:47). This commissioning is confirmed in Acts when Jesus especially enjoins an inclusive mission on the apostles: "You shall be my witnesses in Jerusalem and in all Judea and Samaria and to the ends of the earth" (Acts 1:8).

In the Lukan gospel, however, Luke does not wait until the Resurrection to describe Jesus as engaged in a world-wide mission. The prophet Simeon blessed God at Jesus' Presentation in the Temple and prophesied about Jesus: "A light for revelation to the Gentiles and for glory to thy people Israel" (2:32). In his inaugural appearance at the synagogue in Nazareth, Jesus compared his mission to that of the prophets Elijah and Elisha. In the comparison, Luke indicates that not only is Jesus a prophet who mediates God's healing blessings, but, like Elijah (who was sent to the pagan woman in the gentile town of Zarephtha) and like Elisha (who healed the Syrian Namaan), Jesus is engaged in a mission that will include Gentiles too. And so, Luke indicates in the most rhetorically significant places of his narrative — beginning and ending — that Jesus considers his mission as an ecumenical mission, inclusive of all people, Jew and Gentile alike.

As regards the membership of the Lukan community, it would likewise appear to be pluralistic and inclusive. From the gospel, we learn that:

1. *Observant Jews* accept Jesus: Simeon and Anna are prophets and highly traditional Jews who see in Jesus "the consolation of Israel" (2:25) and "the redemption of Jerusalem" (2:38). Paul, a member of "the strictest party of our religion...a Pharisee" (Acts 26:5), becomes a follower of Jesus.

2. *Other Jews,* perhaps not so observant, likewise join the covenant-in-Jesus. For example, Peter, Andrew and others became Jesus' followers (5:1-11), as did certain women (8:1-3). And in Acts, the apostolic preaching leads thousands of Jews to accept Jesus (2:41, 47; 4:4).

3. *Marginal Jews,* whom the orthodox and observant would place on the fringes of the covenant, also find a place in the covenant-in-Jesus. Jews, who were "unclean" by virtue of a defiling illness, are ministered to by Jesus: lepers (5:12-16), cripples (5:17-26), and the blind (7:21). And in tandem with Mark's narrative, Luke records how Jesus performed exorcisms on the possessed (4:31-37), healed a menstruating woman (8:42-48), and touched dead bodies to revive them (8:49-56).

4. In Luke, Jesus gives specific instructions to invite the marginal people of Jewish society to one's feasts, thus indicating their full acceptance and complete status as first-class members of the covenant: "When you give a feast, invite the poor, the maimed, the lame and the blind" (14:13). The inclusive vision of Jesus is carried over into Acts where the lame are healed in Jesus' name (Acts 3:1-10; 9:32-35; 14:8-11), the blind are given sight (13:8-12), and the dead are raised by the touch of the prophet (9:36-43; 20:9-10). Deformed people, who would be on the margins of Temple and worship, are evangelized by Christian missionaries, viz., the Ethiopian eunuch (Acts 8:26-38).

5. Besides these marginal people, Luke records that Jesus conducts a special mission to *sinners.* Infamous public sinners are favored with Jesus' evangelical attention. For example, Zacchaeus, the rich chief tax collector, received Jesus into his home (19:5-7). Jesus justifies his uncommon attention to Zacchaeus with the claim that "the Son of Man came to seek and save the lost" (19:10). Jesus likewise called Levi, a tax collector, to be an associate (5:27). He regularly ate with such people (5:29; 15:1-2). In a striking parable, a tax collector praying in

the Temple was declared acceptable to God (18:10-13). All of Jesus' association with sinners is interpreted best in the twin parable of the search for the lost sheep (15:3-7) and for the lost coin (15:8-10).

6. *Apostate Israelites*, like the Samaritans, are included by Jesus in the covenant. Besides favorably using a Samaritan's act of kindness in a teaching story (10:33-36), Jesus later healed a Samaritan leper (17:14-18). These stories are clarified in Acts when Jesus commands a mission which would include the Samaritans (Acts 1:8), a mission which is realized through the ministry of Philip the Deacon (Acts 8:26-38).

7. *Gentiles and pagans* are welcomed by Jesus in the covenant. As we noted above, Jesus himself is said to extend favor and blessing to them. But it is in Acts that we find the initiative of Jesus for a mission to the Gentiles formally begun. During his vision of a sheet full of "unclean" animals descending from heaven, Peter hears from heaven the proclamation that God considers no thing or person "unclean" (Acts 10:15, 28). And in light of that vision, Peter preached to Cornelius, the pagan centurion. The story in Acts 10-11 indicates that divine initiative is clearly expressed in the conversion of Cornelius, upon whom God poured the Holy Spirit (10:45-47; 11:15-17). This pivotal incident becomes a powerful argument at the Jerusalem council in favor of including the Gentiles precisely in their Gentile state. Peter insists that "God made choice among you that by my mouth the Gentiles would hear the word of the gospel ...God made no distinction between them and us" (Acts 15:7-9).

And so, according to Luke, Jesus is a saving figure for Jews and Gentiles alike. God desires it; Jesus commissions it.

OLD TESTAMENT

Luke makes it abundantly clear that Jesus is an official interpreter of God's word to Israel in the way he presents

Jesus preaching and teaching the meaning of the Scriptures. In Jesus' inaugural visit to Nazareth's synagogue, he reads from the prophet Isaiah a passage about God's plan of salvation for Israel:

> The Spirit of the Lord is upon me, because he has anointed me to preach good news to the poor. He has sent me to proclaim release to captives and recovering of sight to the blind, to set at liberty those who are oppressed, to proclaim the acceptable year of the Lord (4:18-19/Isa 61:1-2 and 58:6).

This passage is classified by Jesus as a "prophecy," a prediction which "has been fulfilled in your hearing" (4:21). The event at Nazareth is intended by Luke to be programmatic for his portrait of Jesus. For Jesus is the fulfilment of the Old Testament Scriptures: he will engage in a healing mission to the poor, captives, blind and oppressed. But it is Jesus who is the prime exegete of the Scriptures; for the covenant which gathers around him, Jesus develops a distinctive way of understanding the Hebrew Scriptures. They are basically prophecies of which he is the fulfilment.

At the very end of the gospel this pattern is once more vividly presented. The most consistent thing about the Lukan resurrection account is the insistence on the teaching activity of the Risen Jesus. When Jesus engages the two disciples who are drifting to Emmaus away from the Jerusalem group of Jesus' followers, he conducts a bible study class for them. To prove that Jesus is really God's holy prophet and Christ, Jesus "began with Moses and all the prophets and interpreted to them in all the Scriptures the things concerning himself" (24:27). Likewise to the Eleven gathered in Jerusalem, Jesus gave a detailed interpretation of his death and resurrection from the Scriptures: "Everything written about me in the law of Moses and the prophets and the psalms must be fulfilled" (24:44). But the evangelist insists that this is no novel teaching, but part of Jesus' regular instruction of the disciples: "These are my words which I spoke to you while I was still with you . . ." (24:44a).

Jesus, then, is the prime interpreter of the Scriptures. He is the prime teacher of God's word. He reads the Scriptures, however, differently from his fellow Jews, for he sees them not as a legal document but as prophecy which heralds and legitimates his own mission (4:18-19) and which interprets his death and resurrection (24:27, 44). Jesus' basic pattern of interpretation can easily be fleshed out in light of other passages in the gospel. Mary and Zechariah both see the wonderful events of Jesus' and John's birth as the fulfilment of the ancient prophecies to Abraham (1:55 & 72-73); Jesus' birth is explicitly proclaimed as the fulfilment of the covenant promises to David (1:32-33; see Act 13:22-23). Jesus is "the stone rejected by the builders who has become the cornerstone" (20:17; see Acts 4:10-12). Jesus is the Lord's Anointed One against whom the Gentiles raged and against whom the kings and rulers gathered (Acts 4:25-28 / Ps 2:1-2). It is important to remember that it belongs to Jesus to interpret the Scriptures in a new and correct way, and so this is an important element in Luke's portrait of Jesus.

The prophetic interpretation of the Old Testament serves many functions in Luke's narratives. First and foremost it lays down the foundation for the basic portrayal of Jesus as God's prophesied Savior. This is both an evangelical as well as an apologetic move: Jesus is no Johnny-come-lately figure who surprisingly appears on the scene to claim false honors. Rather he is the focus of all of Israel's ancient history, the person in whom all of God's long-standing covenant plans are being realized. And so this use of the Old Testament serves basically to undergird the legitimacy of Jesus. The promises to Abraham and David are realized in him; the salvation of Israel is prophesied of him. Even his death and resurrection are accounted for in the "plan and foreknowledge of God," which is the Scriptures, proving him to be a genuine prophet (see Acts 3:22; 8:30-35).

Because the Old Testament Scriptures were accepted by Jews and Christians alike as God's inspired word, eternally valid and true, it was imperative that Luke show how the very sources of biblical faith all point to Jesus, heralding him, explaining his mission, and interpreting his significance. By seeing the Scriptures as heralding Jesus, Luke insists that Jesus is no novelty, no ne'er-do-well, no whimsy, no surprise. Jesus' appearance, rather, has been God's plan and intention from of old. "According to the definite plan and foreknowledge of God" (Acts 2:23), Jesus came on the scene; his career was to do "whatever thy hand and thy plan had predestined to take place" (Acts 4:28). God's consistency as found in the Scriptures is the legitimation of Jesus. All one needs to know about Jesus can be found in the Scriptures. And Jesus himself is the first and best exponent of them.

But even as Luke emphasizes the prophetic character of the Old Testament, he presents Jesus as fulfilling many of the legal prescriptions commanded in the Scriptures. Jesus is circumcized like all observant Jews (2:21); as firstborn, he is dedicated in the Temple to the Lord (2:22-23); he makes the required pilgrimages to Jerusalem for feast days (2:41-42). Luke is not inconsistent here, preaching a legal interpretation of the Scripture's cultic laws as well as a prophetic interpretation. Rather, Luke insists that by keeping these laws and customs, Jesus and his followers are *not* "uneducated, common men" (Acts 4:13), who do not know God's Scriptures. They are *not* decadent, sinful, unobservant Jews who were always on the fringes of Israel's religion. Rather, they start within the framework of Israel's faith; they are pious, zealous, and observant worshippers of God. The many appearances of Jesus and his followers in the Temple (24:53; Acts 2:46; 3:1ff; 4:1; 5:20, 25; 21:26-30) are all calculated to assert that they are holy people, not mavericks from Israel's faith and its God. Jesus' orthodox upbringing, then, serves an apologetic purpose to silence slander that he was a demonic person.

Neither Jesus nor his disciples maintain the continuing validity of the legal or cultic portions of the Old Testament. On the contrary, the covenant-in-Jesus comes to realize that several of the most important Jewish customs mandated in the Scriptures are no longer valid. The famous dietary laws, which prohibit the eating of unclean foods, are declared invalid (Acts 10:15, 28). Nor is circumcision any longer required for admission to the covenant (Acts 15:1). Such customs are declared by Peter to be an intolerable "yoke which neither our fathers nor we have been able to bear" (Acts 15:10). As regards the very temple building and its cult, the prophet Stephen argued that the Jews misunderstood the Old Testament when they established a temple in the first place. God indeed promised Abraham that after a sojourn in a foreign land, the covenant people "shall come out and worship me *in this place*" (Acts 7:7). But "this place" is *not* the temple, for God "does not dwell in houses made with hands" (Acts 7:48), as Isaiah 66:1-2 proves (see Acts 7:49-50). And so all of the materials in the Scriptures about the temple and its cult are shown to be misguided and erroneous interpretations of God's will. The correct "place" for worship is no place but Jesus. Being with him means having access to God, for he is the mediator of God's blessings and mercy to the covenant people.

The figure of Moses is specially interpreted in Luke's narrative, not as a source of law for the people, but as the prophet of the Christ who is to come. Moses' basic significance, then, is not as the mediator of a covenant, but as prophet. Luke several times calls attention to Deut 18:19 as summing up the importance of Moses in the Scripture; for in this passage Moses makes a prediction of great importance to Luke and the church: "God will raise up for you a prophet from your brethren as he raised me up" (see Acts 3:22 and 7:37). No, for Luke the Scriptures are basically a prophetic document, not a legal or cultic handbook. The way to live and worship are found in Jesus.

ESCHATOLOGY

In Luke's gospel, Jesus speaks many of the traditional sayings about the future coming of the Son of Man (e.g. 17:22-35; 21:20-33). Juxtaposed to the references about a future age of salvation is the Lukan note that in Jesus salvation is already present.

1. At Jesus' birth, for example, the angel proclaims to

the shepherds: "To you is born this day a Savior, who is Christ the Lord" (2:11).

2. At Jesus' first visit to Nazareth's synagogue, he tells the assembly, "Today this scripture is fulfilled in your hearing" (4:21); the "Scripture" here is the prophecy of Isaiah that the poor will hear the good news, that captives will be set free, that the blind would see — all prophecies of salvation.

3. To Zacchaeus Jesus proclaims: "Today salvation has come to this house" (19:9).

4. And on the cross, Jesus tells the repentant criminal: "Today you will be with me in paradise" (23:43).

Jesus, then, tells those who accept him that God's salvation is a present reality, found in Jesus then and there.

The proclamation by Jesus that salvation is had "today" does not necessarily mean that a new eschatological scenario is introduced. Rather, these remarks of Jesus should be seen in conjunction with the previous comments about faith and belonging to the covenant-in-Jesus. Finding Jesus means finding salvation. Being part of the covenant-in-Jesus means being part of God's covenant of blessing and power. These statements are true enough as they stand, but they serve an apologetic function as well. By having Jesus' offer salvation "today," Luke underscores the legitimacy and value of the Christian covenant community in his day. Not Israel, but the covenant-in-Jesus is the authentic covenant; not in Israel, which only hopes for redemption in the future, but in Jesus one encounters God's blessing and redemption "today." The eschatology of present salvation in Jesus serves to contrast the church with the synagogue and to undergird the significance of Jesus as the unique agent of salvation.

In another vein, Luke most clearly calls Jesus "the Judge of the living and the dead." Twice in Acts, both Peter (10:42) and Paul (17:31) proclaim Jesus as the universal judge of every person, Jew and Greek, living and dead. This, of course, is a very traditional confession about Jesus (see 1 Peter 4:5; 2 Tim 4:1). But in Luke this theme is quite well developed. We noted above that in reaction to Jesus there is usually a *schism*; some acclaim him, as others reject him (see 2:34). Luke portrays Jesus as a prophetic judge, constantly proclaiming woe and ruin on those who reject him as God's prophet and anointed one. Although Jesus speaks a word of mercy to sinners, there comes a time when lines are drawn and judgment separates believers from unbelievers.

Examples of Jesus' judgment are numerous.

1. Judgment is pronounced against the cities of Jesus' ministry for their unbelief: "Woe to you Chorazin, woe to you Bethsaida" (10:13-15).

2. The door will be shut on those who refuse to enter the door of Jesus' covenant through acceptance of his word; "I do not know you!" (13:25) the householder says to these "workers of iniquity."

3. Those who refused the first invitation to the great feast are condemned in Jesus' parable for their refusal: "I tell you none of those who were invited shall taste of my banquet" (14:24).

4. From Mark's account, Luke repeats Jesus' quid-pro-quo judgment on unbelievers: "Whoever is ashamed of me and my words, of him will the Son of Man be ashamed..." (9:26//Mk 8:38).

5. Likewise from Mark come the parable of the vineyard, in which Jesus tells that judgment will come on those who repeatedly reject God's messengers, especially for the killing of the "Beloved Son": "He will come and destroy those tenants" (20:16//Mk 12:9).

6. Special Lukan material on judgment occurs in the Lukan redaction of the Parable of the Talents. Of the nobleman in the parable Luke asserts that "his citizens hated him and sent an embassy after him saying, 'We do not want this man to reign over us'" (19:12-14). This rejection brings a severe judgment: "As for those enemies of mine who did not want me to reign over them, bring them here and slay them in my sight" (19:27).

7. To this list could be added the oracles of Jesus

against Jerusalem for rejecting God's prophets (11:47-51; 13:34-35; 19:41-44; 21:20-24; and 23:27-31).

This substantial body of judgment material, which forms an essential part of Jesus' portrait, must be put in its proper perspective. I view the function of this material as the correlative of the proclamation of "Salvation...today...in Jesus." If salvation is truly found in faith in Jesus and in belonging to his covenant, then non-salvation comes upon those who would *not* believe and join. The judgment language, although traditional, serves to confirm the view of Jesus as the only authentic word of God, as the only Way, as the only locus for contacting God. Apart from Jesus one finds judgment; but with Jesus is salvation.

ETHICS

Like other gospels, the action which is valued most by Jesus is acceptance of him, faith, and consequent association with the covenant-in-Jesus. The theme is sounded at the beginning of Jesus' life, when the prophet Simeon predicted of him: "This child is set for the fall and rise of many in Israel: and for a sign that is spoken against" (2:34).

Although faith may be the most important activity of genuine covenant members, Luke sees that some believe and some do not. Luke keeps a careful record of who accepts and who rejects Jesus, probably to keep indicating who is in God's covenant and who is not. For example:

> 1. The Pharisee who invited Jesus to dinner gave Jesus no respect or mark of hospitality; but the sinner woman watered his feet with tears, wiped them with her hair, and anointed his head with oil (7:44-46). Contrasting attitudes to Jesus!
> 2. Zacchaeus the sinner welcomed Jesus into his home, but the crowds stood in judgment on Jesus' association with sinners — contrasting attitudes to Jesus (19:1-10).
> 3. The fates of the seeds sown in diverse soils are

carefully noted; the seed is "the word of God" and so acceptance or rejection of Jesus is reflected in the receptivity of the soils (8:11-15).

4. The two thieves crucified with Jesus react differently to him, one reviling him and the other asking for remembrance in his kingdom (23:39-43).

This pattern, already clear from the gospel, is developed still further in Acts where Luke records that at the preaching of the apostles "the city was divided" (14:4). And Acts contains many examples of this.

5. Great success attended the initial preaching (4:4), but it is juxtaposed with rejection by the priests and Sadducees (4:1-3).

6. A favorable reception of the apostolic preaching in 5:12-16 is balanced with official rejection by the Sanhedrin (5:17-32).

7. Persecution of the church in Judea (8:1-3) is followed by new missionary success in Samaria (8:4-8).

8. The Pauline mission experiences both favorable and negative responses: at *Antioch,* some believe (13:44-47, 50-51) and some reject Paul's word (13:42-43, 48-49); at *Thessalonika,* some are persuaded (17:2-4, 12), but some fight against Paul (17:5-9, 13); at *Corinth,* many in the synagogue accept Paul's preaching (18:7-11), while others persecute Paul (18:12-17).

9. Finally, Pharisees and Sadducees split over Paul's preaching of the resurrection (23:6-9).

Truly Jesus is set for the rise and fall of many. The value, moreover, of faith or rejection lies in its results: believers join the true covenant of God but unbelievers formally dissociate themselves.

The importance of belief in the word preached lies in the covenant which is formed out of those who so believe. Believing in Jesus' or the apostles' preaching results in being gathered around Jesus as the legitimate covenant leader. Failure to believe or rejection of the preaching means that one is an outsider of God's true covenant, viz., the covenant-in-Jesus. The results of the preaching, then, are of great importance, as the parable in 13:24-30 explain. Hearers of the word are told to *enter* the *narrow door,* that is, to believe and become a covenant "insider." For the householder will shut the door and some will find themselves "outsiders." Of them he will say "I do not know you" (13:27), a severe form of judgment; and they will find themselves "thrust out" (13:28). By tracing the importance of the theme of belief in Jesus' preaching, Luke insists in his own way that there is no salvation outside of the covenant-in-Jesus.

Luke has carefully shown all through the gospel that the most important thing which people can do is to believe the word spoken to them by God's messengers: angels, prophets, and especially Jesus. Compare Zechariah and Mary; both receive angelic messengers who announce the birth of their children. Zechariah cannot believe, while Mary is praised for her acceptance of God's word: "Blessed is she who believed that there would be a fulfilment of what was spoken to her from the Lord" (1:45). At the end of the gospel, the angel at the tomb pressed the women visitors to remember and believe what Jesus had continually told them: "Remember how he told you, while he was still with you, that the Son of Man must be delivered into the hands of sinful people and be crucified, and on the third day rise" (24:6-7). Belief, then, is tantamount to canonization.

Besides belief, Jesus commands his disciples to follow the law of love (10:25-28). Basically, this means keeping the Ten Commandments (18:19-20), but it implies something more in Luke's portrait of Jesus. Luke specifically censures those who are judgmental of sinners, of "outsiders," and of marginal Jews. Those with a highly restricted sense of who belongs in God's covenant (e.g. only the pure, those learned in the Law, the observant, etc.) are corrected and told to practice a more inclusive acceptance into the covenant of those whom God elects to lead into it. So "love" takes on a special meaning: inclusiveness and respect for less honorable and less perfect members of God's covenant. This is made evident in Jesus' instructions on who should be invited to share one's table. The elite tend to accept only other elite as companions at table, as covenant sisters and brothers. But Jesus commanded a more open table and so a more open covenant: "When you give a feast, invite the poor, the maimed, the lame, the blind" (14:13). Jesus himself dramatized this openness by repeatedly eating with sinners and offering them covenant fellowship with himself:

1. He ate with Levi and other tax collectors (5:29).
2. He received tax collectors and ate with them, a thing which aroused the ire of his enemies (15:1-2).
3. He ate with Zacchaeus, the chief tax collector (19:5-7).
4. And he ate with the Emmaus disciples who lost faith and left the group of his followers (24:29-30).

In a comparable way, Jesus is said to proclaim God's acceptance of a publican who prays meekly, contrasting God's acceptance of this sinner with the Pharisee's rejection of him (18:9-14). This is probably the attitude which is behind the parable of the Good Samaritan: one should accept a neighbor in need, and not judge that neighbor by one's own purity code or elite standards (10:36-37). Love, then, involves the issue of who is my covenant neighbor. According to Jesus, "love" means inclusive acceptance of those whom God has called to covenant fellowship, especially the non-elite, sinners, and marginal people.

Jesus gives special instructions on the correct use of wealth, a unique characteristic of the portrait of Jesus in the Third Gospel. For example, the rich estate owner who experienced a bumper crop resolved to hoard the crop and "take my ease, eat, drink and be merry" (12:19). It never entered his mind to share that wealth with his poor covenant brothers and sisters. He is severely reproached by God ("You fool!" 12:20) for he laid up treasure for himself but was not rich with God (12:21). "To be rich with God" is a code phrase used by the Lukan Jesus for sharing wealth with others, and so honoring the less fortunate or the non-elite with full status as covenant members. Comparably, the wicked steward was told to face a severe audit by his land-lord (16:1-2). He began dispensing his commission on the produce he had collected from the tenent farmers who worked his master's great estates. For this wise use of his money, he was praised (16:8). For he fulfilled Jesus' command to "make friends with/by means of mammon" (16:9); he spent his riches and surplus on covenant members in need. This principle is dramatized most clearly in the subsequent parable of Lazarus and the Rich Man. They are neighbors; Lazarus is at the Rich Man's very gate; he begs for crumbs, for succor, and for basic covenant love from a fellow member of the covenant. The Rich Man is very, very rich: he is clothed in purple and feasts sumptuously every day. But he gives *nothing* to Lazarus: no money, no crumb, no care for his sores, no respect, and no covenant fellowship. He is cast into hell at his death, whereas Lazarus is taken by God to heaven. This shows that God regarded Lazarus as a full member of the covenant, although the Rich Man did not; for this failure of practical love, God did *not* regard the Rich Man as a member.

Jesus' instructions on the right use of money, then, are a further extension of his command to love the sinner, the non-elite, the non-observant person. One must be friends with those whom God regards as friends, especially the poor of the group, lest we treat them as second-class citizens and as marginal covenant members. Peter said it most accurately when he proclaimed that "God has made no distinction between us and them" (Acts 15:9).

There is, then, a centrality to the actions which are urged by Jesus in this gospel. Faith and acceptance of the preaching of Jesus and his disciples are most important; they constitute membership in the covenant-in-Jesus. Belonging to that covenant is a matter of life and death. Second, one must show openness, respect, and love to other covenant members whom God elects and draws to this group. This especially concerns a new attitude to sinners, tax collectors, the unclean and other folk formally considered marginal to covenant membership. God's judgment of them must become one's own evaluation. Finally, one must show practical help for the covenant members who are poor, sick or marginalized. Through all of these commands, Jesus enjoins on his followers an inclusive openness to other covenant members, especially a new pluralism which replaces the elitism or perfectionism which tended to characterize the rich, the pious, the educated and the elite. Inclusive membership is supported by special commands from Jesus that hedge against any factionalism in the covenant.

Conversely, the vice most condemned by Jesus in Luke's narrative is rejection of Jesus or unbelief. Jesus' initial preaching is met with hostility (4:24-30), a bitter note which sets the tone for his ministry. There follows a long string of reports about people rejecting Jesus' word.

1. Scribes and Pharisees reject Jesus' forgiveness of sins, and so dismiss Jesus as well (5:21).

2. They criticize his eating with sinners (5:30).

3. They object to his Sabbath observance (6:1-11).

4. Missionaries are forewarned about rejection and so given instructions about it (10:10-12).

5. A parable tells of people who knew Jesus intimately, but who refused to enter the narrow door and join him (13:14-26).

6. Jerusalem failed repeatedly to accept God's prophets, and so "did not know the day of its visitation" (19:41-44).

7. Another parable tells of citizens who reject a certain man being appointed king, a reference to the Jews' rejection of Jesus (19:12-14).

8. Finally, in his trials Jesus is rejected first by the whole assembly (22:66-71) and later by all the people (23:13-25).

Luke situates this terrible act of rejection of Jesus in terms of the pattern of Jewish history in which Israel's prophets have always been rejected. "Jerusalem, Jerusalem, killing the prophets and stoning those sent to you!" (13:34). Thus Luke repeatedly records that prophets like Jesus have always been rejected: 11:47-50; 19:14; 20:10-12. Even Moses is presented primarily as a prophet rejected by his own people (Acts 7:27, 35, 39-40).

Unbelief and rejection mean that people are refusing to accept Jesus as God's appointed covenant leader. And so in rejecting Jesus, they are also rejecting God:

> Who hears you, hears me
> and who rejects you rejects me
> and who rejects me rejects him who sent me   (10:16).

And so, unbelief makes one an outsider to the covenant of God's love and favor.

Likewise, to reject those whom God has called to covenant fellowship is also censured by Jesus. The Pharisees and other elite Jews never seem to come under censure except when they despise those to whom Jesus ministers. They think he should distance himself from the sinful woman (7:39), from tax collectors (5:30; 15:1-2), from sinners (5:21), and from the unclean (19:1-6). The priest and Levite who did not stop to help the wounded man on the road are criticized because in their elite sense of maintaining distance from all uncleanness they failed to show covenant love to a needy covenant brother (10:30-32). In the parable about the two men praying in the temple, the Pharisee is censured, not because of his alleged legalistic piety, but because he despised the publican and broke covenant faith with him (18:9,11). He could not accept as covenant brother a person whom God accepted. Jesus, then, censures elitist attitudes which would split God's covenant. Those who do not judge by God's standards will find themselves judged by Jesus and by God.

GROUP SELF-UNDERSTANDING

In the Third Gospel, Jesus does not herald his mission as the founding of a "new" or different covenant. Rather he proclaims continuity with the traditional covenant. For example, Jesus repeatedly points to Old Testament texts as prophecies which he is fulfilling, thus maintaining his continuity with the history of God's covenant people. A few pertinent examples amply illustrate this:

1. Isaiah's prophecy, "The Spirit of the Lord is upon me..." (Isa 61:1) is said by Jesus to be "fulfilled today in your hearing" (4:21)

2. About his rejection and resurrection, Jesus claims that he is basically fulfilling the prophecies of Scripture: "And beginning with Moses and all the prophets, he interpreted to them in all the Scriptures the things concerning himself" (24:27; see 24:44-47).

The covenant-in-Jesus, then, is in direct continuity with God's word to Israel.

In Jesus' assertion that he and his covenant group are the authentic Israel, we find a search of the Old Testament Scriptures to justify the inclusion of non-Jews in the covenant, for they are traditionally outsiders to God's covenant. Jesus' explanation of his mission at Nazareth's synagogue is a programmatic text for the gospel, including many of Luke's major themes (such as, anointing by the Spirit, mission to the poor, rejection of the prophet, and prophecy-fulfilment). In that passage, Jesus cites as models for his own ministry the careers of Elijah and Elisha. He calls attention to the fact that these prophets included Gentiles in the scope of their mission: "Elijah was sent to Zarephtha, in the land of Sidon, to a woman who was a widow" (4:26) and Elisha cleansed Namaan, the Syrian leper (4:27). The covenant ministry of Israel's prophets, including Jesus, has always embraced Gentiles in its scope. This is confirmed in Acts 15 where the issue of the inclusion of Gentiles in the authentic covenant was resolved. At that council, James, the leader of the Jerusalem group, cites the prophecy of the prophet Amos (9:11-12):

> After this I will return and I will rebuild the dwelling of David, which has fallen; I will rebuild its ruins, and I will set it up, that the rest of men may seek the Lord, and all the Gentiles who are called by my name (Acts 15:16-17).

This text functions for Luke as a conclusive proof that God had destined long ago that non-Jews be included in the "re-building" of the authentic covenant people. Israel's history and its Scripture both validate the Lukan self-understanding of the covenant-in-Jesus as the authentic covenant which included Jews and Gentiles alike.

But what kind of covenant? The priests, Scribes and Pharisees of Israel would point to the covenant with Moses as the true model of the covenant. Like other first-century Christians, Luke sees the covenant-in-Jesus as based on a different model of what the covenant should be — the covenant with Abraham and David. As we noted earlier, the covenant with Abraham and David is characterized as

> 1. an act of God's free election,
> 2. as based on God's promises
> (which are now fulfilled in Jesus),
> 3. and requiring "belief" in God's word for its realization, not careful observance of a code of covenant law.

Luke has repeatedly called attention in his gospel to the covenant with Abraham and David in such striking ways that the reader clearly begins to see how the covenant-in-Jesus is understood according to that model. In regard to the birth of Jesus, Mary prophetically acclaimed that in Jesus, God "remembers his mercy, as he spoke to our fathers, to Abraham and his posterity forever" (1:54-55). Zechariah prophesied at John's birth that God is now fulfilling the covenant promise "to perform the mercy promised to our fathers, and to remember his holy covenant, the oath which he swore to our father Abraham" (1:72-73). Jewish covenant members, of course, would also identify themselves as "Sons of Abraham." For being a "Son of Abraham" was synonymous with being in the covenant of Israel. But who is an authentic "Son of Abraham"? Luke records that "Son of Abraham" is not synonymous with pious and orthodox Jews, but includes all who do God's will. To the assembled crowds whom John lectured about God's coming judgment, he told them not to pride themselves on *already* being in God's covenant: "Do not begin to say to yourselves, 'We have Abraham for our father' for I tell you, God is able from these stones to raise up children to Abraham" (3:8). Membership in God's covenant is not confined to purity-conscious Jews, for even the crippled woman "whom Satan has bound for thirteen years" is a "daughter of Abraham" (13:16). She may be an outsider to the synagogue, one of those marginal people in Israel, but Jesus proclaims her an insider. Thus the appeal to the covenant of Abraham as a model for the covenant-in-Jesus stresses that non-Jews and marginal Jews are included as well as the elite and orthodox Jews. This type of covenant is characterized as an inclusive covenant.

The self-understanding of Luke's Christian group may be characterized as follows: a) the covenant-in-Jesus is the authentic covenant of God with Israel; b) it is based on the Abraham model of covenant, not the Mosaic model; and c) it means an inclusive covenant of Jews and Gentiles. Jesus, then, is the patriarch of God's covenant people; he is legitimated as the fulfilment of God's first and best covenant plans, through Abraham and David. In him the Gentiles find a share in God's blessings.

EXPERIENCE

What are the events which shaped the Lukan community and its portrait of Jesus? What is the daily experience of the Lukan group, its *Sitz im Leben*? We may confidently say that Luke is writing late in the first century. He is aware of other versions of the Jesus story, as he tells us in the prologue of his gospel: "Inasmuch as many have compiled a narrative of the things which have been accomplished among us..." (1:1). Without specifically naming Mark's gospel, a comparison of Luke and Mark indicates that Luke knew it and was deeply influenced by Mark's story and its perspective of Jesus. Luke and his community, then, are first and foremost influenced by Mark's story of Jesus.

Many have described Luke's community as an *ecclesia pressa*, a church hassled and attacked. It is true that the gospel and Acts both stress how prophets to Israel are rejected and even killed. Furthermore, the covenant-in-

Jesus in Acts is constantly being arrested, investigated, and tried. The following list brings this element to the fore:

Text	Persons	Place
4:3-23	Peter & John	Jerusalem
5:17-40	Peter & John	Jerusalem
6:9-7:60	Stephen	Jerusalem
16:19-30	Paul & Silas	Philippi
17:5-9	Jason	Thessalonika
18:12-17	Paul	Corinth
21:27-22:30	Paul	Jerusalem
22:30-23:10	Paul	Jerusalem
24:1-26	Paul	Jerusalem
25:5-12	Paul	Caesarea
25:24-26:32	Paul	Caesarea
28	Paul	Rome

It is unclear, however, if the "trial" motif is an exact record of history or a literary motif used by Luke. If it is a literary motif, it would serve to give an artificial platform for the church's vindication of itself and to give one last opportunity for Israel to judge correctly the word of God.

Jesus in the gospel and the church in Acts are both in intense conflict with Israel. But no Lukan scholar today suggests that the Lukan community is actually being hassled by the synagogue, being condemned by it, and excommunicated, as was the case with the Johannine church. Luke's group is generally said to be composed of Gentiles, as well as Jews, and to be on non-Jewish soil. It is a group which has consciously split with the Jewish interpretation of their common parent faith. Perhaps it would be safer to describe the Lukan group as going through an extended period of self-definition.

Self-definition is achieved in several ways. It is important for the followers of Jesus that they be understood as the covenant, as the true fulfilment of God's promises, as the authentic and continuous link with the core of the Scriptures. Legitimacy then leads Luke to stress the ties with Israel, its history and its Scriptures. Not only does this tack validate the covenant-in-Jesus, it becomes the occasion to assert the illegitimacy of those who reject Jesus as prophet, as Messiah and as covenant Lord. Hence Luke repeatedly records Israel's continual rejection of God's prophets throughout its history (see 11:47-51; 13:34-35; 20:10-12; Acts 7:35, 39-40 and 51-52). As Israel's history continually shows, disobedience to God has always resulted in ruin and exile for the disobedient covenant people (see Acts 3:23-26; 7:42-43; 13:40-41). This phenomenon takes on great significance for Luke because of the recent Roman-Jewish war of 70 AD. Thus Luke's basic theme of prophecy-fulfilment and his insistence on the continuity of the covenant-in-Jesus with the true Israel basically function to clarify the self-identity of the group as the legitimate covenant.

But self-identity can also be shaped by pointing out the sharp discontinuities between the self and others, or by accentuating whatever differences exist as a way of distinguishing the self from others. We would expect to hear arguments such as "We are *not* like you in these ways...we are different." Luke seems to exemplify this aspect of developing self-identity by pointing out how Jesus differs from prevailing Jewish postures and values. When we ask how *Jews* typically defined themselves vis-à-vis non-Jews, we find a traditional list of rules and practices which specifically identify them, which separate them from others:

1) they keep strict dietary rules,
2) they observe the Sabbath,
3) they are circumcized,
4) they actively separate themselves from sinners and unclear people,
5) they keep the Law of Moses (more or less strictly).

Jesus and his covenant followers take stands on these issues which are radically different from the prevailing Jewish attitudes.

1. No dietary restrictions govern Jesus' group: all foods are clean (Acts 10:15; 11:19).

2. Jesus "violates" the Sabbath by healing on it, distinguishing his practice from that of other Jews (6:1-11; 13:10-17).

3. Circumcision is not required for members of the covenant-in-Jesus (Acts 15:1, 5, 28).

4. Jesus does not separate himself from sinners (7:39; 15:1-2; 19:1-10), lepers (5:12-16), menstruating women (8:43-48) or dead bodies (7:11-17; 8:49-56). According to Acts, "God has shown me that I should not call any person common or unclean" (Acts 10:28; see 15:9).

5. Jesus' followers criticize the law of Moses: it is a "yoke which neither our father nor we have been able to bear" (Acts 15:10). Keeping the law of Moses, says Paul, could never cleanse or free its observers from sin (Acts 13:39).

I suggest that Luke's frequent mention of "trials" of Christians is a literary motif which allows Jesus and his covenant followers to work out the issue of Christian self-identity, both by the claim of legitimate fulfilment of Israel's Scriptures and by contrast with the Judaism of Luke's day. In positive and negative ways, the Lukan covenant-in-Jesus sees itself accurately and confidently as the authentic covenant. The distinctiveness of Jesus' followers is dramatized by the constant drawing of differences between them and the Jews in the synagogue. The "trials" serve to make this distinctiveness and difference all the more apparent. This enterprise obviously occupies the bulk of Luke's time and effort. This is the formative experience which shaped his narrative and consequently his portrait of Jesus.

We can point to few specific events that impinged on Luke's consciousness. Rather we can be much clearer about his attempts to see things in a large, historical perspective, in terms of biblical patterns and prophecies. In this vein, Luke is very optimistic and upbeat about Jesus and the covenant in his name. The precise *Sitz im Leben* may be difficult to pin down, but not the mood or vision of the author. Luke's experience is one of confident self-understanding, of finding one's true place in the patterns of salvation history, of surviving death, crisis, and trial. In this, Luke's experience is very future oriented, for he sees his covenant-in-Jesus as being firmly established as the authentic covenant vis-à-vis Israel.

We ask now what contribution all of this information makes toward a full portrait of Jesus? Since Jesus is always more than the mere names and titles ascribed to him, we can learn a great deal about Luke's portrait of Jesus from the attitudes and positions ascribed to him by the evangelist. Jesus himself is credited with practicing an inclusive mission. He enjoined the same on his followers; and so the *de facto* presence of Gentiles in Luke's own group is validated by this aspect of the portrait of Jesus. Jesus, then, is a *universal* savior, universal in terms of *all* peoples, especially Gentiles, and universal in terms of the *kind of people* to whom he ministered (saints and sinners, elite and unclean). Jesus is credited with teaching his followers to read the Old Testament in a distinctive way. Seeing the Scriptures as prophecy served to legitimate Jesus as their fulfilment and to validate the covenant-in-Jesus as the authentic Israel. Jesus himself ministered to sinners and unclean folk, and he commanded to his followers acceptance, mercy, forgiveness, and charity to such people. This surely reflects the composition of the Lukan group. Jesus' inclusiveness is an ethical posture which he insists must characterize his followers as well. Jesus acts as a prophet, proclaiming salvation to those who accept him and join themselves to him, but he is also judge of those who reject him as God's prophet. Jesus, then, is presented as a covenant prophet with an authentic word of God. Jesus' word has to be taken with utmost seriousness, for one's standing with God depends on it. Acceptance of him means that one joins the covenant-in-Jesus but rejection of him means that one is an outsider to God's plan. And the covenant he gathers is an inclusive covenant, a group legitimated by God's own promises and correctly inclusive of all peoples, Jews and Gentiles. Jesus heralds a behavior appropriate to this: inclusive acceptance of all whom God elects. Inclusiveness, then, becomes a key element in Luke's portrait of Jesus.

CHRISTOLOGY

The portrait of Jesus in Luke's gospel receives fresh clarity and definition when we ask what identity names or titles Luke used to describe Jesus. Of course Luke describes Jesus according to traditional categories used by other evangelists and their communities, such as "Son of God," "Son of David," "Son of Man," etc. But there are some special categories used exclusively by Luke and there is often a special Lukan meaning given to older, traditional titles.

1. *Prophet.* Clopas, one of the Emmaus disciples, described Jesus as a prophet: "Concerning Jesus of Nazareth, who was a prophet mighty in word and deed" (24:19). This is balanced with Jesus' own self-identification in his inaugural synagogue appearance, when Jesus cited in his own regard the saying that "no prophet is acceptable in his own country" (4:24). Although 4:24 is a flexible proverb which may apply to any person rejected by his own, Luke follows that up with Jesus' comparison of himself with two of Israel's greatest prophets, Elijah and Elisha (4:25-27). Thus at the beginning and at the end of Jesus' career he is aptly described as a prophet.

Prophets, moreover, have typical things to do and to say. Primarily Jesus the prophet is a figure who does mighty deeds. When Jesus raised to life the son of the widow of Nain, the crowds rightly acclaimed him as a prophet: "A great prophet has arisen among us!" (7:16; compare with 1 Kings 17:17-24 and 2 Kings 4:32-37). When Jesus tells the synagogue crowd that the Spirit of the Lord has anointed him "to proclaim release to captives and recovering of sight to the blind" (4:18), he is describing himself as a man of God (a prophet) who does mighty acts of healing. These healing acts, like those of Elijah and Elisha, are not confined to Israel, but are offered to Gentiles as well. A prophet, then, is a healer and wonder worker, even of non-Jews.

Prophets, moreover, speak God's authorized word to the covenant people. They are the authorized messengers who call to repentance the wayward people or who invite the covenant people to obedient relationship with God. John the Baptizer was the epitome of this, "a prophet and more than a prophet" (7:26). As a prophet, he preached "a baptism of repentance and forgiveness of sins" (3:3); he condemned sin (3:10-14) and urged Israel to prepare for God's judgment (3:9 and 17). As a prophet, Jesus was authorized to spot sin, name it, and demand repentance. It is under this rubric that the pious Pharisee is surprised to see Jesus *not* condemning the sinful woman who came and anointed his feet: "if this man were a prophet, he would have known who and what sort of woman this is who is touching him, for she is a sinner" (7:39).

Prophets who are critical of Israel's waywardness have traditionally been rejected by Israel for their criticism. In several places Luke retains traditional remarks about rejected prophets (11:47-51; 13:34). In truth, the proof that one is an authentic prophet may lie precisely in being rejected. In this regard, Luke occasionally speaks of Jesus as a " prophet like Moses"; for Moses predicted in Deut 18:19 that the Lord would raise up a prophet like him. And Luke shows that Moses was repeatedly and consistently rejected by the Israelites (Acts 7:37, 39-40, 52). An authentic prophet, then, ought to be rejected, and so prove to be a genuine prophet.

"Prophet" is a major Lukan title for describing Jesus. Not only does it point to *what* Jesus does (healing, judgment), but the title "prophet" functions in four important ways for Luke's narrative.

a) The model of the rejected prophet from the Old Testament Scriptures serves as a useful apologetic category to argue for Jesus' acceptable status with God. Rejection and death do not of themselves mean that such-and-such a prophet is a fraud. On the contrary, such rejection serves to link Jesus with the great religious figures of old, whom Israel always rejected. Such is a fate of authentic prophets.

b) Prophets need credentials, and their wonders and mighty acts are observable credentials that God stands with them. Prophetic miracles not only describe the quality of the prophet's ministry, but they are self-validating credentials for the prophet. Jesus' miracles should tell the hearer that he is "a man attested to you by God with signs and wonders" (Acts 2:22). Thus Jesus' miracles in the gospel and Acts are proof that God authorized him; they are indisputable proof of his status (see Acts 4:14, 16, 21-22).

c) Jesus' being a prophet served Luke's purpose of showing the intimate connection between the covenant-in-Jesus and God's plan of salvation in the Old Testament. "Prophet" is a category which links Jesus to the main-stream of Israel's tradition, and legitimates Jesus and his followers in the tradition, even if they are rejected (Acts 7:52).

d) If a prophet, then prophets are expected to have a word on how God's people are to live and think as cove-nant members. Jesus' word on the kingdom of God, on God's visitation of his people, and on Jesus himself as God's covenant leader, are thus underscored. The "Way" of Jesus as Torah for the covenant is thus legitimated.

The prophetic identity of Jesus constitutes a major, cohesive element in Luke's portrait of Jesus.

2. *Christ*. Luke builds on the traditions which call Jesus "the Christ" (see 9:20; 20:21; 23:2). He frequently links the title "Christ" with "Lord," thus asserting that Jesus is the unique Lord of the covenant, God's "anointed" agent. The angel proclaimed him thus at his birth: "A savior is born to you who is Christ, the Lord" (2:11). And Peter repeated the proclamation in his Pentecostal speech: "God made him Lord and Christ" (Acts 2:36). Paul likewise speaks of Jesus as "our Lord Jesus Christ" (Acts 20:21; see 28:31). But Luke adds a certain nuance of his own to the title "Christ." He uses it again and again in an apologetic vein to affirm that Jesus is God's *holy* agent, "anointed" with God's Spirit. Jesus described himself in this way at Nazareth: "The Spirit of the Lord has 'anointed' (*christ*ened) me..." (4:18). This meaning is confirmed in Peter's preaching in Acts: "...how God anointed (*christ*ened) Jesus of Nazareth with the Holy Spirit and with power" (10:38). "Christ," then takes on the

special Lukan meaning of God's holy, authorized covenant leader. Where there was intense competition for leadership in the synagogue among Pharisees, Scribes, Sadducees and Priests, Jesus' "anointing" would set him apart as the one whom God authorized for leadership.

3. *Savior*. One of the most original and striking titles which Luke uses to name Jesus is "Savior." The angel at Jesus' birth tells the shepherds: "Today is born to you a savior, who is Christ the Lord (2:11). The angel's word is God's word: God designates Jesus as savior. At the end of the gospel we find other references to Jesus as savior, although they are put in an ironic mode. To Jesus' enemies, the Savior seems to be in need of salvation himself: "He saved others..." (23:35), and "Save yourself and us!" (23:39).

Yet Savior he is. Like the beneficent rulers of classical empires, Jesus is called "Savior-Benefactor." What, however, constitutes the "salvation" which Jesus brings? A wide range of items is included here:

1. the "consolation of Israel" (2:25),
2. the "redemption of Jerusalem" (2:38),
3. the healing of illness and disease, such as the ancient prophets brought to God's covenant people (8:36, 48; 17:19),
4. forgiveness of sins (7:50; Acts 13:38-39).

The full range of God's covenant benefactions, diverse and many as they are, are the acts of salvation which come through Jesus.

But "Savior" has a still wider range of meaning. Salvation can mean becoming a member of the covenant-in-Jesus, the true people of God. One can "save oneself from this crooked generation" (Acts 2:40) by believing in Jesus and so joining his group. The way of Jesus is also a "way of salvation" (Acts 16:17).

There is even a stronger meaning to this title in Acts, where Luke affirms that Jesus is the unique, necessary, and universal savior of the world. In Peter's commentary on the healing of the crippled beggar, he proclaims of Jesus: "And there is salvation in *no one else,* for there is *no other name* under heaven given among us by which we must be saved" (4:12). Jesus is unique savior! In Paul's preaching to the Antioch synagogue, he proclaims forgiveness of our sins in Jesus: "By him every one that believes is freed from everything from which you could not be freed by the law of Moses" (13:38-39). Jesus is the necessary and universal savior!

As savior, Jesus tells the dying thief that "Today you will be with me in paradise" (Lk 23:43). As savior, Jesus appears to Stephen in his hour of execution (Acts 7:55-56). And so, Jesus is identified as savior who can offer eternal life (Paradise) and eternal vindication to dying people. Salvation in Jesus, then, includes eschatological salvation from sin and death.

"Savior," then, is an extremely rich title for Luke, one which identifies Jesus as a ruler of God's people, a Benefactor. Jesus' salvation is ecumenical, for Gentiles as well as Jews. His salvation touches every aspect of the lives of covenant members: their sins, ill health, dying, as well as their resurrection and standing before God. Yet Jesus alone is savior; salvation can only be had through him and in union with him.

4. *Ruler of the Covenant People.* There are several other titles given to Jesus which all basically affirm him as the ruler and leader of God's covenant people: "King," "Son of David," and "Lord." At the very beginning of Luke's narrative, God's angel proclaims Jesus as the successor of David and as the fulfilment of God's covenant promise of a Shepherd to guide God's chosen people:

> He (Jesus) will be great and will be called
> the Son of the Most High;
> and the Lord God will give to him
> the throne of his father David;
> and he will rule over the house of Jacob forever.
> And of his kingdom there will be no end (Lk 1:32-33).

King and ruler of the covenant people, of course, are no mere honorific titles for Jesus. Not with Israel standing in opposition to the church. These titles identify Jesus as ruler and shepherd and validate his actions of gathering a covenant people around himself. People beg a boon from him, just as they begged a favor from a monarch: "Jesus, Son of David, have mercy on me" (18:38-39). For the ruler is seen as a person close to God and so with access to God's saving power. Benefaction toward his people is the job of a shepherd-ruler. And so as the crowds "praise God for all the mighty works they had seen" through Jesus' hand (19:37), they acclaim him their king: "Blessed is the King who comes in the name of the Lord" (19:38). The gospel closes as it began, with the identification of Jesus as King. One of the charges before Pilate is that Jesus "says that he himself is Christ a king" (23:2). This is repeated on the cross where people taunt Jesus with being a "savior," the King of the Jews: "He saved others, let him save himself if he is the Christ of God, his chosen one" (23:35) and "If you are the King of the Jews, save yourself" (23:37). At the beginning and the end of his narrative, Luke affirms for his community Jesus' identity and role for them as the authentic, promised Son of David, King of the Jews. Functionally, this gives special meaning to Jesus' miracles and saving actions, for such benefactions are characteristic of God's shepherd of the covenant people.

But if, in calling Jesus "King" the gospel stresses his saving miracles, the Acts of the Apostles takes a much wider view of Jesus' executive leadership of God's covenant people. The climax of Peter's first speech is the solemn affirmation of Jesus as covenant Lord of Israel: "Let the whole house of Israel know assuredly that God has made him both Lord and Christ, this Jesus whom you crucified" (2:36). Luke then begins to catalogue the range of beneficent actions of this "Lord and Christ":

> 1. As covenant Lord, Jesus poured out the Spirit of God on God's people: "Having received from the Father the promise of the Holy Spirit, he has poured out this which you see and hear" (2:33).

2. In his name healing miracles continue to be performed: "In the name of Jesus of Nazareth, walk!" (3:6; see 4:10-12; 9:34).

3. As ruler of the covenant, Jesus guides the mission of the prophets of that covenant, sending them to "Judea, Samaria and the ends of the earth" (1:8). And so Jesus sends Phillip to evangelize the Ethiopian eunuch (8:26), and has Paul and Barnabas set aside for mission (13:1-3); Jesus calls Paul across from Asia to Europe to continue the mission (16:9).

4. As chief executive, Jesus calls a new emissary to himself to carry his message abroad (9:4-6, 15-16).

5. As Lord of all, Jesus rescues his followers from prison (12:6-11; 16:25-26; 18:9) and from catastrophe (27:23-26).

6. He consoles and vindicates those who die on his behalf (7:55-56).

7. He raises up prophets, especially prophets who predict coming disaster, and so hedge the covenant people from famine and ruin (11:27-30).

In Acts, then, Luke presents the picture of genuine covenant people, ruled by a powerful, present and active "Lord and Christ."

5. *Judge.* As we noted in regard to eschatology, Jesus acts vigorously as "judge." The depiction of this in the gospel is somewhat fluid, for one might see Jesus' pronouncements against sinners as woe oracles of a typical prophet against sinful Israel (esp. 10:13-15). It belongs to a prophet to uncover sin and condemn it. A quick survey of Jesus' judgmental statements would surely include: 3:17; 10:13-15; 11:47-51; 13:34-35; 19:27; and 23:27-31. The Lukan portrait of Jesus as "prophet," especially as judging prophet, is compounded with the presentation of him as "Son of Man." This title, we recall, speaks of one who was rejected on earth by men but vindicated in heaven by God (see 7:34). In the paradox of the gospel, the rejected one is the judged one; but in his vindication, the judged one becomes the Judge of those who judged him. And so judgment is attributed to Jesus under the rubric of "Son of Man," as the following Lukan text illustrates:

> "Whoever is ashamed of me and my words of him will the
> Son of Man be ashamed when he comes in his glory and
> the glory of the Father and of the holy angels" (9:26).

The gospel, then, attributes the function of judgment to
Jesus in terms of faith. Those who reject Jesus, especially as
God's prophetic messenger, are condemned; those who
judge the "Son of Man" are judged in turn by him.

As usual, Luke reflects in Acts a much fuller portrait of
Jesus' role as Judge. He is the universal judge of all people,
Jew and Greek, living and dead (Acts 10:42; 17:31). Indeed,
in Acts Luke begins to speak of an eschatological scenario
which will embrace all people. Paul, for example, speaks to
Felix, his judge, about the basic Jewish dogma of resurrection and judgment. In his defense on trial, Paul first affirms
his acceptance of the orthodox position: "According to the
Way, which they call a sect, I worship the God of our
fathers, believing everything laid down by the law or written
in the prophets, having a hope in God which they themselves
accept, that there will be a resurrection of the just and the
unjust" (24:14-15). This "resurrection" is, of course, a resurrection unto judgment (see Jn 5:29). Later in private conver-
sation with Felix, Paul speaks further about "justice,
self-control, and future judgment" (24:25). In this context,
we can appreciate the proclamation of Jesus as the one "by
whom God will judge the world in righteousness" (17:31).
Jesus' universal judgment is now functionally linked with
his being the Lord of the covenant and the Ruler of God's
people. Judgment is a function of ruling power, a role which
Luke clearly ascribes to Jesus in Acts.

The role of Judge, like so many aspects of Luke's portrait
of Jesus, is inclusive. Jesus is Lord of *all* God's covenant
people, Gentiles included. He is the unique savior of the
world. And he is the Judge of *all*. Although there is a strong
note of inclusiveness in Jesus' judgment, that is moderated
by the remembrance that his judgment serves to fix and
determine who is in/out of the covenant, and who is finally
included/excluded. Judgment is universal, inasmuch as the
Christian mission is universal, "to the ends of the earth"

(Acts 1:8). But judgment is essentially a narrowing process in Luke-Acts by which unbelievers and sinners are thrust out, just as the chaff is winnowed from the wheat and cast into the furnace (Lk 3:17). Nevertheless, the role of Judge fills out the portrait of Jesus in Acts as the cosmic and eternal Lord of God's covenant people, "of whose kingdom there shall be no end" (Lk 1:33).

6. *The Ever-present Jesus.* Luke is the only evangelist who narrates Jesus' ascension (Lk 24:50-51; Acts 1:9), which suggests at first blush Jesus' absence from the covenant followers gathered in his name. Although Luke formally describes Jesus' ascension, his absence is *not* intended. In fact, one of the distinctive features of the Christology of Luke-Acts is the proclamation of the active presence of the Risen Jesus in the life of the church.

Jesus' active presence is never more evident than on Easter. Acting as the Good Shepherd (see Lk 15:3-7), Jesus goes in pursuit of two straying followers who were making their sad way to Emmaus (Lk 24:13-33). He teaches them, feeds them, enlightens them, and so restores them to communion with his other disciples (24:33). Luke then tells how Jesus came to the Eleven in Jerusalem (Lk 24:36-49) to convince, strengthen, and commission them. Jesus, then, is actively present on Easter, continuing his ministry of reconciliation and proclamation.

Acts confirms this. In two places Luke tells us of Jesus' active presence during the forty days after his resurrection. In a summary at the beginning of Acts, Luke notes that "To them he presented himself alive after his passion by many proofs, appearing to them during forty days, and speaking of the kingdom of God" (Acts 1:3). Jesus' presence has a ministerial purpose, for his "appearing" serves to confirm the Eleven as formal witnesses of his resurrection: "God made him manifest, not to all the people, but to us who were chosen by God as witnesses" (Acts 10:41).

Although Luke narrates Jesus' ascension, he does not see this event as Jesus' absence from the church. On the contrary, Jesus' ascension is his enthronement as "Lord and Christ" of God's covenant people (Acts 2:36). "Lord and

Christ" is a summary formula in Luke-Acts which expresses Jesus' full governing function over God's covenant people as its prophet, judge, and ruler. Jesus, enthroned in heaven, is actively present in the history and affairs of his followers on earth.

Examples of Jesus' active presence in the affairs of the covenant community abound in Acts, as the following list indicates:

1. The enthroned Jesus pours out God's Holy Spirit on his covenant followers: "Having received from the Father the promise of the Holy Spirit, he has poured out this which you see and hear" (Acts 2:33). Not only is Pentecost Jesus' gift, but by this inaugural act, Luke indicates that all other outpourings of the Spirit are to be attributed to Jesus as he governs God's covenant people (see Acts 4:8; 6:5; 8:15-17; 9:17; 13:2-4; etc.).

2. Jesus continues to heal the sick in Acts through the invocation of his name by his apostles: "In the name of Jesus of Nazareth, walk" (Acts 3:6, 16); "Aeneas, Jesus Christ heals you" (Acts 9:34).

3. Jesus actively recruits new leaders to witness to him and to serve his people. The classic example is Jesus' appearance to Paul on route to Damascus: "Saul, Saul, why do you persecute me?" (Acts 9:4). Through Jesus' Spirit, he indicates seven Deacons to serve the Hellenists' widows (6:7), and three missionaries to preach in his name (13:3-4).

4. Jesus actively intervenes in the ministry of his preachers and missionaries. Jesus regularly appears to his preachers to support and uphold them in their crises. He manifested himself to Stephen on trial (Acts 7:55-56) and to Paul in crisis (17:9; 22:17-21; 27:23-26).

5. As he announced in Nazareth's synagogue, Jesus' role includes the "release of captives from prison" (Lk 4:18). Jesus continues this role in Acts when he sends an angel to free Peter from prison: "Now I am sure that the Lord has sent his angel and rescued me from the hand of Herod" (Acts 12:11). In this light, all of the rescues from

prison in Acts are to be attributed to Jesus' intervention (see Acts 5:18-21; 16:25-26).

6. Jesus actively supervises the direction of the mission of the church. Paul is chosen by Jesus for a Gentile mission: "He is a chosen instrument of mine to carry my name before the Gentiles and kings and the sons of Israel" (Acts 9:15). When the proper time arrives, Jesus sent a dream to Paul authorizing him finally to cross from Asia to Europe (16:9).

Luke indicates that in his church there is no sense of a golden age in the past when Christians saw and heard Jesus in the flesh. Luke never looks back nostalgically on a blessed time which is not accessible to his own church. For there is no sense in Luke-Acts of Jesus' absence from his followers. On the contrary, Luke portrays Jesus actively present to his followers as the "Lord and Christ" whom God has set over the church.

Chapter Five

THE CHRISTOLOGIES OF JOHN'S GOSPEL

Modern scholarship on the Fourth Gospel has been exceptionally creative, and its major results should be borne in mind. I have tried to summarize in four points the significant contributions to our reading from contemporary study.

First, contemporary studies of the Fourth Gospel tend to focus on the community which gave rise to this document, its history, character and development. The axiom on which these studies are based states that the story of Jesus in the gospel is also a cipher for or a symbol of the story of the Johannine group. No one seriously thinks that the composer of the Fourth Gospel is a more detailed or accurate historian of Jesus than the authors of the other gospels; rather he is recording the story of his church. (N.B. Raymond Brown's exciting book on the relationship of the Fourth Gospel to the Letters of John is called "The *Community* of the Beloved Disciple".)

Second, since the foundational work of J.L. Martyn, it has become necessary to pay special attention to certain traumatic events in the group's history as the important historical background of the gospel, namely its excommunication from the synagogue. Data for this event abound: a) threats of excommunication are repeatedly noted (9:22; 12:42; 16:2); b) ch 9 tells of the de facto excommunication of the blind man: "and they cast him out" (9:34). The excommunication, which did not fall unexpectedly on the Johannine group, had powerful and lasting effects on it. Just as one cannot study Jewish theology since 1940 without assessing the effects of the Holocaust, so study of the Christology of John's community must take into account the circumstances which led up to its excommunication and the subsequent effects which this had on the Johannine group.

Third, serious historical studies of John's group tend to point out how the portrait of Jesus developed over time from "low" christology (titles about the special status and role of the human, earthly Jesus) to "high" christology (confession of Jesus as a heavenly figure, as "equal to God," and as "Lord and God"). No other gospel explicitly confesses Jesus as "God" or "equal to God"; so we are curious about why and how this group began to confess Jesus in this way.

Fourth, more and more studies are being done on the sectarian character of the Johannine group. The group makes exclusive claims for itself and its cult leader: it repeatedly claims to have the true worship of God, the true doctrine, and the true bread; it claims to be the true vine. Unless one submits to its practices and confesses its confession, one cannot enter into God's kingdom or have access to eternal life. In a strict sense it is claimed that "there is no salvation outside the Johannine church." The Christological confession of the Fourth Gospel must be assessed vis-à-vis the growing sectarian character of the group, for this experience was singularly influential in the shaping of the portraits of Jesus in the gospel.

These four contributions of modern Johannine studies have blazed trails through the gospel which careful students will follow. In general it can be said that the diverse Christological portraits of this gospel grew and developed vis-à-vis the changing experiences in the group's history. In fact, one of the best ways to grasp these portraits is through an appreciation of the changing experiences and history of the Johannine group. The proclamation of Jesus was definitely not a static confession but was influenced by community developments, and represents a series of pastoral adaptations of the Christian kerygma to changing circumstances.

I.
Stage One: Missionary Christology

MISSION AND MEMBERSHIP

This early group of Johannine Christians was very missionary oriented. Preaching about Jesus seems to be its favorite activity. We see this dramatized in the first events of the narrative of Jesus' ministry in ch 1, where a series of disciples are catechized and led to faith in Jesus. John the Baptizer preaches about Jesus to two of his disciples (1:35-40); one of these converts then seeks out Peter (1:41-42); finally Philip preaches to Nathanael (1:45-46). The Samaritan woman fits into this pattern. After she herself is evangelized by Jesus, she preaches to the people of Sychar: "Come and see a man who told me all that I have done" (4:29-30, 39). As we shall see below (under *Ethics*), the gospel concludes with this pattern on the closing day of Jesus' ministry. The gospel, then, is framed with preaching about Jesus.

Jesus' "signs" are one form of missionary propaganda. Their purpose is to lead people to accept Jesus as God's authorized prophet or covenant leader. The editorial comment after the first sign clearly expresses this missionary purpose: "This, the first of his signs, Jesus did at Cana in Galilee, and manifested his glory; and his disciples believed in him" (2:11). Balancing this is a comment at the end of the gospel about the missionary value of Jesus' signs: "Now Jesus did many other signs in the presence of his disciples, which are not written in this book; but these are written that you may believe that Jesus is the Christ, the Son of God"

(20:30-31). Signs, like preaching, serve a missionary purpose.

The preaching of the early Johannine missionaries could also take a more academic turn, as they tried within the synagogue to preach that Jesus is "the one of whom Moses in the Law and also the prophets wrote" (1:45). Jesus' identity and mission, they claim, were already predicted by God in the sacred writings of Israel. Yet this preaching meets with resistance. Nathanael, an astute student of the Scriptures, raises objections to this early preaching when he points out that in the Scriptures Nazareth is not fertile ground for prophets (1:46). Other Jews in the synagogues where Christians preach also raise comparable objections to this line of preaching. Jesus cannot be the Christ: "Is the Christ to come from Galilee? Has not the Scripture said that the Christ is descended from David and comes from Bethlehem, the village where David was?' (7:41-42). Leaders of the synagogue dismiss the Christian preaching, "Search and you will see that no prophet is to rise from Galilee" (7:52). Nathanael, therefore, stands out as a type of hero of this period of Johannine history; for, although he too raised objections to the Christian preaching about Jesus from the Scriptures, he does "come and see" Jesus. And Jesus lavished praise on him, "an Israelite without guile" (1:47) — a statement of praise which canonizes him as a Johannine saint. From this we gain some sense of the character of missionary preaching in the early Johannine group.

The flip side of this intense missionary activity is the question of the membership of the Johannine group. The bulk of its members seem to be Jews who still attend the synagogue. But the Christian preaching seems intended for a much wider audience. Samaritans, with whom the Jews have no truck (4:9, 27), are evangelized; and they confess Jesus, not just as a Jewish leader, but a universal figure of salvation, even as "Savior of the world" (4:42). The title over Jesus' cross is in three languages, "Hebrew, Latin, and Greek" (19:20), suggesting the universal significance of Jesus' mission. And his death is interpreted "not for the nation only, but to gather into one the children of God who are scattered abroad" (11:52; see 10:16 & 12:32). In the early stage of its history, the Johannine group engaged in enthusiastic missionary preaching, which was aimed at all peoples: Jews, Samaritans, and Gentiles.

OLD TESTAMENT

As we noted in regard to the contents of the early preaching, the Old Testament was interpreted by these Christians as a valid and sacred document, whose function was to predict the coming of Jesus, Prophet and King. We often find Christians interpreting events in Jesus' life as "fulfilling the Scriptures." For example, when Jesus' seamless garment is made the object of a game of chance, the evangelist remarked that "This was to fulfil the Scripture, 'They parted my garments among them, and for my clothing they cast lots'" (19:24/Ps 22:18). Again, in regard to the non breaking of Jesus' legs and his pierced side, the evangelist remarks: "These things took place that the Scripture might be fulfilled, 'Not one bone of him shall be broken' (Ex 12:46), and again another Scripture says, 'They shall look on him whom they have pierced' " (19:36-37/Zech 12:10). The Old Testament is a valid book of God's revelation for Christians; but it is basically a prophetic document which foretells Jesus' identity and career (see 2:17; 5:39 & 46).

ESCHATOLOGY

Scholars are uncertain whether in this developing period there is a preferred word from Jesus about eschatological realities. If one compares John's traditions with those found in other early Christian groups, we find a complex word from Jesus about the importance of accepting his preaching. Acceptance could mean that one is either *prepared* for the coming judgment of God or *already* in God's favor because of faith in the word of God's prophets. Although it is difficult to be certain of this, I would hazard a guess that Johannine Christians would emphasize the *already* quality of eschatology, supporting the importance of belief in Jesus' revelation. To believe is *already* to enter God's kingdom; to believe is *already* to possess eternal life.

ETHICS

Consistent with the missionary activity of this group is its insistence that faith in Jesus is the premier virtue which Jesus praises. This is evident in Jesus' first public appearance, where a succession of preachers preach about Jesus and convert a host of people to their preaching:

> 1. John the Baptizer preached Jesus: "Behold, the Lamb of God, who takes away the sin of the world" (1:29)..."I have seen and borne witness that this is the Son of God" (1:34). John evangelized two of his disciples, who followed Jesus and became his disciples (1:37). They believed John's preaching.
>
> 2. One of these first disciples, Andrew, then spoke a word about Jesus to his brother, Simon Peter: "We have found the Messiah (which means Christ)" (1:41). Simon believed Andrew.
>
> 3. Another convert, Philip, himself evangelized Nathanael: "We have found him of whom Moses in the law and also the prophets wrote, Jesus of Nazareth, the son of Joseph" (1:45). Nathanael proved to be a difficult convert, but in the end confessed Jesus as "Son of God... King of Israel" (1:49).

This episode has a programmatic function in John for it describes a process whereby a convert evangelizes others about Jesus. The hearer has no direct access to Jesus, but must believe the word of another. This pattern also concludes the gospel where we find another series of evangelists speaking about Jesus:

> 4. Mary Magdalene, commissioned by Jesus to tell the disciples of his resurrection and ascension, announced

Jesus' word to them: "She told them that he had said these things to her" (20:18).

5. The disciples then tell the absent Thomas of their experience with the Risen Jesus, a word which he refuses to accept without proof (20:25).

6. Jesus himself comes to Thomas and reproaches him for his unbelief in the church's preaching. In the process, Jesus canonizes this belief: "Blessed are those who have not seen and yet believe" (20:29).

The beginning and ending of the gospel, then, indicate that the premier action which leads to life is belief in the word which is preached, whether Jesus' own word or the word of his disciples.

Examples of this abound in the gospel. This is seen first in the way John the Baptizer is transformed from a fiery prophet to a witness who testifies about Jesus. He is officially labeled a "witness" and he repeatedly gives "testimony" about Jesus (1:7, 15, 32; see 5:32-34). The Samaritan woman fits into this pattern; for after she is evangelized by Jesus, she becomes his herald in her city: "Come and see a man who told me all that I ever did. Can this be the Christ?" (4:29). We can see the importance of faith for this group in the way in which belief is spoken of as a matter of life and death: "Who believes in him (Jesus) is not condemned; who does not believe is already condemned" (3:18). Again, "who hears my word and believes him who sent me, has eternal life, s/he does not come into judgment, but has passed from death to life" (5:24). These very statements indicate that the converse is true. If belief is the premier virtue, then unbelief is the worst sin.

GROUP SELF-UNDERSTANDING

These early Johannine Christians had no distinct sense of themselves as a new religious group. They stayed in the synagogue. As they always had, they still acclaimed Israel's monotheistic belief in one God (see Deut 6:4); they accepted God's word in the Scriptures alongside other pious Jews.

Yet they see all of Israel's history and its literature as pointing to Jesus and fulfilled in him. The idiom of Johannine preaching is taken completely from Jewish tradition. And so they implicitly claim to be "authentic Israelites" (1:47) because they believe in Jesus. The early Christological confession, then, is fully coherent with the life-situation and experience of the early Johannine group which was still part of the synagogue.

EXPERIENCE

The action characteristic of this stage of John's history is missionary preaching on Jesus' behalf. It should not be surprising that in a community in a missionary mode, faith and belief in the group's preaching would be valued as the premier virtue. Nor is it surprising that such belief would be hyped as an eschatological blessing whereby the believer already enjoys God's favor and has passed to life.

This missionary group is not aggressively seeking to overthrow the synagogue and its structures, but to re-focus them on a new prophet whose word is now definitive for it. And so, we hear little from Jesus about how one lives from day to day as a true member of God's covenant people; this is presupposed in the Old Testament and in the synagogue's traditions. Belief constitutes one a member of God's kingdom and covenant group, and so there is a corresponding awareness of evangelization as the major experience of the Johannine Christians.

CHRISTOLOGY

We begin as far back in the history of the Johannine group as we can. And we find early, traditional materials acclaiming Jesus as (a) the Messiah, the Christ (1:41; 4:25-26 & 29; 7:26), (b) as the one predicted by Moses and the Prophets (1:45; 5:39; 7:52), (c) as Son of God (1:49), and (d) as King of Israel (1:49; 12:13-15). These titles describe Jesus functionally as God's authorized and holy agent, who is sent to be the newest leader of God's covenant people. These titles, moreover, constitute what in Johannine studies is called "low Christology," the proclamation of Jesus as a special, even as a unique agent of God, albeit as a thoroughly human, earthly figure. Even "Son of God" refers here to Jesus as the leader like Israel's kings, who were also called sons of God (see Ps 2).

These titles, which tell of Jesus' leadership of God's covenant people, are firmly attached to the "signs" of Jesus in the Fourth Gospel. In John, Jesus' miracles are distinctively labelled "signs," that is, events which manifest Jesus' glory (2:11) and which serve as his credentials (compare with Lk 24:19; Acts 2:22). A person who sees these signs ought to conclude that the one who performed them is a special person sent from God: "If this man were not from God he could do nothing" (9:33); "When the Christ appears, will he do more signs than this man has done?" (7:31). Sinners can make no claim to be God's agent or to have access to God's power; Jesus' signs, therefore, argue that, although Jesus did not keep the Sabbath in the traditional way, he *cannot* be a sinner:

> We know that God does not listen to sinners; but if anyone is a worshiper of God and does God's will, God listens to him... If this man were not from God, he could do nothing (9:31-33). Can a demon open the eyes of the blind? (10:21).

When people are open to God's revelation, they tend to interpret correctly the sign-miracles of Jesus as his credentials, and so conclude to a true Christology. After Jesus multiplies the loaves (6:1-13), the crowd recognizes this as a "sign" and correctly concludes, "This is indeed the prophet who is to come into the world" (6:14). Signs, then, attest to Jesus as a holy figure sent to teach God's covenant people (i.e. prophet) and to shepherd them as their covenant leader (i.e. king). The crowd in ch 6 who ate the multiplied loaves would make Jesus their leader; they were about to "make him king" (6:15). Later, the crowd that greeted Jesus on his entrance into Jerusalem as "King of Israel" (12:13-15) did so because "they heard that he had done this sign" (12:18), viz., the raising of Lazarus from the dead.

This Christology is similar to that found in the synoptic gospels. Jesus goes about doing miracles; he heals the sick, multiplies food, and raises the dead. And the crowds interpret these deeds correctly. When Jesus asks about their impressions of him, his disciples record that the people say that he is "Elijah or one of the prophets" (Mk 8:28). The disciples themselves conclude that his miracles give ground for calling him God's Christ, that is, God's anointed leader of his covenant people (Mk 8:29). He does "the deeds of the Christ" (Mt 11:2).

There is a strong sense of coherence between the formal Christological confession of Jesus and other aspects of Jesus' portrait. As missionaries within the synagogue, Johannine preachers announced Jesus as the fulfilment of Israel's Scriptures. Faith in Jesus as the new prophet like Moses constitutes salvation; authentic membership in God's covenant depends on confession of Jesus as leader of that covenant. The setting is a synagogue of Israel; the preaching is from Israel's Scriptures; the Christology is expressed in titles and images from Israel's history. Stage one of the Christology of the Fourth Gospel, then, is characterized as missionary Christology where enthusiasm and success abound.

II.
Stage Two: Aggressive Christology

At a later stage in the group's history, we find new and different confessions being made about Jesus. Instead of seeing Jesus as another Prophet, even as the authentic leader of the covenant, he is heralded as a figure greater than the Prophets and Patriarchs of Israel's history. He is acclaimed as "greater than" Jacob (4:12, 13-14), Abraham (8:53, 56-58), and even Moses (1:17; 3:13-15; 5:36, 46; 6:31-32). Implicit in these confessions is the claim that in Jesus a newer and better revelation is offered than Moses offered; in Jesus a newer and better covenant people is formed than was formed through Abraham; in Jesus a newer and better revelation about worship is offered than came through Jacob. It is not enough to see Jesus as the latest and best of the line of prophets and founding figures; now radical and exclusive claims are made that Jesus is superior to older prophets and leaders. In fact, he replaces them and makes their revelations obsolete. Jesus is the revealer of *new* things — a new place to worship, a new way of worship, and new rites. Jesus is confessed as the ultimate word from God who surpasses and replaces all previous words. We must now try to appreciate this Christological confession in the context of the experience of the group which espoused it.

MISSION AND MEMBERSHIP

One senses a change in the mission of the Johannine group. Although there is little hard evidence that it stopped evangelizing or that it began to restrict membership to certain nations or races, one detects a shift in its apostolic energies. There is less preaching of Jesus as the fulfillment of the Scriptures and more assertion of him as the replacement of Israel's revelation. The argument is now *against* the Jews; and it is just that, an argument, a debate — not a preaching. The thrust of its missionary endeavor seems to have turned inward. The group's energy is now directed toward Christian self-definition, that is, how Christians are different from synagogue Jews. And so exclusive claims on behalf of Jesus and his teaching are being made. Debate replaces missionary propaganda.

The membership is open to all who would accept Jesus. Inasmuch as the stakes are raised by the new and exclusive claims of the absolute superiority of Jesus, membership will effectively be limited. For the Christian claims are very off-putting; they are bound to be offensive to synagogue Jews. And this will effect membership.

OLD TESTAMENT

We can detect a major shift in the way that the Old Testament is used in this stage of the history of the Johannine group. Previously it was a valid body of sacred writings whose function was to prophesy about Jesus. In that view, however, one finds the seeds of further development. If the Scriptures are but a foreshadowing of Jesus, when the prophesied object comes, then the prophecy is of diminished value. The Old Testament is but a shadow of the reality which is now present. At this new stage of Johannine experience, moreover, the Old Testament is being systematically replaced. As we saw above, Jesus supplants Jacob, Abraham and Moses as Prophet, Revealer and Source of Knowledge. The value of the Old Testament passages which speak of these figures is relativized, for they are now replaced.

Jesus begins to speak of the replacement of all the sacred aspects of Israel's history. At the marriage feast at Cana (2:1-11) Jesus fills the water jars with wine; those jars originally held water "for the Jewish rites of purification" (2:6). Jesus now gives a fluid which is admittedly "better than" the former fluids in which the Jews delighted. The steward makes this clear when he tells the bridegroom that instead of serving the best fluid first and then the poorer, "You have kept the good wine till last" (2:10). Because they are superior, Christian fluids replace Jewish purification fluids. This miracle is immediately followed by Jesus' activity in the temple (2:13-22). First we are told that Jesus chased out of the temple oxen and sheep (2:14), animals which are used for purificatory sacrifice. Second, Jesus makes a claim that his risen body is the new temple ("He spoke of the temple of his body," 2:21). Thus chapter two proclaims that Jesus replaces purificatory rites (washings and sacrifices) with Christian purifications; he replaces the temple too. These issues obviously touch the core of Israel's faith.

In ch 3, Jesus is face to face with Nicodemus, a ruler of the Jews, in what seems like a first-century summit meeting. Jesus tells Nicodemus that being born from above is necessary to see the kingdom of God (3;3, 5). A typical Jew understood that membership in the kingdom of God's covenant people came through circumcision, which might also be accompanied by a form of proselyte baptism. But Jesus declares these rites obsolete and invalid; they are replaced by Christian baptism. Likewise in ch 4, Jesus speaks of a new place to worship and a new mode of worship. Samaritans claimed that Mt. Gerizim in Samaria is the correct place to worship because God appeared there to Jacob (see Gen 28:12, 16-17); Jews claimed that Jerusalem is the legitimate place for God's temple. Jesus, however, invalidates both claims: "Neither on this mountain nor in Jerusalem will you worship the Father" (4:21). The temple is replaced. And Jesus says further that there is a new and true form of worship: "True worshipers will worship the Father in spirit and truth" (4:23-24). The old Jewish worship with animal sacrifices and other such rites in the temple is declared invalid and replaced.

Jewish feasts, too, are replaced. Jesus multiplies his loaves on the occasion of Passover (6:4); he then claims that there is a new bread come down from heaven which is "the *true* bread" (6:32). In the Fourth Gospel, moreover, Jesus is killed on the same day and about the same hour when the passover lambs were traditionally slaughtered. His own pierced body is compared to a passover lamb when the evangelist comments about it with a sacred phrase used to describe the passover lamb, "not one bone of it shall be broken" (19:36/Ex 12:46). Jesus replaces the Unleavened Bread and the Lamb of Passover. Jesus goes to the feast of Tabernacles (7:2). There he replaces the two key elements of that feast which were the prayer for rain (water) and sun (light). Jesus himself claims to be the true water (7:37-39) and the true light (8:12).

Christian claims for the superiority of their cultic practices and their assertion that Jewish rites etc, are replaced can only be seen as a radical devaluation of the Old Testament as a source of authentic revelation. Whatever its past value, it is replaced by new revelation in Jesus: "He bears witness to what he has seen and heard...he whom God has sent utters the words of God" (3:32-34). And the the new wine is definitely better than the old.

ESCHATOLOGY

Accompanying this view of Christian sacraments as replacements of Jewish rites is a distinctive view of eschatology. Three points can be made. First, whereas Jewish rites offered "life," Christian rites are said to offer "everlasting life." Whoever drinks the physical waters of Jacob's well will thirst again; but "whoever drinks of the water that I will give him will never thirst again" (4:14a). For Christian waters will "become a spring" within the believer, "welling up to eternal life" (4:14b). Christian Eucharist is superior to the Unleavened Bread and Manna of the Jews: "Who eats this bread will live forever" (6:58; see 6:49-50). Second, Jesus is clearly not the judge of the Jews: "God did not send the Son into the world to judge the world" (3:17); "You judge according to the flesh, I judge no one" (8:15); and again, "If anyone hears my words and does not do them, I do not judge him; for I did not come to judge the world, but the save the world" (12:37). Third, the "judge" is the very believer; the "judgment" is the decision which one makes about Jesus and his revelation. "This is the judgment: the light came into the world and men loved darkness rather than the light" (3:19). At this stage of Johannine experience it is possible to speak of realized eschatology: the believer, when confronted with Jesus, judges him to be God's authentic word and so is presently in possession of eternal life and passes even now beyond judgment. This is most clearly seen when Jesus states:

> Amen, amen I say to you: who hears my words and believes him who sent me has eternal life; he does not come into judgment, but has passed from death to life (5:24).

Christian sacraments and confession, then, are superior to Jewish customs because they offer immediate access to life which never ends, even eschatological life.

ETHICS

Belief in the Christian preaching continues to be the premier virtue of the Johannine group. As Christian claims to be the fulfilment and replacement of Jewish rites accelerated, acceptance of those Christian claims became all the more important.

In the early stage, we seem to have had stories only of the success of Christian preaching (see 1:35-49; 4:28-29). In this later stage of development, we begin to find stories of failure to believe. In fact, John's narrative begins to tell of a *division* among the crowds over Christian preaching: some believe and others reject the word.

1. When the crowds heard Jesus' word, "Some of the people said, 'this is really the prophet.' Others said, 'is the Christ to come from Galilee?' So there was *division* among the people over him" (7:40-43).

2. After the healing of the man born blind, John again records contrasting reactions: "Some of the Pharisees said, 'This man is not from God, for he does not keep the Sabbath.' But others said, 'How can a man who is a sinner do such signs?' There was a *division* among them" (9:16).

3. In another case, John records: "There was a *division* among the Jews because of these words. Many of them said, 'He has a demon, he is mad; why listen to him?' Others said, 'These are not the words of one who has a demon. Can a demon open the eyes of the blind?'" (10:19-21).

4. Other examples would be the contrasting reactions to Jesus' weeping over Lazarus's death (11:36-37), to Jesus' raising of Lazarus (11:45-46), and to Jesus' entry into Jerusalem (12:13-19).

Conversely, the Johannine pattern of *division* among

hearers of Jesus' word indicates that many do not believe. These are censured as sinners who "see but do not believe." Although it was earlier stated that Jesus did not come for judgment (3:17), that is qualified as more hostile reactions to Jesus occur. In a controversy setting, John remarks that indeed Jesus has come for judgment: "For judgment I came into the world, that those who do not see may see, and that those who see may become blind" (9:39). Unbelief remains the number one vice in the Johannine community.

GROUP SELF-UNDERSTANDING

The self-understanding of the Johannine group likewise undergoes change. The group is evidently in the process of distinguishing itself from the synagogue, a process it undertakes by clarifying how correct and superior Jesus' revelation is to the Torah of the synagogue. The Johannine group is beginning to build a wall between itself and the Jewish synagogue by making exclusive claims on its own behalf, claims which may be grasped under four rubrics. First, Jesus reveals newer and better cultic practices than the old and invalid ones of Israel: a newer and better place to worship, newer and better purificatory rites, as well as newer and better feast days. Second, Jesus begins to use the tag "true" of his revelation and doctrine, a tag which implies that what the synagogue has is "false." For example, Jesus is the "true light" who illumines everyone (1:9); Christians are the "true worshipers" (4:23); Jesus is the "true bread come down from heaven" (6:23); Jesus' testimony and judgment are "true" (8:16); Jesus is the "true vine" to which one must belong (15:1). Third, Jesus begins to make exclusive claims that "Unless one is born again of water and the spirit, one cannot see the kingdom of God" (3:3,5); or "Unless you eat the flesh of the Son of man and drink his blood, you do not have life in you" (6:53). Access to God's life and kingdom is exclusively through Jesus. Finally, the old prophets, revealers and founding fathers of Israel's covenant are inferior to Jesus and obsolete; for Jesus is "greater than" Jacob (4:12), Abraham (8:53), or Moses (1:17). The Johannine group is effectively claiming to be the only authentic covenant group, with the only adequate Torah and the only genuine worship. Outside of this group there is no salvation.

EXPERIENCE

The Johannine group still resides in the local synagogue; it still engages in propagandistic preaching on Jesus' behalf; it still claims that belief in Jesus leads to eternal life. But its experience is not simply that of a missionary group. The Johannine group is now making bold and exclusive claims on Jesus' behalf, claims which flat out negate the synagogue's traditional beliefs. The activity of the Johannine group has taken on a decidedly aggressive quality in its claims that Christian rites replace Jewish rituals, that Christian interpretation of the Old Testament supplants Jewish traditions, and that Jesus replaces Moses and the Patriarchs. The Johannine group is not so much reacting to events, but controlling them. They are shaping their own experience by the content of their preaching. Their claims and their preaching are rapidly creating a polarization of the synagogue; they are forcing a division to be made.

CHRISTOLOGY

The Christological confession of this group cannot be appreciated except in the context of the experience of the group which confessed it. That Jesus is "greater than" Israel's prophets and patriarchs and that he replaces them makes sense in terms of the new claims that Christian sacraments and worship replace inferior Jewish rites. The full extent of what Jesus means at this stage of Johannine history is clear when we see that Jesus himself *is* the temple; his flesh and blood *are* life; his fluids *give* purification; confession of him *is* worship of God. No Old Testament figure could claim that his person or his teaching was purification, sacrifice or holiness. Jesus claims that those who accept him in faith even now "have eternal life," not just life such as Moses' manna might give, but eschatological life.

The group's exclusive claims to have the truth, the whole truth, and nothing but the truth are tied ultimately to their claims that Jesus is in every way superior to all previous religious figures. An exclusivist Christology, then, corresponds with an exclusivist sense of church.

Appreciation of this context enables us to situate the next step in the group's confession of Jesus, even if we cannot fully explain its origins. At a certain point in time, the Johannine Christians began making still more exclusive claims on Jesus' behalf. 1. He is the Word of God (1:1), the unique and only revealer of God's revelation: "No one has ascended to heaven but he who descended from heaven, the Son of Man" (3:13). This statement claims some startling things on Jesus' behalf: a) no other Old Testament mystic or prophet has ever ascended to receive God's revelation — not Enoch, not Elijah, not Moses; b) Jesus alone has God's revelation or word (3:32, 34); and c) Jesus is first and foremost a heavenly figure who originally descended from heaven. According to 3:13, then, Jesus is the unique revealer of God's word; he replaces all previous revealers in Israel's history.

2. One begins to find a refrain in John, "No one has ever seen God" (1:18; 6:46; see 3:13). Taken seriously, this calls into question all of the Old Testament theophanies to Abraham (Gen 12; 15; 18), to Jacob (Gen 28; 31), to Moses (Ex 20; 34), to Elijah (1 Kg 19), to Isaiah (Isa 6), and to Ezekiel (Ezek 1). The Johannine claim is clear and absolute: no! the patriarchs and prophets did *not* see Israel's God, for *"No one* has ever seen God."* Then is the Old Testament in error? No, for according to the Fourth Gospel, the patriarchs and prophets saw Jesus, the heavenly figure who has always revealed God's name and word to Israel throughout its history. Thus we find the claim that "Abraham rejoiced that he was to see my day" (8:56); when Abraham showed hospitality to the three heavenly figures who visited his tent at Mamre in Gen 18, he received and saw Jesus (see 8:39 where "hospitality" is the great virtue of Abraham). Isaiah, it is claimed, "saw his glory and spoke of him" (12:41), when Isaiah saw the vision of God's presence descend on the

temple in Isa 6. He did not see God/Yahweh, but Jesus, the appearing heavenly figure. By implication, neither Moses (5:37-38) nor Jacob (1:51) saw Israel's God, but rather Jesus.

Perhaps it will help to clarify this claim of the Johannine group if we compare it with an identical claim made by Justin Martyr. In his debate with a Jewish adversary, Trypho, Justin claims that all of the Old Testament theophanies were in reality Christophanies — appearances of the heavenly, divine Jesus:

> Neither Abraham, nor Isaac, nor Jacob, nor any other man, saw the Father and ineffable Lord of all, but saw him who was according to his will his Son, being God, and the angel because he ministered to his will *(Dial.* 127).

Justin and the Fourth Gospel agree: 1) no one has ever seen God, 2) but Scripture says that patriarchs and prophets saw someone; 3) they saw Jesus, a heavenly and divine figure.

3. In relation to this we can begin to make sense of certain passages in the Fourth Gospel where reference is made to the special name of God, "I AM." Jesus refers to himself in four places as I AM (8:24, 28, 58; 13:19); in these places the phrase I AM has the status of a name or identification. The Jewish Scriptures say that when Moses asked the figure who appeared to him at the burning bush what his name was, he was told "Say this to the people, 'I AM has sent me to you'" (Ex 3:14-15). Certainly by the time the Hebrew Scriptures were translated into Greek, it was becoming more common to name Israel's God by the sobriquet I AM. For example, the Hebrew text of Isa 51:12 merely says "I, I am he who comforts you"; the Greek translation of this says more: "I am 'I AM' who comforts you." Again, Isa 52:6 merely says, "They shall know that it is I who speak" whereas the Greek translation of this says more: "My people shall know that 'I AM' is the one who speaks." There are ample grounds, then, for taking Jesus' self-identification of "I AM" as reference to the special name of God.

This helps us understand certain remarks of Jesus in ch

17. Jesus repeatedly states that "I have manifested *thy name* to them" (17:6); "keep them in *the name* which you have given me" (17:12) and "I have made known to them *thy name* and I will make it known" (17:26). The "name" of God which Jesus manifested is the "I AM," the name of the appearing deity in Israel's Scriptures. God granted Jesus to bear that name and to use it of himself in his Christophanies in the Old Testament.

The established confession of Jesus as the replacement of Jewish ritual and cult and as "greater than" Israel's patriarchs and prophets is the appropriate context from which to assess this new confession of Jesus as the unique and only figure who has seen God and descended from heaven with God's word. Not only is Jesus "greater than" Abraham, Jacob, and Moses in virtue of his superior revelation, but also because they never saw God and Jesus has (1:18; 6:46). Jesus is greater than them because he is originally a heavenly figure who descends to earth; he is greater than them because it was Jesus who appeared to them in their theophanies in the Old Testament. So Jesus is "greater than" the patriarchs and prophets in a qualitatively new way. He is beginning to be acclaimed as a heavenly figure who descends to earth. This tendency will reach its climax in the statement that God's heavenly word entered this material world and became flesh, pitching his tent among us (1:14). The assertion of Jesus's superiority to all things in Israel's sacred history, then, is the context in which Jesus' uniqueness as a descending heavenly revealer develops. Perceptive synagogue critics might well begin to say the Christians are trying to replace Yahweh with Jesus.

4. We are now in a position to assess still greater claims made by the Johannine group that Jesus is "equal to God." In 10:33 we read that the Jews wanted to kill Jesus "because you, being a man, make yourself God"; and in 5:18, the Jews are reported to be seeking to kill Jesus because he "made himself equal to God." This new and bold confession obviously created a crisis and so we find full and careful explanation of this claim given in 5:19-29. In one sense it is incorrect to allege that Jesus "makes himself" anything; he is

no pushy person who vaingloriously claims honors and powers (no Napoleon complex here!); he is no thief who has stolen God's secrets. Rather, as 5:19-29 clearly assert, God has made Jesus equal to Himself. First, it is argued that "the Father loves the Son and *shows him* all that he himself is doing" (5:20). Second, it is urged that "the Father *has given* all judgment to the Son" (5:22); third, "the Father *has granted* the Son to have life in himself" (5:26). It is wrong, then, to state that Jesus *makes himself* anything; rather, God loves, shows, gives, and grants Jesus certain powers. This is God's doing! And the purpose of God's benefactions to Jesus is clear "... *so that* all may honor the Son, even as they honor the Father" (5:23). It is God's will, then, that Jesus be acclaimed as "equal to God" and given equal honor.

If part of the charge in 5:18 is false ("he makes himself..."), part of it is true. For Jesus is truly "equal to God." We know of God from God's effect in the world, his powers. Jewish theology summed up all of God's working in the world in two basic powers, a creative power and an executive (or judmental) power. John 5:19-29 tries to show that Jesus has these two complementary powers to the full. First, it is important to remember that in ch 5 Jesus healed a man on the Sabbath (5:1-9) and he justified this technical violation of the Sabbath by claiming that "My Father is working still, and I am working" (5:17). Although Gen 2:2-3 states that God "rested on the Sabbath," it was popularly argued in Jesus' time that God in fact kept working, for the Creator must always keep working to maintain the creation he has made [Philo, *Leg. All.* I.5, "God never leaves off making, but even as it is the property of fire to burn and snow to chill, so it is the property of God to make."] Jesus' healing on the Sabbath, then, is considered by the Johannine group as a "creative act"; it shows that Jesus has creative power. And the apology in 5:19-20 expands on this to show that Jesus has God's *full* creative power, "The Father shows him *all* that he himself is doing" (5:20); "*whatever* he (God) does, the Son does likewise" (5:19). It is argued in the gospel's prologue, moreover, that Jesus exercised this creative power at the genesis of the world: "He was in the beginning, all things were made through him and without him was not made anything that was made"(1:2-3). Jesus, then, is "equal to God" because he has God's creative power, as both creation and Jesus' signs attest.

Second, the continuing explanation in 5:21-29 shows that Jesus likewise has God's second power, the judgmental or eschatological power. It is argued first that "as the Father raises the dead and gives them life, so also the Son gives life" (5:21). Then the text claims that "the Father has given all judgment to the Son" (5:22); third, "as the Father has life in himself, so he has granted the Son to have life in himself" (5:26). Fourth, it is repeated that God gave judgment to the Son, because he is the Son of Man (5:27). Fifth, the Son will execute this judgment at the general resurrection, for "those in the tombs will hear his voice and come forth...to the resurrection of life...and to the resurrection of judgment" (5:28-29). The Son, then, has full eschatological power. And so the Christians are justified in claiming that Jesus is truly "equal to God" because he fully possesses God's two basic powers, creative power (5:19-20) and eschatological power (5:21-29).

In Jewish theology distinctive names are associated with each of these two powers respectively. When Israel's deity acts as creator, he is called "God" [the Greek word for "god" (*theos*) is said by the ancients to be etymologically related to the word used for the verb "to create" (*tithemi*).] When the deity exercises judgmental or executive power, he is called "Lord." Philo, an Egyptian Jew and a contemporary of Jesus, explains this link between the two powers of God and God's two names:

> His creative power is called God (*theos*), because through it he placed and made the universe, and the kingly power is called Lord (*Kyrios*), being that by which he governs and rules steadfastly with justice (*Mos.* II. 99).

This association of power and name may help us to understand why in the prologue, when Jesus creates, he is called

"God" (*theos*). "The Word was 'God'...all things were made through him" (1:1-3). And when Jesus performs creative miracles on the Sabbath, he exercises this power again and so is "equal to God." According to the gospel, Jesus has demonstrated over and over again that he has God's creative power and so he is appropriately called "God" or "equal to God." Jesus is only unambiguously called "Lord" after he has demonstrated eschatological power. In 5:21-29, he is only credited with this power. We begin to see him exercise this power in subsequent chapters. First, he calls Lazarus out of the tomb (11:43-44), demonstrating the claim made in 5:25, 28-29 that all who are in the tombs will hear his voice and come forth. Second, Jesus proves that just as God raises the dead and gives them life, so the Son gives life (5:21); after all, he told Martha that "I am the resurrection and the life" (11:25). Third, Jesus claimed "to have life in himself" (5:26), power which he demonstrates at his death and resurrection. For he claimed that "I have power to lay it (my life) down and I have power to take it up" (10:18), power which he received from his Father. And so, after demonstrating that he can raise the dead, even raise himself, he is credited by his disciple, Thomas, with full eschatological power. And Thomas appropriately confessed him by the name associated with that power, "Lord," in his confession "My Lord and my God." By the end of the gospel Jesus has demonstrated that he has God's two powers and so he is acclaimed by the two names associated with those powers: creative power = "God" and eschatological power = "Lord."

This latest Christological claim of the Johannine group represents a threshold. The synagogue could tolerate claims that Jesus was a prophet, Israel's King, even its Messiah; we know from texts such as Acts 5:35-37 that there were other persons in Jesus' time claiming to be such. The synagogue might disagree, but it could tolerate these claims. Up to a point, the synagogue could also tolerate claims to reform Israel's cult, for such claims had been made in its past and were being made even at Jesus' time by the members of the Qumran community. That, too, could be tolerated. Even the claim that Jesus was a heavenly messenger descended from heaven was not totally out of line; for Israel's Scriptures record that angels came to patriarchs etc. with messages; the Archangel Raphael came to Tobias and instructed him (and see Lk 1:26-38). But the claim that Jesus was "equal to God" and that he could rightly be called "God" and "Lord" and that he had a right to call himself by the name of "I AM," crossed a threshold in the synagogue's theology. Granted that the most sacred dogma of Jewish faith was the Shema (Deut 6:4), the proclamation of monotheism, the Christological claim of the Johannine group would seem to compromise that faith. The new confessions of Jesus by the Johannine group could easily be understood by the synagogue as proclaiming a second God. It was a claim not to be tolerated. It was sure to provoke a strong and decisive reaction from the synagogue.

III.
Stage Three: Sectarian Christology

Our world is shaped by experiences which challenge old ideas and force us to re-evaluate our world anew. For example, after the discovery of the telescope and the astronomical revolution of the sixteenth century, the world was forced to interpret a universe where the earth was not the center, but a small planet orbiting the sun. As a result of this, the place of humankind in the world needed to be revalued; no longer was the Renaissance image of "man as the measure of all things" valid. Such experiences forced us to reassess old ideas and accommodate ourselves to these experiences. John's group suffered several such experiences which challenged its old ideas and necessitated adjustments in its views.

EXPERIENCE

Since this is the dominant factor in the analysis of this stage of the development of John's portrait of Jesus, we must begin with it. The Johannine community underwent two traumatic experiences which forced a radical revision of its portrait of Jesus: excommunication from the synagogue and dropouts leaving the Johannine group.

1.*Excommunication*. As the Johannine Christians became bolder and bolder in their confession of Jesus, as they acclaimed him more and more as a heavenly being, as "equal to God," there was bound to be a reaction from the synagogue. Their Christological confession crossed a theological threshold where orthodox Jews who recited the *Shema* could not tolerate the Christian confession. The monotheistic confession of "God is one!" was not only the cardinal doctrine of Jewish piety but served a useful function of distinguishing true worshippers of the covenant from pagans. To acclaim the one, living and true God distinguished Jews in antiquity from pagans who worshipped many gods. The high Christological confession of the Johannine group sounded to the synagogue like ditheism (2 gods), that is, like heresy. This, of course, could not be tolerated in the synagogue; and so we find evidence of a massive and radical Jewish rejection of the Christian group. They were excommunicated. The texts in the Fourth Gospel are clear that excommunication from the synagogue was a genuine and traumatic experience. The cured blind man kept on acclaiming Jesus during his trial and so he was "cast out" (9:34). We know that this was a formal, religious reaction to his testimony. His parents refused to get involved in any way ". . . because they feared the Jews, for the Jews had already agreed that if anyone should confess him to be Christ, he was to be *put out of the synagogue*" (9:22). In another place we are told that there were many people attracted to the Johannine proclamation, "but for fear of the Pharisees they did not confess it, lest they should be *put out of the synagogue*" (12:42). In the Farewell Address, Jesus is said to predict this crisis, "They will *put you out of the synagogue*. . ." (16:2).

2. *Dropouts*. At some point in the history of the Johannine group, the proclamation of Jesus became a "stale" saying which former members of the group found hard to chew. They abandoned Jesus and walked away. We read in

6:66 that after the Bread of Life discourse "many of his disciples drew back and no longer went about with him." We would call these people dropouts. But why did they drop out? and what effect did this have on the confession of the church?

Although we have scanty data, we may conjecture that the dropouts were people who were attracted to Jesus by the signs which he did (see 6:14-15). But this faith seems meagre and insufficient in view of the claims about Jesus in stage two of the history of this group. Jesus criticizes such meagre faith: "You seek me, not because you saw signs, but because you ate your fill of the loaves" (6:26; see 4:48). Jesus then proceeds to tell them about the true Bread from Heaven, that is, about himself as the one who has descended from heaven, as the one who alone has seen God (6:42, 46), and as the one who alone can give eternal life (6:40). Such claims are equivalent to the high Christological confession of Jesus: 1) as a heavenly descending figure (1:14, 3:13); 2) as the only one who has seen God (1:18); and 3) as the giver of eternal life (5:21-22). For some this new aspect of Jesus' portrait is "stale" bread and hard to swallow: "This is a hard saying" (6:60). And some refuse to accept it.

These two experiences had a significant impact on the Johannine group. They occasioned a re-evaluation of values and ideas previously held. This re-evaluation did not necessarily issue in a confession totally new to the group, but it had an impact on what was confessed, how that confession was understood, and why it was so important. This means that as a result of excommunication and dropouts, a re-evaluation took place: some stocks went up dramatically in value and others plummeted.

MISSION AND MEMBERSHIP

It is fair to say that in this stage of John's community, there is a radical shift in energy. As the attacks on the group mount and culminate in excommunication, the missionary thrust of the early period seems to vanish. The covered wagons no longer advance, but are drawn into a circle for defensive purposes. In fact, as pressure is put on Christians to drop out and abandon their beliefs, the new mission field is properly the group itself. All efforts are made to preserve the faith of the Johannine members. The flow of energy, then, is no longer outward in preaching to new members, but inward in apology and defense.

The membership of the Johannine group at this stage is not only smaller but more elitist. Its smallness is due in part to the crisis, for some people are afraid to join (12:42) and others seem to be dropping out. It is now possible in the Johannine group to rank members according to their belief; such a ranking would yield the following list:

> 1. authentic members publicly confess Jesus as "equal to God," even at the risk of excommunication;
> 2. other members still confess Jesus according to a less perfect confession;
> 3. others are crypto-believers who are inclined to confess faith in Jesus, but do not do so publicly for fear of being cast out of the synagogue;
> 4. dropouts once confessed faith in Jesus, but no longer; they are outsiders;
> 5. all others, who do not believe in Jesus, are outsiders and enemies.

The gospel is written from the point of view of full-confessing, courageous believers, and so they see that true membership in the Johannine group is limited to "authentic believers" (see # 1 above).

In this context, it is not surprising to find an elitist strain developing in regard to membership. Jesus states that his only authentic followers are those *chosen by God:* "No one can come to me unless it is granted by the Father" (6:65; see v. 44). Jesus said this on the occasion of dropouts leaving the group, indicating by it that they never were true members, for they were not chosen by God. This harkens back to other remarks of Jesus in the Bread of Life Discourse, that membership is a matter of divine election, and so necessarily limited to the elite few. In one place, Jesus remarked: "All that the Father gives me will come to me" (6:37); and in another place, "Every one who has heard and learned from the Father comes to me" (6:45). Jesus implies by these statements that membership is not a matter of a hearer being convinced and freely choosing Jesus, but a matter of divine election. Authentic members, therefore, are chosen by God and taught by God; they are necessarily the elite few. The dropouts, who seemed to have accepted Jesus, were ultimately shown to be outsiders whom God did not choose. Unbelievers as well are not chosen. The dual crisis of excommunication and dropouts from the group has shaped the way this community understands its mission and membership. New experiences lead the group to portray Jesus discoursing on these topics in a new way.

OLD TESTAMENT

The synagogue naturally contested the Christian claims to interpret the Scriptures in the light of Jesus' replacement of Jewish rites, feasts, and revelation. The Old Testament, then, became a highly contested document, too controversial to be of probative use by the Johannine group any longer. That group, moreover, relativized it in its insistence that the Old Testament was but a type of things to come, a prophecy which is now fulfilled in Jesus. The Scriptures, then, tended to lose positive value in the course of development. As revelation, they are replaced by Jesus' words.

ESCHATOLOGY

The importance of faith in Jesus and membership in his group continued to be emphasized by Jesus' insistence that believers are already beyond judgment and into life. But new experiences of the Johannine group urged development and nuancing of this basic eschatological message.

In the course of time "beloved disciples" such as Lazarus died (Jn 11). Since he is repeatedly called a "beloved one" (11:3, 5, 11), Lazarus presumably was baptized, ate the Bread of Life, and firmly believed in Jesus' words. He was an insider, and elite member of the group. Yet he died. This crisis occasioned Jesus' formal catechesis to Lazarus' sister about future resurrection and its relationship to present life in Jesus. Jesus does not deny the future resurrection unto judgment (see 5:29), but tells Martha that "Whoever believes in me, though he die, yet shall he live" (11:25). Jesus proves that his words have power by raising Lazarus; he proves the utility of belief in himself by calling Lazarus from the tomb then and there. Not all of Jesus' close associates who died were thus raised; a special point is made via Lazarus' case. Johannine Christians, moreover, should not naively believe that they will *never* die (see 21:23). They have a life already which brings them beyond judgment; and should they die, they are sure that Jesus has God's great power to raise the dead (see 5:25-29). The facts of living forced a development of future eschatological thinking even for the elite circle of disciples in John's gospel.

The crisis of excommunication likewise occasioned further development. Early Christian eschatological teaching insisted that believers were beyond death and judgment. They already possessed God's blessing and were already in God's kingdom. What a rude shock, then, for a believer to be hated and excommunicated; what a crisis of faith to hear Jesus called a demon (8:48; 10:10) and to find oneself the object of powerful forces bent on one's destruction (16:1-2). How can a believer who is beyond judgment and into eternal life still experience such hostility? At the very least, the crisis called into question the immediacy of the victory which Jesus proclaimed. It demanded some reconsideration of the eschatological timetable. A new word from Jesus is necessary because of the new situation.

This crisis led to fresh developments in eschatological thinking. On the one hand, Jesus is presented as still proclaiming complete control over the turbulent events. After all, did he not predict these crises (Jn 15-16)? His prophetic announcements are precisely intended to allay fear: "I said all this to keep you from falling away" (16:1) and "Now I have told you before it takes place, so that when it takes place, you may believe" (14:29). Jesus' enemies, moreover, are linked with God's traditional enemy, so that in the ensuing crisis the Evil One or Satan is seen as continuing his age-old battle (13:2, 27; 17:15). Nevertheless, Jesus proclaims victory over this "Prince of the World" (12:31; 14:30; and 16:11). By elevating the crisis to cosmic proportions, the evangelist can conceptualize it as a God-Satan conflict which God must eventually win. But the victory obviously lies in the future.

Although it would seem that the group's enemies have the upper hand at present, Jesus predicts a judgment upon them. The community's Advocate, the Holy Spirit, will "convict the world of sin, of (false) righteousness, and of (false) judgment" (16:8). Most assuredly there is a future judgment for Jesus' enemies: "The word which I have spoken to you will be his judge on the last day" (12:48). And so, reflection on the significance of the present crises forced the Johannine community to portray Jesus uttering a new eschatological word appropriate to the situation. The portrait of Jesus has been shaped once more by the experience of the group.

ETHICS

Belief in Jesus and the fullness of the group's confession of Jesus remain the prime virtue in this troubled period. But as the crisis deepened, faith was joined by faithfulness as the most prized actions. This took many complementary forms:

First, if confession of Jesus as "equal to God" brings excommunication, then such bold and public confession becomes the highest act of faith. In unmistakeable ways, John praises those who publicly acknowledge Jesus:

> 1. the man born blind becomes a new Johannine hero for his confession of Jesus, knowing that it would cause his excommunication (9:17, 30-34);
> 2. the crowds publicly acclaim Jesus on his entry into Jerusalem (12:13-15);
> 3. the Beloved Disciple openly acknowledges Jesus at the

cross under the most hostile of circumstances, thus proving himself as true leader of the group (19:26-27).

These public acts of faith are all the more heroic in light of the explicit threats mentioned in 9:22 and 12:42-43.

Second, we begin to find statements from Jesus about the need for willingness to suffer for one's faith. When Greeks come to him as potential disciples, Jesus beings to scrutinize them — a move quite unlike the enthusiastic missionary activity of earlier times. These potential followers are asked whether they could give their lives for his sake? Like the grain of wheat, they must be willing to die so as to bring forth fruit: "Who loves his life loses it; who hates his life in this world will keep it for eternal life" (12:25). There are now stiffer entrance requirements for Jesus' followers than those asked of Nicodemus (3:3, 5). The threat of excommunication has occasioned new teaching by Jesus for potential disciples.

Third, scholars now speak of the celebrated footwashing in Jn 13 as having symbolic meaning in the gospel. Footwashing, it is argued, becomes a metaphor for suffering and martyrdom. Evidence for this comes from several places.

1. From studies of footwashing in contemporary Jewish literature, we know that it is associated with preparation for sacrifice and with authentic discipleship.

2. Washing suggests a form of "baptism," which in other gospels means Jesus' passion. Jesus asked: "Are you able to drink the cup that I drink, or to be baptized with the baptism with which I am baptized?" (Mk 10:38).

3. The controversial figure in the footwashing in John 13 is Simon Peter. This is not accidental, for Peter is known in the tradition as one who shirked public confession of Jesus and so avoided suffering with Jesus. Of all Jesus' disciples, Peter is most in need of aid and encouragement to confess Jesus and die with him (see Jn 13:37 and 21:18-19).

Like Jesus' scrutiny of would-be disciples in 12:20-26, Jesus' request that Peter allow his feet to be washed should be seen as a symbolic demand for his authentic following of Jesus and his preparation for sacrifice in confessing Jesus unto death.

Fourth, as the crisis deepened, we find Jesus exhorting the group more and more to "love." But a careful look at Jesus' command to "love" in John 15 shows that it is juxtaposed to "hate" and must be seen in that context.

> 1. The second half of Jn 15 speaks of being hated. The world hates Jesus and hates his disciples as well (15:18). The world hates them precisely because they are not of the world (15:19). "Hatred," moreover, is but a synonym in this passage for persecution: as they persecuted Jesus, so they will persecute his disciples (15:20). Jesus' enemies hate not only him, but his Father as well (15:24); in this they fulfil the scriptures which prophesied: "They hated me without cause" (15:25/ Ps 35:19). Hate, then, describes the intensely negative, social experience of the Johannine group.
>
> 2. Juxtaposed to hatred from the world is Jesus' exhortation to love one another. The context suggests that we see "love" as symbolic of faithfulness to Jesus in times of hatred and persecution. This is borne out by observing that the talk about love is intertwined with exhortations to "abide" in the vine, that is, Jesus (15:4-7). Love means faithfulness. And as one abides in the vine, Jesus' Father will prune the vine (15:2), clearly a reference to times of persecution and hatred. "Love," moreover, is basically defined as "laying down one's life for one's friends" (15:13). Love, then, means fidelity to Jesus in crisis, abiding in him, being pruned by God, and laying down one's life for one's friends. "Love" (15:1-17) describes the social antidote to the public "hate" (15:18-25) which will rage against Jesus' followers.

Faith in Jesus and belief in the Christian preaching is now supplemented with concern for fidelity in faith, boldness of confession in crisis, and willingness to suffer and die for the faith. New experiences prompt a new word from Jesus appropriate to the circumstances. Experience again shapes the portrait of Jesus in this gospel.

Conversely, we now find bitter censure of those who will not publicly confess Jesus and endure the harsh consequences of that confession. The parents of the blind man are treated as timid cowards by the author of the gospel, for they will not even speak up for their son, much less for Jesus: 'Ask him; he is of age, he will speak for himself.' His parents said this because they feared the Jews, for the Jews had already agreed that if any one should confess him to be the Christ, s/he was to be put out of the synagogue" (9:21- 22). Many of the authorities also seem to have believed in Jesus, but they did not confess it: "For fear of the Pharisees, they did not confess it, lest they should be put out of the synagogue" (12:42).

GROUP SELF-UNDERSTANDING

The excommunication of the Johannine group from the synagogue would normally be a painful experience. The split was not just over membership in the synagogue, but touched every aspect of life. Radical social dislocation would accompany the excommunication: one's place in the family, clan and village could be strongly affected. Families could be split; sons disinherited; marriage alliances canceled; businesses boycotted (see Mt 10:34-39). As one lost one's place in family and clan, one lost wealth, status and honor in the village. Oddly enough, one finds scant evidence in the Fourth Gospel of a sense of pain as result of the excommunication. At times the mood is just the opposite; it is almost as though the group were saying "You did not throw us out, we left" or "You can't fire me, I quit."

For some time now the Johannine group has been developing a sectarian or dualistic view of the world. Earlier "the world" was viewed quite favorably. Jesus was the light of the world (1:9; 8:12; 9:5); he was sent to save the world (3:16-17); he was heralded as savior of the world (4:42). But as the Johannine group met with debate, harassment and rejection, this view of the world soured. As the Johannine Christians became more sectarian, they claimed that they alone were right, the rest were wrong; they alone had the light and the truth, the rest were in darkness and could not see. Jesus alone is the Way, the Truth, and the Life. This inevitably led them to see the world which did not believe in Jesus as a dark, hostile place filled with ignorant, sinful, and even demonic people. Being rejected by such a world was no loss then. In fact, separation from it would be welcomed.

Neither Jesus nor the Johannine group belonged to "this world" — they are aliens in an alien land. Jesus, after all, was basically *not of this world*. It was said of unbelievers "You are of this world, I am not of this world" (8:23). Of Jesus' disciples it was said, "They are not of the world, even as I am not of the world" (17:16). Jesus and his followers both experience hostility in this world; their common experience leads the evangelist to portray them both as aliens in an alien world. Neither Jesus nor his followers are of this world.

In the very prologue to the gospel we read of irreconcilable hostility between the Word and the world, "The true light that enlightens everyone was coming into the world. He was in the world yet the world received him not" (1:9-10). It is surely an understatement to say that "the world received him not"; it positively hated him. "The world hates me because I testify of it that its works are evil" (7:7). And this hatred spills over against Jesus' true followers: "If the world hates you, know that it has hated me before it hated you. If you were of the world, the world would love its own; but because you are not of the world, but I chose you out of the world, therefore the world hates you" (15:18-19). Jesus and his disciples, then, are hated by the world because they are not of the world: "The world has hated them because they are not of the world, even as I am not of the world" (17:14).

It is fair, therefore, to say that the members of the Johannine group are aliens in an alien world. And this colors their assessment of Jesus himself as an alien figure. As the group made bolder and more exclusive claims on Jesus' behalf, they came to stress more and more his status as a heavenly figure, as one who had existed in glory and subsequently descended to earth, and as one who had returned to that former glory. Stress was put increasingly on Jesus' otherworldliness, his being *"not* of this world." We saw earlier that Jesus is acclaimed as the Son of Man, a figure who was originally in heaven and who descended to earth (3:13). Jesus is the true Bread which has literally come down from heaven (6:33, 41-42). In fact, a constant joke is maintained in the Johannine group over knowing the correct "whence " of Jesus — whence he really came. Some say he has earthly origins: Joseph and Mary are his parents (6:42); he was born in Nazareth (7:27). But these answers are challenged by the claims that Jesus' true origin, his true "whence" is heaven (see 7:28-29; 9:29-33). It is, then, a sign of a true believer to know the secret of Jesus' origin. He is a heavenly figure who descended from heaven; he is truly alien in this world.

This same heavenly figure may pitch his tent here temporarily (1:14), but this world is not his home or his permanent dwelling place. As 1:1-18 and 13:1-3 indicate, the descending Son of Man ascends back to heaven. That return, however, seems to become more and more welcome to the Son of Man as he meets greater and greater rejection on earth. As his alienation increases, he seems to yearn to leave this alien world and return home. And so, when Jesus is rejected as the true Bread from Heaven, he remarks that proof that he first descended from heaven will be found when "the Son of Man ascends to where he was before" (6:62). His leaving and returning to heaven will silence his critics and constitute proof of his heavenly origin in the face of rejection and alienation. And when Jesus utters his Farewell Prayer in ch 17, he prays that God will vindicate him in the alienating conflict in which he finds himself: "Glorify me in thy own presence with the glory which I had with thee before the world was made" (17:5). The alien figure seems to yearn to leave this alien land and to return to his true home.

CHRISTOLOGY

The excommunication from the synagogue seems to have

had four discernible effects on the Christological confession at this stage of the Johannine group's history. First, it sharpened the perception and confirmed the fact that Jesus was "not of this world," but that he was truely alien. The group also experiences itself as alien, just like its leader. Second, since Jesus is truly alien, then his otherworldliness is all the more to be acknowledged and confessed. The full force of the fact that Jesus is "not of this world" develops and the value of his otherworldliness is re-valued upward. It becomes the most valued thing one can say about Jesus.

Third, even as this re-evaluation takes place, a corresponding devaluation is under way. Where Jesus was born, who his parents were, and many other earthly facts about Jesus tend to become insignificant. Since he is truly "not of this world," there is little value attached to his earthly career or even to the confessions of low Christology that he is King, Prophet, or Son of God.

There has been a longstanding principle operative in the Fourth Gospel which distinguishes flesh and spirit. Nicodemus seemed to understand Jesus' words on a literal or fleshly level. When Jesus said, "Unless one is born *anothen*, one cannot see the kingdom of God" (3:3, 5); *anothen* is an ambiguous word, for it may mean "again" or "from above." Nicodemus understands this word quite literally in terms of a second, physical birth, "How can a man be born when he is old? Can he enter a second time into his mother's womb and be born?" (3:4). Nicodemus misses the spiritual meaning of Jesus' words (see 3:31). Using the flesh vs. spirit dichotomy, the evangelist applies this principle to people. "What is born of flesh is flesh, what is born of spirit is spirit" (3:6). Nicodemus thinks literally; he interprets things in a fleshly way; he is radically of this earth and so understands things in an earthly way (see 3:12). He is contrasted with spiritual people who understand the inner or spiritual meaning and who are capable of accepting heavenly knowledge (3:12, 31).

Flesh vs. spirit and earth vs. heaven — these dichotomies have existed all along in the Johannine vocabulary. Now with the great emphasis on Jesus' otherworldliness, this opposition of flesh/spirit and earth/heaven is applied to

Jesus himself. What is valuable is that Jesus is heavenly, that he is spirit, and that he is "not of this world." We find a shocking statement in 6:63, which has bearing on this devaluation of flesh and earth. When the dropouts reject Jesus' claim to be the true bread from heaven, they are told, "It is the spirit that gives life, the flesh is of no avail; the words I have spoken to you are spirit and life." This unmistakably re-values spiritual or heavenly things upwards and devalues fleshly and earthly things, which are "of no avail." This re-evaluation also applies to confessions about Jesus. re-valued upward is all confession of him as heavenly or otherworldly; devalued is all understanding of him as fleshly or of this world.

Evidence of this re-evaluation of Jesus comes from the 1st and 2nd Letters of John. Modern scholarship considers these letters as later commentaries on aspects of the gospel. As such they record that certain people in the former gospel community radically devalued "Jesus in the flesh." 2 Jn 7 identifies former members of the Johannine circle "who will not acknowledge the coming of Jesus Christ in the flesh." It is not that they deny his incarnation or the reality of his body, but that these have any value or significance in their theology. Likewise in 1 Jn 4, we read again that some spiritual people do not confess "Jesus" (4:2). They do not reject all allegiance to the Son, but devalue the fleshly or earthly aspects of the person, Jesus. These former members are contrasted with people in the Johannine group who confess "that Jesus Christ has come in the flesh" (4:2). The 1st and 2nd Letters of John present evidence which suggests that some people took seriously the principle enunciated in Jn 6:63 that "The spirit is life; the flesh is of no avail." Carried to its logical conclusion, it means a revaluation of Jesus as heavenly or otherworldly and a precipitous devaluation of Jesus, the fleshly or earthly figure who pitched his tent here. The excommunication which confirmed that Jesus was "not of this world" occasioned the radical re-evaluation of confessions about Jesus.

A fourth effect of the excommunication may be seen in the crisis which it precipitated within the Johannine community itself. The Johannine group was rent asunder by this event. We know of people, seemingly followers of Jesus, who feared excommunication and so refused to confess Jesus in any way that would lead to their expulsion from the synagogue. The parents of the blind man will not talk about Jesus at all, for fear of being cast out of the synagogue (9:22). And many, even of the authorities, secretly believed in Jesus; but they, too, did not confess him lest they be expelled (12:42). One senses that considerable pressure is building up within the Johannine group for believers to make bold, public confessions of their faith in Jesus. Some do, and they are praised (11:27; 12:13-15); others refuse, and are severely criticized. Of those who refuse it is said, "They loved the praise of men more than the praise of God" (12:43). The confession of Jesus as a heavenly figure becomes the touchstone of authentic membership. It becomes, in fact, required for salvation, "Unless you believe that 'I AM,' you will die in your sins" (8:24). The emotional and social value of the confession of Jesus as a heavenly figure has been affected by the excommunication. It is the only, best, and necessary confession. And it functions to separate the Johannine group from the synagogue and to distinguish authentic believers from psuedo-believers within the group.

When members began to drop out of the Johannine group, this occasioned a severe crisis within the Christian group. The crisis is not about the loss of some members, for all groups suffer attrition in membership. Rather, the crisis involved ideology and confession; and it touched the question of who was a true member of the group. Since it is presumed that these dropouts were formerly members ("many of *his disciples* said 'This is a hard saying,' " 6:60), they had been baptized and entered the kingdom of God. They had received the Johannine rites which were said to give the recipient eternal life. The water which Jesus gives "will become a spring of water welling up to eternal life" (4:14); who eats Jesus' flesh and drinks his blood "has eternal life" (6:54). Inasmuch as such a view of the Johannine sacramental rites entails a belief in realized eschatology (i.e., present possession of God's life and favor or present membership in God's kingdom), the crisis of dropouts who had received these rites touched the very meaning of these rites. Did the dropouts who had received the rites actually cross the boundary from death to life? did they have eternal life within them? were they in God's kingdom and favor? According to the catechesis surrounding these sacramental rites, they indeed should be judged to have eternal life and to belong to God's kingdom. But this is thoroughly repugnant to the fact that they subsequently dropped out of the group. Hence the importance and value of the sacramental rites were called into question. To be more accurate, they were reconsidered and judged as *not* infallibly conveying God's favor, life or inclusion in the kingdom. The sacraments, which were so highly valued in stage two of the history of this group, are now radically devalued.

The devaluation of the sacramental rites can be seen most clearly in the comments which follow the notice of dropouts leaving the group. A new principle is stated as a result of the defections: "It is the spirit that gives life; the flesh is of no avail" (6:63). The mere reception of fleshly or earthly rites is of *no avail!* Only spiritual things give life. To be more precise, "My words are spirit and life" (6:63b). Jesus is the heavenly revealer of God's word; to accept him as such and to confess this is now *the* source of life. Thus a primacy is put on faith and the correct confession of Jesus as the rite which determines authentic membership in God's kingdom and having God's life and favor.

But will any faith in Jesus produce eternal life? Is any confession adequate? True to the principle enunciated in 6:63, mere faith in the fleshly Jesus as King, or mere confession of this earthly figure as the Prophet of God's covenant is not enough. *THE FLESH IS OF NO AVAIL.* The correct faith is faith in Jesus as a spiritual or heavenly being (see 6:62); the adequate confession is the acknowledgement of him as the unique revealer come down from heaven.

The experience of dropouts from the Johannine group, then, occasioned changes in the group's evaluation of its sacramental rites and its Christological confession. No new title of Jesus is proposed; no new explanation of his heavenly character is brought forth. Rather, the high christological confession takes on a different value and a different function. It becomes the supreme, exclusive, and necessary way to salvation. It functions now as the authentic touchstone, determining who is truly a member of the group. Experience has led to a new judgment.

The problems raised by the experience of excommunication from the synagogue and by pseudo-believers dropping out of the group are similar and have similar effects. They both led the group to a new appreciation of its distinctive christological confession. And they both led to a corresponding devaluation of former confessions or rites. In both cases what is spiritual is superior to what is fleshly; what is heavenly is preferred to what is earthly; and what is otherworldly takes precedence over what is of this world. Thus the content of the high christological confession, while not new, takes on new value and meaning. And they function in a new way as well. The high christological confession serves to dintinguish Christians from the synagogue, even as its bold expression distinguishes authentic Johannine Christians from pseudo-believers.

The following chart is offered as a convenient summary of the previous discussion. It shows how the different experiences and crises of the Johannine church form the contexts in which new portraits of Jesus arise. New experiences require a new word from Jesus.

TOPIC	STAGE ONE	STAGE TWO	STAGE THREE
1. *Mission & Membership*	very missionary;	more argumentative & less missionary;	little external mission but strong defensive activity;
	membership open to all peoples	narrower membership because of intensified claims	very narrow membership: only those chosen by God

2. *Old Testament*	Scriptures valued as prophetic of Jesus	Scriptures devalued because of Jesus' replacement of OT rites, feasts, and revelation	highly contested document; Scriptures devalued because Jesus gives new, true revelation
3. *Eschatology*	belief in Jesus means present possession of life	intensified emphasis on present possession of *true* life	supplement: new emphasis on future because of 1. death of group members and 2. hostility from the synagogue
4. *Ethics*	belief in Jesus as key saving activity	intensified emphasis on belief; fullest confession of Jesus required	supplement: 1. faith requires faithfulness 2. new demand for public confession 3. willingness to suffer for the faith is urged
5. *Group Self-Understanding*	still in the synagogue, claiming to be the realization of synagogue's Scriptures	radical challenge to the synagogue; claims to replace old & inauthentic traditions with new & true rites, feasts, & revelation	excommunicated from synagogue; dualistic view of church & world: church alone is God's vine & kingdom—all else is Satan's realm
6. *Experience*	mission, success, enthusiasm	argument, mixed reception, aggressive self-confidence	excommunication & dropouts, hostility, crisis of faith

7. *Christology*	Israel's expected prophet & king	greater than Jacob or Abraham; re-placement of all Israel's rites, heavenly revealer, appearing OT deity, 'I AM,' equal to God	alien, heavenly figure in an alien world; heavenly character over-shadows earthly identity & activity

IV.
Stage Four:
Moderated Christology

The history of the Johannine group went through one more stage, a period accessible to us through the Letters of John. As we observe this last stage in the development of the portrait of Jesus in the Johannine community, we must immediately take note of an experience which had a significant impact on the group's thinking and its confession of Jesus.

EXPERIENCE

At a period subsequent to its excommunication from the synagogue, the group experienced a bitter internal crisis, a radical split over ideology and the correct confession of Jesus. As a result, we are told: "They went out from us...if they had been of us, they would have continued with us; but they went out" (1 Jn 2:19). These "secessionists" did not leave amicably, for we find them called all sorts of derogatory names. They are "antichrists" (1 Jn 2:18, 22; 4:3; 2 Jn 7), "false prophets" (1 Jn 4:1), and "deceivers" (1 Jn 2:26; 3:7; 2 Jn 7). The secession of an elite part of the community had a strong impact on the way the loyal remnant viewed itself and Jesus.

MISSION AND MEMBERSHIP

The energies of the group were not directed in missionary activity, but were internally focussed on the crisis which had just split the group in two. Membership in the group is now smaller and more uncertain. Will others leave? Besides the enemies who persecuted it, the secessionists are now also outsiders. Only a small, loyal remnant remains.

OLD TESTAMENT

There is hardly a reference to the Hebrew scriptures in the Johannine letters. This community seems not to have spent its time interpreting the Scriptures and searching them for revelation and exhortation. Rather they were replaced by Jesus' revelation and words. And so the focus of authority for this stage of Johannine Christians is on correct under-standing of Jesus' words and authentic interpretation of the gospel tradition about Jesus.

ESCHATOLOGY

Two streams of eschatology emerge in 1 John. Like the gospel, there is a sense of the *already*. Eternal life is already revealed in Jesus (1 Jn 1:2); God already abides in the believer (4:15); and the Evil One is already conquered (2:13-14). Yet there is also a strong sense of future eschatology. God's future appearance is predicted, which is a time of judgment and scrutiny (3:2-3). On that day, those who abide in love "have confidence for the day of judgment" (4:17). Because of love, loyal hearts are reassured before God, for "if our hearts do not condemn us, we have confidence before God" (3:20-21).

What has changed in this later stage is the sense that all judgment is *not* over. The exit of the secessionists in 1 John had the same effect as the departure of dropouts from the gospel group in Jn 6:60-65. It called into question the claims of group members to have passed from judgment into eternal life (see Jn 5:24). True eternal life consists in belonging to the correct covenant group and confessing the correct faith about Jesus. But if members keep leaving the covenant group and keep confessing Jesus according to a different confession, how can anyone know who has assuredly passed beyond judgment into life. This Johannine group firmly asserts that it is the correct group and that it has the correct confession; but it is short on proof. It remains for God to appear and reveal who is right and who is wrong. The fluidity and instability of the times make it impossible to know who is persevering in the true vine and who is truly believing in Jesus. This can only be resolved with more time, especially with the future scrutiny and judgment of God, who alone reads hearts.

ETHICS

If belief was the premier virtue of the gospel community, "love" is its counterpart in the Johannine letters. Whereas "love" in Jn 15 had a contextual meaning of perseverance and willingness to die for another, it has a more normal ethical meaning in 1 John. A splendid collection of sayings on "love" occurs in 1 Jn 3:11-18, where it means: a) group loyalty (3:13-14), b) amicable community relations (3:15), c) loyalty unto death (3:16), and now d) practical charity to needy group members: "If any one has the world's goods and sees his sister or brother in need, yet closes his heart against them, how does God's love abide in him?" (3:17). And so, the group is exhorted to love "in deed and truth" and not only in word and speech (3:18).

Yet "love" does not extend to one's enemies and certainly not to the secessionists who have left the group. They are outsiders; they are the "antichrists" (2:18-19), and one should *not* love Satan or his minions. Love, then, is limited in scope. One prays for sinful members whose sin is not mortal (5:16a), but *not* for serious sinners; "There is a sin which is mortal; I do not say that one is to pray for that" (5:16b).

GROUP SELF-UNDERSTANDING

The dualistic viewpoint of the final stages of the gospel group remains. Members of the community in 1 John see themselves alone as God's chosen ones, God's "children" (3:1-2). In this they are totally separated from everything outside their group, that is, from "the world." Christians do not love the world or the things of the world: "If anyone loves the world the love of the Father is not in him" (2:15).

This group also spends considerable energy in trying to distinguish itself from the secessionists. We find a string of statements in the document which distinguishes two contrasting positions on various topics. For example, according to 1 John, loyal Christians distinguish themselves from the secessionists by insisting that they are still sinners in need of Jesus' blood and prayer for their forgiveness (1 Jn 1:8-2:2). They distinguish themselves from the secessionists in their confession that Jesus has "come in the flesh" (4:1-3). They are different from the secessionists in linking love of God with love of neighbor, which they claim is not the case with others (4:20). And they insist that water, blood, and spirit are joined together (5:6-10), which is not the case with the secessionists. While more moderate on positions such as ethics, eschatology and Christology, this group is still quite sectarian in character and consequently spends considerable energy in defining itself as different and better than its rivals who left the group.

CHRISTOLOGY

The bitter fission of the Johannine group was occasioned by radical differences of opinion among the members, one major difference being the Christological confession of each group. We recall the particular slant given to the high Christological confession in stage three, when Jesus' otherworldliness was revalued upward and his fleshliness was devalued. In the Johannine Letters we are twice told that such was the opinion of the "secessionists." First, it is recorded that "many deceivers have gone out into the world, people who will not acknowledge the coming of Jesus in the flesh; such a one is the deceiver and the antichrist" (2 Jn 7). As we saw earlier, this view of Jesus does not flatly deny that Jesus became flesh, but rather devalues his incarnation. Second, we find the secessionists' confession contrasted with that of the group which remained:

> By this you know the Spirit of God: every spirit which confesses that Jesus Christ has come in the flesh is of God; and every spirit that does not confess Jesus is not of God (1 Jn 4:1-3).

Again, the issue is the relative value and importance given to the humanity of "Jesus," the earthly figure. The secessionists, who are false prophets (4:1) and antichrists (4:3), place no value in Jesus-come-in-the-flesh, whereas those who remained in the Johannine group greatly valued it. Obviously the debate was no minor squabble, but a question of determining "the spirit of truth and the spirit of error" (4:6).

Our interest is centered on the confession of the group which remained, that is, the group which placed great value on the humanity of Jesus. The secession of many of its members constituted for it a traumatic experience which occasioned its new and distinctive confession. It is not so much a question of a brand new confession (i.e., new titles or new claims), but rather of a shift in context and a change in certain values in the group's theology which made this newest confession consonant with the group's point of view and experience.

1. *Jesus' Death*. There are few and scattered references to Jesus' death in the Fourth Gospel as an event of saving significance. In a richly ironical passage, we are told by Caiaphas that "It is expedient for you that one man should die for the people and that the whole nation should not perish" (11:50). Or, in predicting his own death, Jesus said, "And I, when I am lifted up, will draw all people to myself" (12:32). These texts, which imply some saving significance

to the death of Jesus, are balanced by a flood of other texts in the gospel which speak of Jesus' death in quite different terms. His death is a "lifting up," an "exaltation" (3:14-15; 8:28); it is his "glorification" (7:39; 8:54; 12:16 & 23; 13:31; 16:14; 17:1). His death is a "going back to where he was before" (6:62; 13:1-3), a "return to former glory" (17:5,24). This stream of material about Jesus' death focusses on that event as the moment when Jesus resumed his heavenly life with God. But it says little about the saving significance of Jesus' death. This is not surprising, for if we recall from the discussion of stage two, salvation is not attached to Jesus' death but to the sacraments. Unconditional demands were made: "Unless you do X or Y or Z, you do not have life." "Unless one is born again of water and the spirit, one cannnot see and enter the kingdom of God" (3:3, 5). But if one partakes of Jesus' special waters, the believer has a spring within himself which wells up to eternal life (4:14). And if one eats the Bread of Life, one has eternal life (6:54). Salvation, then, was consequent to reception of Christian sacramental rites. In stage three of the group's history, salvation was subsequently located, not in the sacraments, but in belief and in having the right confession: "Who hears my words and believes him who sent me, has eternal life; that one does not come to judgment but has passed from death to life" (5:24). As Jesus said, "My words are spirit and life" (6:63). It is common to speak of soteriology in the Fourth Gospel as salvation through revelation, through faith, and through the right confession. Salvation is not generally attached to Jesus' death.

But in 1 John, we find a re-evaluation of Jesus' physical death as a saving event. If we walk in the light and hold to the truth, then "the blood of Jesus, His Son, cleanses us from all sin" (1:7). Or, sinners are told that they have an advocate with the Father, "Jesus the righteous, the expiation for our sins" (2:1-2). "Expiation" is a technical Jewish and Christian term for the saving significance of a sacrificial death (see Rom 3:25 & Heb 2:17). Genuine love was shown us by God, when God "sent his Son to be the expiation for our sins" (4:10). According to 1 John, then, Jesus' death was a saving sacrifice, an expiation which not only took away past sins but cleanses us of all subsequent sins as well. Significant value, then, is put on Jesus' blood and on the spiritual effects which came through that flesh and blood, even through his death on the cross.

2. *The Earthly Jesus.* A second line of inquiry into the Christology of 1 John will further our delineation of that group's confession. 1 Jn 4:2, the author insists that Jesus "came in the flesh." But this leads us to another set of texts which have to do with how Jesus "came" to us. In 1 Jn 5:5-6, the author exclaims of Jesus that "Jesus Christ, this is the one who came by water and blood, not in water only, but in water and blood." The debate, as we have noted, is not about whether Jesus was incarnate, but about the value of his humanity. But this text leads us to still another passage where it is argued: "There are three witnesses, the Spirit, the water, and the blood; these three agree" (5:8). Although these two texts are notoriously difficult to interpret, they admit of a certain range of meaning. In general they mirror the theological controversy between the secessionists and those who remained in the Johannine group; and they indicate where value was affirmed and where it was denied.

When it is urged that Jesus came in water only, or that as a witness the Spirit is to be preferred to water and blood, we get a series of hints as to the position of the secessionists. a) "Coming in water" suggests baptism; the witness of the Spirit likewise suggests this (Jn 1:31, 33; 3:3, 5). b) But according to the logic of the gospel, baptism relates to the very early part of Jesus' earthly career, even to his initial manifestation to John the Baptizer. c) Baptism, moreover, means entering and seeing God's kingdom. d) And baptism implies a realized eschatology: by it one is *now* in the kingdom; one *now* sees or has heavenly enlightenment; one *now* has God's spirit; one *now* enters judgment by the faith choice that is made (3:19). e) We may then conclude that "coming in water" and the "witness of the Spirit" place great, if not absolute, value on Jesus' initial actions and on the initial actions of a believer. Salvation is tied to baptism and its enlightenment. f) But this orientation, we noted in stage three, correspondingly tends to devalue the terminus of Jesus' saving career, his death. For in this perspective, his death has little or no saving significance.

In contrast to this perspective we find the author of 1 John arguing that Jesus "came by water *and blood*, not in water only, but in water *and blood*" (5:6). And the author insists that "there is *agreement* between "the Spirit, the water and the blood" (5:8). These affirmations clearly indicate that his confession of Jesus is radically different from that of the secessionists. Let us see how broadly that difference is contained in the cryptic phrases "come in water *and blood*" and in the agreement of "Spirit, water, *and blood*." In general these phrases reaffirm important aspects of Jesus' earthly career. a') "Coming in blood" suggests Jesus' death (see 19:34). b') Jesus' death, of course, comes at the end of his earthly career. c') According to 1 & 2 John, Jesus' death means cleansing from sins by his blood and expiation. Soteriology is not exclusively linked with revelation or enlightenment. d') The ongoing saving significance of his death, especially in the face of the continuing sinful condition of believers (1 Jn 1:7-10; 2:1-2; 5:16-17), suggests a different eschatology than the realized salvation offered through baptism (see also 1 Jn 3:2; 4:17). e') Jesus' coming in water *and blood*" gives value both to his initial manifestation and his final saving acts. His whole earthly career has saving significance. f') This perspective devalues nothing, but is an appreciative re-evaluation of Jesus' flesh, his humanity, and his death, a most human and fleshly event. The cross is not devoid of saving significance.

We have focussed our attention thus far on how the christological confession of the secessionists differed from that of the group which remained in the Johannine church. Those confessions, however, are not isolated slogans but reflect the clash of much fuller theologies and religious cosmologies. It will greatly help us to appreciate the confession of the author of 1 John if we see it in its broadest terms and implications.

1. The Christological confession of 1 John affirms that flesh, matter, and earthly things are of value. Jesus' blood is salvific and gives life. Thus exception is taken to the broad claim that "It is the spirit that gives life, the flesh is of no avail" (6:63).

2. Even Jesus' death is a locus of grace and saving activity. It is not merely his glorification, his way of leaving this alien earth. It was a moment of God's saving power. Therefore, being linked with Jesus' death as well as rebirth in baptism are salvific for believers.

3. Spirit and matter agree. Thus the dualistic perspective which contrasted flesh with spirit and earth with heaven, and which valued only what is spirit and heavenly, needs correction. Spirit can agree with water and blood; there is no inherent opposition.

4. Sensory knowledge of Jesus and eyewitness experience of him are valuable. Thus the 1st Letter begins with a positive reaffirmation of earthly knowledge of Jesus: "That which was from the beginning, which we have heard, which we have seen with our eyes, which we have looked on and touched with our hands..." (1 Jn 1:1). Faith, no doubt, is important; but this does not deny value to our earthly ways of knowing Jesus nor to those aspects of Jesus which are known through the senses: his flesh and his humanity.

5. Corresponding to this re-evaluation of earthly knowledge of Jesus is a revaluing of "tradition," the testimony about Jesus which was given by those who knew Jesus in the flesh. Whereas the secessionists seemed to have favored charismatic knowledge about Jesus' otherworldliness (which, of course, could *not* be gotten through the senses) and devalued whatever could be known about the earthly Jesus (who were his parents? where was he born?), 1 John reaffirms the old tradition about Jesus: "let what you have heard from the beginning abide in you" (1 Jn 2:24; see 2:7, 13, 14; 3:11).

Conclusion

The portrait of Jesus was hardly static in the course of the history of the Johannine community. Jesus' portrait changed from prophet and king, to replacement for Israel's central symbols, to "equal to God." From being at home in this world (1:13), the Word became emphatically "*not* of this world." From being an earthly, human figure, Jesus became primarily known as a heavenly figure whose true importance lies in his otherworldiness.

These changes in the portrait of Jesus are not the abstract speculation of academic theologians. Rather they reflect the changing experience of the Johannine Christians from that of a missionary group to an assertive group attacking the synagogue to a group expelled from the synagogue. More than the other gospels, the Fourth Gospel most fully verifies the hypothesis of this book that new experiences lead to new understandings and issue in new judgments.

The Fourth Gospel illustrates that there is an inner coherence between the way Jesus is portrayed and the attitudes and teachings attributed to him. In the missionary period in the synagogue, when Jesus is heralded as Israel's prophet and ruler, Jesus' Jewishness is stressed. In the period when Jesus' revelation is proclaimed as "greater than" that of Jacob, Abraham or Moses, Jesus is portrayed as the replacement of all of Israel's cherished symbols and rites. In the time of excommunication, Jesus' earthliness is devalued as his alien heavenliness is celebrated. The preaching of Jesus must speak to the experiences of the church. And so Christology must be coherent with experience.

PART TWO

THE PORTRAITS OF JESUS IN THE PAULINE LETTERS

THE PORTRAITS OF JESUS
IN THE PAULINE LETTERS

Introduction

When we turn from the four gospels to the letters of Paul, the shift is truly enormous. On the surface, at least, there was great uniformity in the gospels: each focussed on Jesus, his mission and significance; each told of his career, his miracles, his controversies, his passion and vindication. Each named Jesus by some consistent title such as "Son of God," "Son of David," or "Christ." Each gospel in its own way was concerned to tell its church of the scope of Jesus' opinions on a wide range of issues; and so each gospel presented Jesus' teachings on a variety of topics, which we collected in our "catchbasins." But the letters of Paul are quite different, for they do not focus exclusively on Jesus. Indeed, they offer precious little information about Jesus' earthly career. There is no mention whatsoever of Jesus' miracles and only scant reference to his teachings (1 Cor 7:10; 1 Thess 4:15). Paul does not supply any data for us to gather into catchbasins.

The difference may be summed up in the fact that Paul wrote letters, not gospels. He wrote, not to one church, but to different churches located on different continents: *Asia*:

Galations; *Greece:* Corinthians, Thessalonians, and Philippians; and *Italy:* Romans. Letters, moreover, do not narrate a story, but seek to exhort and persuade; they do not record sayings and deeds of Jesus but address specific, contemporary problems. They are concerned with issues which Jesus did not discuss and touch on problems which were not part of Jesus' experience. In short, Paul's letters have a radically "occasional" quality: they are each uniquely different letters, written under specific circumstances and addressing specific issues to specific groups. Their occasional quality is not unlike the letters we write to our families and friends on specific occasions such as funerals and births, weddings and divorces, promotions and crises. And for these reasons, the procedure for studying the Pauline letters must be different from that adopted for studying the gospels.

In viewing the letters of Paul as occasional pieces, we are adopting the prevailing scholarly consensus about Paul. This represents a change in the way we understand Paul and his letters. Previous generations have tended to view Paul's letters as tracts of systematic or dogmatic theology. Just as a theologian develops his/her system of ideas in a progressive series of books and articles which are coherently related and which continue to refine and develop the author's key ideas, so Paul was thought to be systematically developing his theology over a series of issue-oriented letters. But Paul is no longer viewed this way. Rather he is seen as a preacher-evangelist who responds to *ad hoc* questions and issues. Writing basically in response to specific issues and diverse crises in his respective churches, his letters take on a more *occasional* rather than a systematic character, a *specific* rather than a generalizing tendency, and a *particularity* rather than a timeless quality.

Paul seems to be quite conscious of being so flexible. From his own correspondence, we find him acknowledging the occasional character of his letters and the non-systematic, pastoral approach to the issues of his churches:

> For though I am free from all men, I have made myself a slave to all, that I might win the more. To the Jews I

became as a Jew, in order to win Jews; to those under the law I became as one under the law that I might win those under the law. To those outside the law I became as one outside the law. . . that I might win those outside the law. To the weak I became weak, that I might win the weak. *I have become all things to all people*, that I might by all means save some (1 Cor 9:19-22).

A skillful pastor, Paul adopted the gospel of Jesus in ways that could be heard and appreciated by his hearers. He, indeed, "explicated the message in view of the situation of his hearers."

For all of his alleged independence and originality, Paul knew the traditions of the early church. Despite his hyperbolic claims to be independent of any church tradition (Gal 1:16-17), Paul is steeped in it. He knows the sacred traditions about Jesus' resurrection (1 Cor 15:3-8) and the Eucharist (1 Cor 11:23-26); he records the tradition of Jesus' prohibition of divorce (1 Cor 7:10) and his legitimation of support for an apostle (1 Cor 9:14). The point is, while knowing and accepting the rich traditions of the early church, Paul also shows remarkable ingenuity in adapting those traditions as well as finding new and more appropriate ways of speaking about Jesus to his churches. He is capable of freshness, originality and sophistication in finding ways to speak about Jesus meaningfully to his converts.

For the purposes of this book, I have made a selection of Paul's letters to illustrate his pastoral preaching of Jesus. I propose to study the Jesus portraits in 1 Cor 1:18-25 and Phil 2:6-11. Unlike the diffused portraits of Jesus in the gospels, the Christology of 1 Corinthians and Philippians is found in highly condensed, rhetorical statements. In each letter we may speak of an initial Christological deposit, which is a specific and carefully nuanced proclamation about Jesus, which Paul proceeds to unpack and apply to the situation of the church addressed. The Christology is stated early in these two letters as a fund of images and arguments which is subsequently turned to the problems of each church. We cannot use our previous method of gathering Jesus' sayings in topical catchbasins, for Paul is not interested in so wide-ranging a portrait of Jesus who discourses on *all* the issues of the day. Paul, rather, has already made a selection of what he thinks Jesus means and stands for vis-à-vis each church. It is not Jesus' attitude to many issues, but his relation to a specific, topical issue that interests Paul. It behooves us, then, to be careful in analyzing the selected material which Paul presents in his portrait of Jesus.

The procedure for recovering Paul's Christology in 1 Corinthians and Philippians will entail three steps. 1. We begin by summarizing the situation and experience of Paul and of the church which is addressed. This is the necessary context and horizon against which to undertake the next step, 2. a careful literary analysis of the selected Christological passage which Paul places at the front of the letter as a fund of images and arguments. 1 Cor 1:18-25 and Phil 2:6-11 do not find Paul preoccupied with traditional titles of Jesus; he presents fresh images which require a different form of investigation than that used for study of the gospel titles of Jesus. 3. Finally we will show how the Christology is applied both apologetically and polemically to the situation of each church. These portraits will ultimately be viewed in terms of the specific experience of each church, its situation, crises, and needs. As we shall see, 1 Cor and Phil already represent two totally different experiences; the portrait of Jesus in each letter, then, should be shown to be adapted to the specific experience of each church.

The hypothesis of this part of the book asserts that Paul is "all things to all people" (1 Cor 9:22), that he writes occasional letters in response to particular issues in specific churches. The individual portraits of Jesus found in each letter have been selected and adapted by Paul vis-à-vis the particularity of each church. Paul has, moreover, developed the portraits of Jesus in two ways. 1. The Jesus story is *positively* developed in some instances to echo the experience of the group, to interpret their experience adequately, and to support and encourage converts. 2. Paul also suggests a portrait of Jesus which has a more *negative* or challenging function. The new Jesus story can confront and correct distortions in outlook, values, and the like. It can force believers to adapt to its rhythms and its logic. And so, the pastoral portrait which Paul suggests may confirm or *confront* the experience of the church, *echo* it or *challenge* it.

Chapter Six

1 CORINTHIANS: JESUS "WEAK AND FOOLISH"

I.
The Situation at Corinth

From Paul's first letter to the Corinthian church we catch a glimpse of a group which is highly factionalized. Paul begins the letter acknowledging that there are dissentions and quarreling among his converts. He cites their slogans: "'I belong to Paul,' 'I belong to Cephas,' and 'I belong to Christ'" (1:12), indicating his knowledge of their factions. He challenges their claim to maturity when he notes that there is "jealousy and strife among you" (3:3). He tells them of reports that "there are divisions among you...factions" (11:18-19). The most important piece of information about the Pauline church at Corinth is its factionalism.

We know, moreover, that Paul hears of the situation from diverse sources, giving him conflicting and biased reports about the group. Paul has a letter from the church, as the introduction to ch 7 indicates: "Concerning the matters about which you wrote..." That letter seems to ask Paul's opinion about a wide range of topics such as:

"Concerning marital activity . . . . " (7:1ff)
"Concerning the unmarried . . . . " (7:25ff)

"Concerning food offered to idols . . . . " (8:1ff)
"Concerning spiritual gifts . . . . " (12:1ff)
"Concerning the contribution . . . . " (16:1ff)
"Concerning Apollos . . . . " (16:12)
But Paul also has oral reports from a group in the church,
reports which are from Chloe, a prominent person in the
group: "It has been reported to me by Chloe's people. . ."
(1:11). This oral report seems to contain all the scandalous
news about Corinth, such as the report about factions (1:10-
13), an incestuous marriage in the group (5:1), lawsuits
among Christians (6:1), and misbehavior at the Eucharist
(11:18). This oral report, no doubt, was very critical in tone.
There is still a third group of Corinthian Christians who feel
no need whatsoever to report to Paul or ask his advice. They
are standing tall in the church, claiming to be mature
enough to settle their own problems and to make their own
decisions. And so, we know of three different factions in the
church.

The scope of the factionalization of the Corinthian community can be appreciated by noting how people describe
themselves with tags and slogans. The tags in 1 Corinthians
come in dialectical pairs, contrasting an elite position with
one considered mean and common. I have compiled a quick
list of them to give us a sense of the electric tension which
was splitting the group into polarized factions:

1. wise   vs   foolish (1:27; 3:18)
2. strong   vs   weak (1:27b; 2:1-5)
3. spiritual   vs   fleshly (2:13-14; 3:1-3)
4. adult   vs   babes (3:1-3)
5. those "in   vs   those "*not* in the
   the know"   know" (8:1, 10-11)
6. free   vs   unfree (8:9; 10:29)
7. eye of the body vs ear (12:16)
   head "   "   vs   foot (12:21)
8. honorable   vs   unpresentable (12:23)
9. greater   vs   inferior (12:24)

The abundance of such dualistic language confirms our sense of a factionalized group and helps us to see the extent of the splits, quarrels, and divisions in the group. One of the upshots from this type of analysis is the emergence of the profile of an elite group of people in the church. Perhaps with a touch of sarcasm, Paul alludes to them as "arrogant" (4:18) and as "kings...rich folk" (4:8). They are the people who probably refuse to write to Paul about the issues in their church; for they are the adult, spiritual, free, knowledgeable people who can settle the issues on their own. They are also probably the people who judge Paul (4:1-5) and who see no sense in his coming back to their church.

Extrapolating from the letter, we can get a composite picture of these elite folk. The profile may not be fully accurate; after all, we have only Paul's version. If we had their own version of the affair, surely the elite folk would describe themselves differently and more favorably than the reports of Chloe's people. But Paul's letter is all we have and it serves to inform us of what *he* thought was going on. Who are these elite Christians and what are they saying?

1. They are *pneumatic* or spiritual Christians (3:1), who received the Spirit powerfully at baptism.

2. They focus on Jesus' *resurrection* as the event which liberated Jesus (and his followers) from all limits: Jesus cannot die again; he is beyond the limits of his body; he is not bound by earthly contraints such as the Law or church rules.

3. They have a sense of *realized eschatology*. They "already" share fully in Jesus' breakthrough (4:8); they are already living the risen life with Jesus and share its full power. They will not face judgment, since they are already "born again."

4. They are *free*. The Spirit comes with Jesus' resurrection and with the Spirit there is freedom (2 Cor 3:17) —freedom from all authority, laws, and even bodily restraints.

5. With the Spirit comes great *wisdom:* knowledge, insight and enlightenment.

6. With the Spirit comes *power*, such as is demonstrated in charismatic gifts.

7. As "spiritual" people, they do not need Paul or any other pastor; they are *beyond leadership*. They can decide for themselves.

And so they are the elite of Corinth, the eyes of the body, those gifted with the Spirit, those "in the know," those who are wise, strong, honorable people.

The source of these attitudes could very well come from Paul's own preaching. The slogans which we find in 1 Corinthians, for example, are often thought to be distortions of Paul's own teaching to that church. Paul celebrated freedom (Gal 5:1) which may be the background for the slogan "All things are lawful for me" (6:12 and 10:23). Paul claimed to know God's mysterious plan, which may explain the origin of "All of us possess knowledge" (8:1). Paul spoke emphatically about the unrestrained presence of the Spirit (1 Thess 5:19). He celebrated Jesus' resurrection (Rom 1:3-4). So it is possible that Paul's own preaching was the clay and straw out of which the elite made their bricks. But Paul does not seem to be responsible for the elitist interpretation of his preaching. He takes great exception to the distortion of his preaching.

One wonders what the elitists thought about Jesus. What portrait did they have of Jesus? What Jesus story or what aspects of that story did they emphasize and make the justification for their position? It is doubtful from the composite profile we have sketched of them that they would give much significance to the story of Jesus the human figure, Jesus the crucified one, or Jesus the supreme authority of the covenant group. These aspects of Jesus do not readily support their emphasis on resurrection, Spirit and freedom. Rather, they would seem to emphasize and promote aspects of the *risen* Jesus: already Jesus is perfected; already Jesus is radically free; already Jesus is beyond human limits, rules and structures; already Jesus is spirit, rather than body. It is possible that the baptismal formula in 10:1-4 mirrors their position (Paul emphatically denies that he baptized at

Corinth, see 1:13-17). Baptism was not seen as participation in Jesus' death and resurrection, but as the occasion in which one gains the Spirit. Baptism is compared to the exodus of the Israelites in which they passed through water and partook of "spiritual" manna and water; and so baptism is the occasion for "eating *spiritual* food and drinking *spiritual* drink" (10:3-4). And so, the present possession of Spirit becomes the keystone of the elitists' position: "Where the Spirit is there is freedom" (2 Cor. 3:17).

This, then, is the situation which confronted Paul. This is the horizon against which he selected what he would say to a community which was factionalized and which had spawned a group of elitist Christians. If he was to succeed in bringing the factions back together and in moderating the anti-church tendencies of the elitists, he would have to find appropriate myths, arguments, images and stories to correct and heal the divisions in the Corinthian church. We turn now to the portrait of Jesus which Paul chose and adapted to meet this situation.

II.
The Portrait of Jesus in 1:18-25

When a preacher or evangelist discourses on Jesus, s/he could focus on any one of several aspects of the complete Jesus story. One could make a point about Christians' adoption as God's children by telling the story of Jesus' baptism; one could speak of God's compassion for our human needs in stressing the miracles of Jesus; one could encourage suffering Christians by discoursing on Jesus' passion; and one could emphasize the radical newness of Christian existence by focusing on his resurrection. In 1 Cor 1:18-25, which is the first mention of Jesus in the letter, Paul selects the crucified Jesus as his focus, a stress not to be taken for granted: "the cross of Christ" (1:17) . . . "the cross is folly " (1:18), and ". . . we preach Christ crucified" (1:23).

Paul immediately notes that "Christ crucified" is an occasion of division and separation. "To those who are perishing the word of the cross is folly, but to us who are being saved it is the power of God" (1:18)—the cross separates humanity into two camps. The "crucified Christ" is "a stumbling block to Jews and folly to Gentiles, but to those who are called... Christ is the power of God and the wisdom of God" (1:23-24) —division again. Jesus' death on the cross, then, becomes an occasion in which distinctions are drawn and groups are divided. One can sense this in the dualistic language which appears in every sentence: wisdom vs foolishness, strength vs weakness, and cleverness vs folly. To a factionalized group Paul depicts a portrait of Jesus which does not heal factions but creates division.

Wise men and debaters of this age are reputed to be able to tell us where wisdom lies and what constitutes strength (1:20). But Christ crucified is seen as an event which in the minds of many does not fit into our normal experience of what is wisdom and strength. To many "wise" people Christ crucified is a stumbling block and foolishness. But Paul calls the crucified Christ the power of God and the wisdom of God (1:24). Clearly there is a division of opinion! But whose perspective is correct? who can tell us where true wisdom lies and genuine strength is found? If there is a fundamental division of opinion, who can judge?

God can judge and decide what is wise and what is foolish. And so we look for God's verdict in the debate over Jesus' crucifixion. Paul's remarks about God in 1:18-25 all pertain to Jesus' crucifixion, and they make two points. First, God clearly declares where wisdom and strength lie. The crucified Christ is "the wisdom of God and the strength of God" (1:24). Second, God formally challenges and reverses the prevailing conceptions of strength and wisdom. Citing Isa 29:14 as indicative of God's actions, Paul argues that God aggressively corrects the worldly view of things:

> "I will destroy the wisdom of the wise and the cleverness of the clever I will thwart" (1:19)

God challenges the prevailing canons of wisdom: "Has not God made foolish the wisdom of the age?" (1:20b). "It has pleased God," Paul notes, "through the folly of what we preach to save those who believe" (1:21). Finally, Paul concludes that God's viewpoint challenges that of others by remarking that "the foolishness of God is wiser than men, and the weakness of God is stronger than men" (1:25). Through this type of rhetoric, Paul indicates a canon of truthfulness: God's will and plan. In valuing Christ crucified as wisdom and strength, Paul obviously stresses his agreement with God and also claims validity for his point of view. In Paul's rhetoric of contrast and reversal, he also implies that there is a wrong position; should anyone at Corinth be holding that pont of view, s/he will find that God is set on thwarting their cleverness and destroying their wisdom. The story of the crucified Christ, then, is intended to function as *apology* for Paul's position and as *polemic* against other positions (probably that of the elitists).

It seems fair to say that "the Cross" in 1:18-25 is a complex symbol for Paul, functioning the way the Resurrection seems to support the position of the elite at Corinth. The Cross includes 1) a reference to Jesus, the pre-risen figure, 2) to his full mortality, 3) to his flesh, and 4) to his state of being weak, rejected and dismissed. The cross denotes here radical victimness, not triumph, complete weakness, and extreme obedience to God's will. Yet, Paul argues, the crucified Jesus is the arena of God's saving activity. Flesh is holy to God; God can favor it, not just Spirit. Suffering and weakness are not necessarily signs of non-inclusion in God's presence, rather they may be precisely the object of God's chosing and the arena of God's transforming activity. God's grace and favor attend the crucified Jesus, even if his cross is folly, weakness and dishonor to others. God is not offended by or distant from the crucified Jesus. The cross, then, implies many important religious values and attitudes for Paul; it is a complex symbol which carries an implicit argument in it. One does not sense glory, Spirit, and freedom in this image. On the contrary, the cross may be the enemy of that complex of ideas.

III.
The Social Functions of 1:18-25

As we noted above, 1 Cor 1:18-25 is cast in a distinctive rhetorical mode. It *affirms* something and it *denies* something. Yet affirmation and censure in this case reverse normal expectations: what is affirmed is something unlikely (death, weakness) and what is censured is something commonly valued (wisdom, strength). 1:18-25, then, seems to function both as an apology and as a polemic.

A. APOLOGY

Paul is no armchair philosopher, reflecting on metaphysical issues in the world, but a pastor of a specific church addressing its genuine and pressing issues. The thrust of his apologetic use of the portrait of Christ crucified in 1:18-25 points in two directions: Paul's own standing at Corinth and the status of the non-elite members of the Christian group there.

As regards Paul's standing at Corinth, we know several things:

> 1. Paul apparently made a modest impression on the group, as he came to them "in weakness and in much fear and trembling" (2:3). In his second letter to Corinth, Paul quotes what is said of him, confirming his less-than-exalted performance at Corinth: "His bodily presence is weak, his speech is of no account" (2 Cor 10:10).
>
> 2. Paul was discredited in the eyes of some at Corinth. Apollos is preferred to him ("I belong to Apollos," 1:12 and 3:4), probably on the basis of Apollos' wisdom, eloquence, and sophistication — qualifications which would make him attractive to many of the elite members of the group (see Acts 18:24-28).
>
> 3. Paul is accused of being a non-elite person; he only gave the Corinthians "baby food" doctrine, not enlightened or sophisticated widom. Paul cites this opinion of

himself, only to disagree with it; but it was the opinion of many about him: "I could not address you as spiritual people, but as people of flesh, as babes in Christ. I fed you with milk, not solid food..." (3:1-2).

4. Paul is "judged" by some at Corinth and found wanting. He tries to shrug this off in 4:1-5, giving a sense of how this nettled him: "With me it is a small thing that I should be judged by you or any human court" (4:3).

Paul, therefore, is considered foolish, weak and despised. His standing at Corinth is in jeopardy.

Yet in his foolishness and weakness, he sees himself patterned after the crucified Christ. As regards "foolishness," Christ sent him to preach "nothing except Jesus Christ, and him crucified" (2:2). Christ sent him to preach "*not* with eloquent wisdom" (1:18; see 2:1). His preaching was *not* eloquent by design: "My speech and my message were *not* in plausible words of wisdom" (2:4). Paul purposely chose this style to match his message with its contents. In doing this Paul affirms the radical transcendence of Christian faith: "...that your faith might *not* rest in the wisdom of men but in the power of God" (2:5). As regards "weakness," Paul claims that his "weak" appearance and performance represent a conscious strategy on his part, in conformity with the message which he preached. He preached the cross without eloquent wisdom "lest the cross of Christ be emptied of its power" (1:18). Thus Paul's personal presence was adapted to mesh with the message he preached. The basic confession of Christ crucified may indeed come from the early church's tradition, but Paul asserts that he adapted his rhetoric to suit the topic. This lays an apologetic foundation for re-evaluating his standing with some of the factions at Corinth.

In Paul's apology for his lack of wisdom and power, he is also defending his authoritative status as the prime teacher of the Corinthian group. In response to the elitists arguments about him, Paul has closely identified himself with the pattern of the central, mythical figure of Christian preaching, Christ crucified. Paul conforms to the pattern of

Jesus in "foolishness" and "weakness." Yet as God reversed the worldly judgment about the foolishness and weakness of Christ crucified, so Paul is claiming to share in God's revisionist judgment as well. "No," he implies, "my weakness and foolishness are affirmed by God to be true wisdom and power." God's judgment of what is truly wise and powerful is obviously different from that of the elitists in Corinth, for God "destroys the wisdom of the wise and thwarts the cleverness of the clever" (1:19). Thus, Paul claims to be judged by God in a certain way, as Jesus was; and he pits God's judgment (1:18-25) against the judgment of men (4:1-5). And so, the portrait of Jesus is crafted to function as an apology for Paul's position and performance against the biases of the elitists in the church.

1 Cor 1:18-25 serves a second apologetic function in regard to the non-elite members of the Corinthian church. Immediately after he presents his rhetorical portrait of Christ crucified in 1:18-25, Paul applies this portrait to the social composition of the group. "For," he says, "consider your call..." (1:26). The conjunction "for" in v. 26 clearly links what preceded with what follows.

The social composition of the group at Corinth was extremely complex. We know that there was an elite wing of the church, who were socially and financially well established enough to eat at elegant funeral services (chs 8 and 10), to eat and drink well at the Eucharist (ch 11), and to appreciate sophisticated preaching (3:1-3). Not only were some Christians socially prominent, but they boasted in their wisdom and knowledge (8:1) and their power (4:8). The danger of this elitism lay in its potential to split the Body of Christ into factions, implying that there is a first-class status of Christians as well as 2nd and 3rd class. We know of Paul's deep horror at the factionalization of the Body of Christ (1:11-12; 11:18-19). And so he constructs an apology for the non-elites in 1:26-31, stressing their likeness with Christ crucified as that is described in 1:18-25.

In 1:26-31, Paul describes the non-elite wing of the Corinthian group.

> Consider your call:
> not many of you were *wise*,
> not many were *powerful*,
> not many were of noble birth   (1:26).

We recognize the terms "wise" and "powerful" from the rhetorical discourse on Christ crucified in 1:18-25. Paul admits that there is a negative value placed on being "not wise" and "not powerful," for he admits that some value "according to worldly standards." But just as God overthrew worldly evaluations of weakness and foolishness in regard to Christ crucified (1:19, 24-25), so God disagrees with the elitists' negative judgment on the weak and powerless status of the non-elite in the church:

> But *God chose* what is foolish...
> *God chose* what is weak......
> *God chose* what is low and despised...   (1:27-28).

We know that *God chose* Christ crucified (i.e., God saw value in him, gave him favor, and exalted him). So Paul applies this judgment of God to the situation of the non-elite. As God reversed the worldly evaluation of Christ crucified, so God confounds the elitists' evaluation of the foolish, weak, and despised members of the church. It is surely a *tour de force* of Paul's argument that he claims that God chose the weak and foolish precisely "to shame the wise...the strong" (1:27) and "to bring to naught things that are" (1:28). On balance, Paul would argue that both wise and foolish are chosen by God; but for the moment, he sees their election as a first attack on the excesses of the elitists' position.

In a later passage, Paul urges "those in the know," who are "free" to eat idol meat, *not* to do so in deference to the weak. A weak member is one who is scandalized at the enlightened behavior of an elite member who displays his/her wisdom and freedom by eating idol meat. In principle Paul does not take issue with the decision of the elite to eat this meal, but only with the scandal it may cause. And so he explains his request that in cases of scandal, the elite member *not* eat: "And so, by your knowledge, this weak person is destroyed, the brother/sister for whom Christ died" (8:11). No longer is Christ himself weak and foolish; rather, the argument functions like that in 1:26-29, affirming the value of the weak member. Whereas "God chose" the weak in 1:26-29, here their importance rests on Jesus' valuing the weak enough to die for them. The cross of Christ now functions as a value statement on its own. But it functions once more as an indicator of where God and Jesus find value. The story of the cross, then, supports the status of non-elite folk as full, worthy members of the Christian covenant group.

B. POLEMIC

Paul's conflict with the elitist wing of the group is also reflected in the rhetoric and function of the portrait of Christ crucified in 1:18-25. The elite are those who are *powerful* because of their possession of the powerful Spirit and *wise* and "in the know" because of their spiritual enlightenment. They are those who "already" claim to share fully in Christ's resurrection. And they see themselves as beyond body and flesh because they are risen with Christ and have his Spirit. It is doubtful if their Christology would make much of Christ crucified; for it represents the "before" stage of Christian transformation, and they boast that they are in the "after" stage. Yet "Christ crucified" is the gospel which Paul preaches to the elitists. This portrait of Jesus has a deliberate polemical function of challenging and correcting the excesses of the elitists' position.

The portrait of Christ crucified in 1:18-25 highly values the weakness and foolishness of Jesus. This automatically contests the power and wisdom of the elitists. The image of Christ crucified and God's accompanying judgment of him challenge a wisdom and power which are *not* rooted in him. God, we noted, acts aggressively to "destroy the wisdom of the wise and thwart the cleverness of the clever" (1:19). This argument is used independently in 3:18-21 to challenge elitist attitudes to preachers and their messages. Paul there echoes the rhetorical tone of 1:18-25 in his warning: "If anyone thinks that s/he is wise in this age, let her/him become a fool that s/he may become wise"(3:18). He echoes the reversing activity of God in 1:25 as he remarks, "For the wisdom of this age is folly with God"(3:19). As he cited Isa 29:14 in 1:19 to illustrate God's reversing judgment, so he cites another passage of Scripture in 3:19 to illustrate God's ways: "For it is written, 'He catches the wise in their craftiness' (Job 5:13) and again 'The Lord knows that the thoughts of the wise are futile' "(Ps 94:11). The close similarities between 1:18-25 and 3:18-19 clearly confirm that Paul sees in 1:18-25 a portrait of Jesus which has relevance for his situation, especially a polemical function against the elitists' claims.

It is surely ironical, moreover, that in addressing those who celebrate the Resurrection, Paul preaches the Cross. To those who celebrate Spirit, not flesh, Paul discourses on body and flesh — not flesh as glorified or ennobled, but flesh in its weakest, most dishonored state. The appeal to Jesus in the flesh and as obedient unto death challenges so many values of the elitists. Their view of body as something neutral (6:12-13) or something to be transcended needs adjustment in the light of the preaching of the Crucified Christ. Their sense of radical freedom from laws and authority (6:12; 8:9; 10:23) needs qualification in view of Christ's obedient death on the cross. For if God's foolishness is wiser than men and if God's weakness is stronger than men (1:25),then God does not give unqualified approval to the elitists' portrait of Jesus as the Risen One. God places great value in the Cross; therefore, all value and importance are not to be placed in the Resurrection, the "already" state of Jesus and the state claimed by the elitists as well. Rather, the crucified Christ is valued by God; his death is important for our salvation (1:21, 30; 8:11). The portrait of the crucified Christ and the rhetorical exposition of it by Paul serve as a powerful challenge and corrective to the excesses which Paul sees in the elitists' position.

In conclusion, we can assess the content and function of

the portrait of Jesus in 1 Cor 1:18-25 in the following way:

1. Paul knows and uses a wide variety of images and portraits of Jesus in his letters. His Christology is not monochromatic.

2. The portrait in 1:18-25 is most probably Paul's own reflection, even though he draws on Old Testament texts as proof of God's ways.

3. His choice of this Christological portrait for 1 Corinthians and his specific articulation of it in terms of weakness and folly are not capricious or idiosyncratic. He chose the image and the imagery for pastoral reasons and he developed them precisely in response to the crisis in Corinth.

4. There is an extremely close relationship between the Jesus story in 1:18-25 and Paul's dealing with the various crises at Corinth.

5. The Jesus story in 1 Corinthians functions in two ways: a) *apology*: to support the cause of the weak and to defend Paul's disputed authority, and b) *polemic*: to correct the excesses of the elitists' position.

6. The Christology in 1 Corinthians is very social indeed, for it implies specific social values regarding membership in the group, specific social behavior, and specific social organization of the group. Christology touches life! Paul's Christology shapes life.

Chapter Seven

PHILIPPIANS: JESUS AS THE NEW ADAM

I.
The Situation of Sender and Addressees

Philippians is rightly called a "letter from prison." Paul openly speaks of "my imprisonment" (1:7, 14), and he tells how his legal problems have given him a platform from which to bear testimony to Jesus: "What has happened to me has really served to advance the gospel, so that it has become known throughout the whole praetorian guard and to all the rest that my imprisonment is for Christ"(1:12-13). There is a prophecy attributed to Jesus in Mk 13:9-13 that Christian preachers would be arrested and arraigned before "governors and kings"; this is to be a time for formal witnessing to Jesus, "to bear testimony before them" (13:9). Paul's remarks in the letter to the Philippians about prison and testimony seem more plausible in light of this gospel prophecy.

We cannot be sure whether this imprisonment coincides with Paul's stay in Rome (Acts 28). The reference to the "praetorian guard" (1:13) and the mention of the "saints, especially those of Caesar's household" (4:22) have led many to conclude that the situation of this letter of Paul is his formal imprisonment in Rome, which legend says led to Paul's martyrdom. But the imperial references in 1:13 and 4:22 may just as well refer to provincial situations, thus allowing one to date the letter earlier than Paul's imminent martyrdom. This particular imprisonment, moreover, may be just one of the many imprisonments which befell Paul. In the list of Paul's hardships in 2 Corinthians, he cites "... with far greater labors, *far more imprisonments*, with countless beatings" (11:23). Clearly Paul was imprisoned more than once.

Paul is most assuredly incarcerated. His imprisonments are scandalous, for they imply to the world (and to some in the church as well) that he is a lawless and revolutionary person who is outside of upright society. Then as now, being constantly "busted" leaves a blot on one's record and impugns one's credibility and standing in the community. Paul seems to have felt the need to give his imprisonment the best interpretation possible and to show how it does not harm the gospel or mean that he is discredited as a preacher. After all, imprisonment is the result of his service to Jesus and it functions to make Jesus even more widely known.

Besides being in prison, Paul speaks in a rather somber tone of the nearness of his death. At least the topic is on his mind. In 1:19-26, Paul seems to allude to the possibility of his death. He begins the section on an upbeat note, remarking that their prayers and God's spirit will aid his deliverance from the present crisis. But then he becomes more somber: "For to me to live is Christ and to die is gain" (1:21) and "My desire is to depart and to be with Christ, for that is far better" (1:23). But he admits that whatever his desire is, there are apostolic considerations: "To remain in the flesh is more necessary on your account" (1:24). "I know that I shall remain and continue with you all, for your progress and joy in the faith" (1:25). To live means apostolic work: "If it is to be life in the flesh, that means fruitful labor for me" (1:22).

Besides these allusions to death, we find a recurring mention of the eschatological "day of the Lord." Paul prays for the Philippians to persevere "at the day of Jesus Christ"

(1:6) and to be pure and blameless "for the day of Christ" (1:10). Later in the letter he urges rejoicing because "the Lord is at hand" (4:5). These traditional remarks would not draw special attention except that they seem to go hand-in-hand with the musing on death mentioned above and with the special comment on Jesus as our eschatological Lord in 3:20-21.

The situation of the writer of the letter is clearer now. Paul is in a restrained, even a somber mood. His present imprisonment seems to have been a sobering experience. His tone is conciliatory and moderate, especially on issues which normally cause him to respond with considerable vehemence.

If Paul's situation is a bit clearer, let us ask about that of the recipients of the letter. If we may consider chapter three as an original part of the authentic letter, then we know of an internal problem in the church at Philippi. Paul urges them to "Look out for the dogs, look out for the evil-workers, look out for those who mutilate the flesh" (3:2). This seems to refer to false teachers who are urging the group to be circumcized ("mutilate the flesh"), and so it would appear that some form of Judaizing is being discussed in the church at Philippi. At least some are saying that perfection before God includes: 1. circumcision, 2. dietary observances (see "their god is their belly," 3:19), and 3. other observances "based on the Law" (3:19).

The mention of this unorthodox doctrine in ch 3 is cryptically done. One senses that those who aired these ideas were proclaiming them as the completion of the Christian catechesis. The observance of certain Old Testament customs was presumably heralded as a "perfection" of one's conversion to Christianity, as a doctrine for "the mature" (see 3:12, 15). It was a way of finding "confidence" with God, for all the required rites could in fact be formally performed (see 3:3-4). One does not find here the same degree of threat that Paul sensed in Galatians and so the letter does not evoke the same vehement response from him. We are not sure that the heresy here is identical with that which infected the churches of Galatia, or only a weaker strain of it. But inasmuch as

Paul counters it with a brag of how orthodox and Jewish he is (3:4-5), we may conclude that the core of this troublesome doctrine was the demand that Christians finish entering God's covenant with Israel by observing all the divine ordinances for the covenant people which are clearly written in the holy Scriptures. Being "Jewish" was the next and complete step in becoming a genuine Christian.

The presence of false doctrine means the presence of false preachers. There is a reference in 1:15-18 to two types of preachers. Paul contrasts good preachers with bad ones; the good preachers "preach Christ from good will and out of love," whereas the bad ones "preach Christ from envy and rivalry" and "out of partisanship" (1:15-16).

Two Types of Preachers

1. from envy and rivalry (1:15a)	1. from good will (1:15b)
2. out of partisanship (1:17)	2. out of love (1:16)
3. in pretense (1:18a)	3. in truth (1:18b)

This seems to indicate Paul's perception that at Philippi there are rival preachers, even some who disagree with Paul's teaching and who were aggressive and polemical in their preaching, especially against Paul. One may speculate that if some people highly value a type of perfectionism, then Paul's imprisonment would certainly put him in disfavor with them. It may well be that we should link 1:15-18 with the formal notice of Judaizers in ch 3. Their doctrine is often described as polemical in content and tone, in that they would argue that Paul did not say enough, that he was immature in preaching, and that he did not keep himself "pure" as God demands. They would, then, be building up their teaching by tearing down Paul and his doctrine. And so we should probably link the remarks about dishonorable preachers in 1:15-18 to the condemnation of false teachers in 3:2-21.

We know how violent Paul can get when he learns of

other preachers (not necessarily unorthodox preachers at that) moving into the churches which he left vacant as he traveled on to new mission territory. 2 Cor 10:13-17 and 11:1-15 record Paul's deep distress at the presence of rival preachers. But that level of anger is not found in Philippians. Nevertheless, non-Pauline preachers are clearly active in the church at Philippi, which is a cause of concern for Paul.

If there is rivalry between Paul and the new preachers, there is also a public feud in the community between two women. Because they are both named and formally addressed, it is assumed that they are influential people in the community, possibly the patronesses of the house churches in which the Pauline Christians gather and worship. Paul writes: "I entreat Euodia and I entreat Syntyche to agree in the Lord" (4:2). These are important figures in the church; for Paul remarks that "they have labored side by side with me in the gospel" (4:3).

The situation of the writer is now clear, as is the situation of the church at Philippi. It remains for us to see what Jesus story Paul selected and used in view of these two situations.

II.
The Portrait of Jesus in 2:6-11

There is no doubt that the celebrated hymnic passage in 2:6-11 is the major Christological reference in the letter to the Philippians. But for all of its beauty and power, the hymn has been surrounded by endless controversy as to its source and meaning. I am relying on the careful studies by modern scholars such as C.H. Talbert, J. Murphy-O'Connor, and R. Martin for a current and critical reading of the passage. The results of these scholars suggest the following conclusions about the passage.

> 1. 2:6-11 is *not* a pre-Christian, gnostic hymn which Paul and his churches adopted for Christian usage; it is a typical Christian preaching about Jesus.

2. It was probably *not* composed by Paul himself, but belongs to the rich tradition of early church preaching and worship.

3. 2:6-11 is structured in 4 stanzas, as the following translation suggests:

I

WHO IN THE FORM OF GOD BEING
DID NOT THINK IT ROBBERY TO BE EQUAL TO GOD
BUT EMPTIED HIMSELF
THE FORM OF A SERVANT TAKING

II

IN THE LIKENESS OF MEN BECOMING
AND (in) SHAPE FOUND AS A MAN
HE HUMBLED HIMSELF
BECOMING OBEDIENT UNTO DEATH

III

THEREFORE, GOD ABOVE-EXALTED HIM
AND GAVE HIM THE NAME
WHICH IS ABOVE EVERY (other) NAME

IV

SO THAT AT THE NAME OF JESUS
EVERY KNEE SHOULD BEND: IN THE HEAVENS,
ON THE EARTH AND UNDER THE EARTH
AND EVERY TONGUE CONFESS
"THE LORD IS JESUS CHRIST"
TO THE GLORY OF GOD

4. There is no reference in stanzas I & II to Jesus' pre-existence and incarnation; the language there is best explained in view of Jesus' likeness to Adam.

5. Jesus' status in stanzas III & IV is considered higher than that in stanzas I & II. He is better off in terms of power and glory at the end than he was in the beginning.

It is time to study the passage more closely. And we begin with a structural analysis of the whole hymn. First, the "therefore" in v. 9 indicates that vv. 9-11 are juxtaposed to vv. 6-8. The hymn, then, is basically structured in two halves: I-II and III-IV. Jesus' life and death (I & II) are contrasted with his life after death (III & IV). The "therefore" in v. 9 indicates a radical shift in perspective from part one to part two.

Second, turning to the first half (I & II), we immediately notice the structure of each of the two stanzas. Stanza I begins and ends with the key word "form": "in the *form* of God being" and "the *form* of a servant taking." Stanza II begins and ends with the phrase "becoming": "in the likeness of men *becoming*" and "*becoming* obedient unto death." The contents of each stanza, moreover, are structured in terms of contrasts and parallelisms. *Contrasts*: the contrasts occur internally within each stanza. a) In stanza I, the "form of God" (v. 6) is contrasted with the "form of a servant" (v. 7b); b) in stanza II, this same "form of God" is contrasted with the "likeness of men" and "shape as a man" (v. 7c, d). *Parallelisms*: despite the contrasts within each stanza, both stanzas are themselves parallel to each other in form and content. a) Stanzas I & II each begin with "in": "*in* the form of God . . . " and "*in* the likeness of men," suggesting parallel form as well as content. And b) "he emptied himself" (stanza I) is parallel with "he humbled himself" (stanza II).

The first two stanzas are parallel in form as well as content. The basic message about Jesus is repeated in each, the focus being the repetition of the *shift* in status. First, "he emptied himself" and "he humbled himself" clearly indicated a radical shift in status. Second, the language of "taking" and "becoming" also echo the shift in status. Third, the contrasts studied above also tell of the shift in status: godlike to human, lord to servant, deathless to mortal. What progress there is in the two stanzas is basically from deathlessness ("equal to God") to "death on a cross." As we shall see, the movement is not from divinity and pre-existence to incarnation and to death.

Third, as regards 2:9-11 we find no contrasts within these

two stanzas, but rather extensive parallelisms. a) Stanza III begins and ends with "above," stressing Jesus' super exaltation: "God *above*-exalted him"..."a name *above* every other name." b) Stanzas III & IV are carefully linked by a series of parallel phrases: a) "God" starts the process in stanza III and "God" is its object at the end of stanza IV: "*God* above exalted him" and Jesus' exaltation is "...to the glory of *God*." b) The "name" of Jesus also links stanzas III & IV. "God gave him a *name* above every other *name*," which name is repeated in stanza IV where the text says "at the *name* of Jesus" and "the Lord (the actual 'name' itself) is Jesus Christ." c) Stanza IV stresses "*every* knee" and "*every* tongue," heralding the universal scope of Jesus' lordship. And this universality links IV with III, where Jesus had a name "above *every* name." This type of analysis suggests that III & IV are basically parallel stanzas. Stanza III states that God exalts and names Jesus as Lord; and in stanza IV God spells out the scope of that Lordship.

In terms of the internal logic of the hymn, Jesus is better off in stanzas III & IV than he was in I & II. Now he is above-exalted and has a name which he did not have before. Now he is established as Lord of all, which was not so before. Now he is Lord of heaven, earth and under the earth, which was not stated in I & II. The final status of Jesus as "Lord" (III, IV), then, is seen as superior to being "equal to God" (I, II). But what does this mean? What is being said of Jesus? One excellent explanation of 2:6-11 from this perspective calls attention to the comparison of Jesus with Adam as the basis for the logic of the passage.

Let us go through the hymn phrase-by-phrase, indicating how Phil 2:6-11 compares and contrasts Adam and Jesus.

A. *In the form of God being* (2:6a)

Adam, of course, was "made in the image and likeness of God" (Gen 1:26-27). Like Adam, Jesus has the same "form."

B. *thought it not robbery* (2:6c)

Here Adam and Jesus begin to be contrasted. Adam, although in God's image and likeness (deathless) was tempted "to be like God" and "to know good and evil" (Gen 3:5). Jesus never sought more; he was always God's faithful and obedient servant. Adam was warned that, although created deathless, he should not try to exploit that gift: "for on the day you eat of that tree, you shall die" (Gen 2:17) and "you shall not eat of it, lest you die" (Gen 3:3). Exploiting the gift of deathlessness, Adam waxed bold and lost his gift by sinning. He died: "Dust you are and to dust you shall return" (Gen 3:19). Jesus, however, did not cling to that gift or exploit it in the face of God's mission for him. He sought only God's will and that will was Jesus' obedient death. He did not exploit his prerogative of deathlessness to avoid God's will and its mortal consequences.

C. ...to be equal to God (2:6b)

In Jesus' time, Adam's "likeness" to God and his equality with God rested on the gift of deathlessness which God gave him. The essential and distinguishing characteristic of deities in the ancient world was their deathlessness, their immortality. Yet it was commonly believed that the first human, Adam, was created immortal and deathless. The Wisdom of Solomon insists that "God did not make death...God created all things that they might live" (1:13-14); "God created man for incorruption and made him in the image of his own eternity" (2:23). As Adam was deathless, so was Jesus; both, then, are "equal to God" as deathless. This is what it means to be "in the form of God" — deathless.

D. he emptied himself (2:7a)

Although blessed with deathlessness and given dominion over all creation, Adam sought more: "to be like God" (Gen 3:5). Adam, then, was involuntarily emptied of his gift of deathlessness. Jesus, although gifted also with deathlessness, sought only to serve God, and so voluntarily emptied himself of this gift at God's request. He was not stripped of this gift, as was the first Adam. He gave it up.

E. *the form of a servant taking* (2:7b)

Although lord of creation (Gen 1:26-30), Adam was still to be God's "servant." "Servant" means no more here than "obedient worshiper," as in the following passages:

1. Abraham: "O offspring of Abraham, his *servant*" (Ps 105:6)
2. Moses: "He sent Moses, his *servant*" (Ps 105:26) "When Moses, the *servant* of the Lord, sent me..." (Joshua 14:7)
3. David: "I have sworn to David, my *servant*..." (Ps 89:3) "By the hand of my *servant* David I will save" (2 Sam 3:18)
4. Any pious Israelite: "Save thy *servant*, who trusts in Thee" (Ps 86:2).

Adam, however, did not remain God's obedient servant; he sinned and became a slave of the earth and of death (Gen 3:17-19). He fell from being creation's lord to its slave. But Jesus ever remained obedient and faithful to God: he was, like the saints of old, truly God's faithful servant. Deathless, he submitted to God's will and "emptied himself" in death. And so he proved to be a true servant, a saint.

F. *in the likeness of men becoming* (2:7c)
Adam, the original "man," was "made of dust and returned to dust" (Gen 3:19). Jesus, by emptying himself of deathlessness, became a man like Adam, viz., liable to death, capable of dying. But his death and his likeness to "the man of dust" is *not* the result of sin.

G. *he humbled himself* (2:8a)
Adam sought to be like God (Gen 3:5); he disregarded God's word not to eat of the fruit of that tree (2:17; 3:3); he sought to know good and evil. In short, he exalted himself. Not so God's servant, Jesus. He sought only and always to be faithful to God's will. And God's will was

that he "humble" himself, viz., that he become a "man of dust" and die like all men of dust.

H. ... *obedient unto death* (2:8b)

Adam died because he sinned: "on the day you eat of it, you shall die" (Gen 2:17; 3:3). Created deathless, Adam died because of disobedience. Jesus, however, died precisely because of his obedience to God. His death was no curse (cf. Gen 3:19); it was an act of supreme worship of God. Like Adam, Jesus died, but not as the wages of his sin; his death is clearly seen as obedience, that is, as an act of holiness, not sin.

I. *God above-exalted him* (2:9a)

In his sinlessness, Adam was exalted by God and given dominion over all creation (Gen 1:26-30). But as a sinner, Adam was cursed and condemned to radical slavery: "you are dust and to dust you shall return" (Gen 3:19). He became earth's slave (Gen 3:17-18) and death's slave (3:19). Jesus, in complete contrast with Adam, was not cursed with death; God, in fact, rescued him from death and exalted him. He is slave of no one.

J. *and gave him a name above every (other) name* (2:9b)

Adam's own name means "clay" or "earth man" — hardly an exalted name. Yet he was given the power to name earth's creatures: "The man gave names to all cattle and to the birds of the air, and to every beast of the field" (Gen 2:20). In contrast, Jesus was given a true name of power: "*The Lord* is Jesus"; his name ("Lord") is above all other names. The one who gives a name has the higher position than the one who is named; in the case of Jesus, he does not do the naming, but is given a name which is the "name of names" and which all in a lower position must acknowledge, including Adam and all powers on earth. No mere "earth man" (Adam), Jesus is now "Lord" and remains such for all eternity.

K. *every knee, in heaven, on the earth, and under the earth* (2:10b)

Adam was given a triple dominion: "over the fish of the

sea and over the birds of the air, and over every living thing that moves upon the face of the earth" (Gen 1:28, see v. 30). Jesus, however, was given a dominion far greater, for he is Lord of heavenly beings (angels), earthly people, and the dead who are under the earth. Adam had dominion over animals, Jesus over human beings and angels. Adam's dominion was limited to living things on earth's surface; Jesus' dominion extends to both living and dead — things on earth and under the earth. Adam, of course, lost his dominion, whereas Jesus was given his as the crowning of his obedience.

ADAM - JESUS COMPARISON IN PHIL 2:6-11

ADAM	*CHRIST*
made in the image/likeness of God (Gen 1:26,27)	who in the form of God being
tempted to go still further and to be "like God" (Gen 3:5)	did not think it robbery
created deathless (Wis 1:13-14; 2:23)	to be equal to God
emptied of deathlessness "on the day you eat it, you shall die" (Gen 2:17; 3:3,19)	he emptied himself
by sin he spurned being God's obedient servant	the form of a servant taking
it belongs to mortals to die	in the likeness of men becoming
ultimately found as mortal man —he returned to the clay of which he was made (Gen 3:19)	and in shape found as a man
Adam exalted himself: "You shall be like God" (Gen 3:5)	he humbled himself
and became disobedient	becoming obedient
and died as a result of sin (Gen 2:17; 3:3,19)	obedient to death on a cross

contrast: previous dominion ...... God above-exalted him
(Gen 1:26) but subsequent
servitude (Gen 3:17-19)

while naming everything else ..... and gave him a name which is
(Gen 2:19-20), Adam's "name"   above every (other) name
means "man of dust"

dominion over sea, sky and ...... every knee in heaven, on earth
earth (Gen 1:26)   and under the earth should bend
                                  and every tongue confess him "Lord"

According to an Adam-Jesus comparison, what does the hymn say of Jesus? First, it builds on the basic kerygma of early Christian preaching: a) Christ has died ("obedient unto death" — I & II), b) Christ is risen ("God above-exalted him" — III), and c) Christ will come again to judge the living and the dead ("every knee in heaven, on earth, and under the earth" — IV). The hymn tells the basic story of Jesus' paschal mystery: death, resurrection, exaltation, that is, the basic stuff of standard, well-known preaching. Second, in Jesus' total obedience to God, he becomes the perfect example of a true servant of God; he is the model for all Christians to imitate. We are all called to be a chip off the old block. Third, Jesus is, as early preaching indicates, "Lord" (see "Maranatha," 1 Cor 16:22; "Jesus is Lord," 1 Cor 12:3; Rom 10:9). The content of the hymn, then, is typical, early kerygmatic preaching.

It is helpful to remember that Paul regularly uses an Adam-Jesus comparison to explain Jesus' role, function, and significance. Rom 5:12-21 most clearly contrasts Adam's sin and death with Jesus' obedience and gift of life. 1 Cor 15:21-28 cities Adam as the model of our own future resurrection, a comparison which is developed in 15:46-49. Under the rubric of "new creation," Gal 3:28 speaks of baptism as a new creation in which all differences are wiped away, and humanity in Christ is now as Adam once was, "neither male nor female, Jew or Greek, slave or free." 2 Cor 5:17 explicitly states, "If anyone is in Christ, s/he is a new creation." Adam, new creation and the Genesis story have always been the preferred metaphor for Paul's preaching of Jesus.

III.
The Use and Function of the Hymn

I suggest that the hymn in 2:6-11 has bearing on the three situations mentioned earlier: a) the internal dissention referred to in 1:15-18; 2:1-5 and 4:2-3, b) the Judaizing heresy discussed in 3:2-21, and c) Paul's own experience of weakness and imprisonment.

A. We noted above that the house church at Philippi was somewhat factionalized. There were rival, competitive preachers (1:15-18); Euodia and Syntyche were squabbling (4:2-3). Paul knew that there was a sense of one-upmanship in the group and his antidote to this is the example of Jesus in the hymn. He explicitly refers to the hymn as the basis for his exhortation in 2:1-5: "Have this mind among yourselves which is yours in Christ Jesus..." (2:5). What is this "mind of Jesus?" Jesus forewent privilege and status; he emptied himself; he became a servant and was obedient even when it was costly to him. He was, in short, the model of Christian humility.

And so, with reference to stanzas I and II, Paul addresses the house church and tells them to "be of the same mind," the mind of Jesus, having the same love, being in full accord, and of one mind (2:2). Jesus' emptying of himself and his yielding to God now become the basis for the next phrase in the exhortation: "Do nothing from selfishness or conceit, but in humility count others better than yourselves" (2:3). Jesus' humility (2:8) is the model for our humility.

Jesus' radical obedience to God and his being God's "servant" become the basis for the next phrase: "Let each of you look also to the interests of others" (2:4). In regard to the factions and fights, stanzas I & II are pastorally used by Paul to correct growing individualism and pride in the church at Philippi. Paul did what any good Sunday preacher would do if s/he used the congregation's hymn as the text for the sermon that day.

B. There is a theological disagreement at Corinth. Judaizing doctrine is being urged, which is hyped as the perfection of Christian initiation and not as something which is over and done with. Yet how to respond? In the hymn in 2:6-11, Paul finds the appropriate language and concepts for his correcting response.

Since the theological disagreement serves to put Paul himself in a difficult position, he must defend himself and his doctrine, even as he seeks to correct the error. We can see the solution to these two, connected issues in the way Paul applies the hymn in 2:6-11 to himself with the express purpose of presenting himself — now modelled on Jesus —as a model to be followed by the church. He models himself after Jesus; and the Philippians should model themselves after him: "Let those of us who are mature be thus minded" (3:15) and "Brethren, join in imitating me" (3:17). So Paul begins his correction of the Judaizing heresy with an explanation of his own experience.

After warning the church about the lurking presence of false teachers (3:2-3), Paul speaks about his own past experience as a perfect Jew. 1. Whatever the Judaizers urge, Paul urged it long ago and stronger: "If any man thinks he has reason for confidence in the flesh (i.e. Judaizing practices), I have more" (3:4). 2. Whatever perfection the Judaizers now value and urge, Paul had that perfection long ago: "circumcised on the eighth day, of the people Israel, of the tribe of Benjamin, a Hebrew born of Hebrews" (3:5). 3. Paul boasts that he himself once was a Judaizer's Jew, a perfect Jew: "as to the law a Pharisee, as to zeal a persecutor of the church, as to righteousness under the law blameless" (3:6). If there was value in Judaizing practices, Paul himself was most rich. He is not ignorant of this tradition. In presenting his past as a perfect Jew, Paul begins to allude to the Christ hymn in ch 2, especially to stanza I. As Christ's former status was an exalted status (equal to God), so Paul's former status under the law was exalted (a Pharisee, zealous, perfect). Jesus was sinless; Paul was blameless.

Then Paul tells us that he voluntarily gave up his former status as a blameless Jew. He revalued whatever good there was in his Jewish past: "Whatever gain I had, I think as loss for the sake of Christ" (3:7). He waxes stronger: "For Christ's sake I have suffered the loss of all things and think of them as dung, in order that I may gain Christ" (3:8). In his voluntary change of status, Paul reflects how Jesus voluntarily changed his status: "he emptied himself" (2:7), "he humbled himself" (2:8). Jesus voluntarily changed from "the form of God" to "the form of a servant." And like Jesus, Paul did not cling to his past, to Judaism; but he voluntarily changed his status as a blameless Jew. Jesus did it in obedience to God; Paul, in obedience to Jesus. Thus 3:7-8 reflect stanzas I & II of the hymn.

Paul then tells us that he sought a new holiness, a new status. As opposed to his past Judaism where he found confidence in his observances ("as to righteousness under the law, blameless," 3:6), Paul now seeks "to gain Christ, and be found in him, not having a righteousness of my own, based on law, but that which is through the faith of Jesus" (3:9). Paul's change of status means that he knows of a new way of holiness, which he considers superior to his former way of holiness in Judaism. In this he is like Jesus who gave up his status as deathless and entered upon a new way of being close to God and being sinless, viz., by being God's servant and by being obedient to God, even unto death (2:7-8). Paul, like Jesus, finds holiness now in obedience to a new divine command.

Paul's new holiness, moreover, is like that of Jesus, for it is based on obedience. We must remember that for a Jew such as Paul, the concept of obedience was very broad: it included *faith* in God (confession of God and membership in God's covenant people) and *faithfulness* to God's word. Obedience to the law, of course, characterized the way of holiness in Judaism; and Paul is playing with that notion of obedience in 3:9, expanding it and showing how obedience includes faith and faithfulness. Of himself he says that he seeks "a righteousness (read: 'holiness') which is through the faithfulness of Christ, the righteousness from God that depends on faith." The basis of his new holiness is obedience-as-faithfulness, which is what Jesus displayed when he became "obedient unto death, even death on a cross" (2:8). It is not obedience to legal observances which is the new way of holiness, but obedience as faith and as faithfulness. The Christ example of faithful obedience is radically different from the Judaizers' celebration of obedience.

Paul states, moreover, that his aim is to be like Jesus and to imitate him. He desires "to share his sufferings, being conformed to him in his death" (3:10). In this, he seeks to be like Christ "obedient/faithful unto death." In the radical self-emptying of Jesus, Paul finds the paradigm of his new way of holiness: faithfulness and likeness to Christ's death.

Paul also knows that death leads to life and that the self-emptying 'death' which we die with Jesus should lead to resurrection. So he makes as his ultimate aim "to know him and the power of his resurrection . . . that if possible I may attain to the resurrection of the dead" (3:10-11). He sees perfection in holiness, then, not in the past or in Judaism, but in the future and in full likeness to the risen Jesus. Of course, Paul is alluding to stanza III of the hymn here, where God raised up the obedient Jesus and gave him heavenly perfection: "Therefore, God exalted him" (2:9).

On the surface we can see a host of similarities between the Christ hymn and Paul's own religious career:

Christ		*Paul*
	A.	
deathless	former status	a Jew's Jew, blameless
	B.	
he emptied himself	voluntary change	I think as loss
he humbled himself	of status	I suffer the loss
	C.	
obedient	new way of holiness	righteousness which is through faith

	D.	
unto death	The Cross	conformed to
on a cross	E.	his death
resurrection	new, better	attain the
	status	resurrection

These surface similarities, however, are quite intentional. For Paul fully understands the pattern of the hymn. As Jesus voluntarily gave up former status and trusted in the future, so does Paul: "Forgetting what lies behind and straining forward to what lies ahead, I press on toward the goal" (3:13). This very pattern, moreover, is a most fitting argument against the Judaizer's claims. Perfection lies not in the past, in former Jewish observances, but perfection lies in a new way of holiness and in the future resurrection which ratifies that new holiness. The pattern of voluntarily changing status and ways of holiness is that of Jesus in the hymn and of Paul as he left Judaism for Christ; it should also be the pattern for the Judaizers and their sympathizers as well.

Paul is indeed conscious of this patterning. He tells those who are fascinated with Judaism's claim to perfection and maturity: "Let those who are mature be thus minded" (3:15), that is, forget the past and strain forward to what lies ahead. Let them understand Paul's experience and follow its pattern. He repeats: "Brethren, join in imitating me" (3:17). He, of course, is imitating Jesus.

The structure of Paul's argument, then, corresponds point-for-point with the pattern of Jesus in the hymn. But that is not the only link between 2:6-11 and the polemic against the Judaizers in ch 3. Paul consciously re-used a host of special and technical terms from the hymn in the argument in ch 3. For example:

1. As Christ "did not *think* (hēgēsatō) it robbery" (2:6), so Paul now "*thinks* (hēgēmai)" of past perfection "as loss" (3:7) and now "*thinks* (hēgoumai) of it as dung" (3:8).

2. As Christ "was *found* (heruetheis) in shape as a man" (2:7c), that is, like us, so Paul desires "to be *found* (heurethō) in Christ" (3:9), that is, like Christ.

3. As Christ "took the *form* (morphē) of a servant" (2:7b), so Paul seeks "to be *conform*ed (summorphizomenos)" to the servant-Christ "in his death" (3:10b).

4. As Paul told the church to imitate Jesus: "have this *mind* (phroneite) within you which was in Christ Jesus" (2:5), so Paul tells the Judaizers to imitate him as he imitates Jesus: "Let those who are mature be *thus minded* (phroneite)" (3:15).

One can safely say, then, that Paul is explicitly using the hymn in 2:6-11 both as the model of his own religious experience and as the pattern which best corrects the errors of the Judaizers.

In 3:17-21, Paul continues to argue against the Judaizers. He describes Judaizing practices in very pejorative terms: "their god is their belly, they glory in their shame" (3:19). This refers to the Judaizing insistence on a) Jewish *dietary restrictions* (no blood, pork or unclean foods), hence their "god" is their belly ; and b) Jewish *circumcision*, where "shame" refers to the penis which, when circumcised, becomes "glory." And so the Judaizers "set their minds on earthly things" (3:19c). By valuing these customs as salvific and necessary for covenant membership, the Judaizers are said to be "enemies of the cross of Christ" (3:18). For, they imply that the cross is insufficient or is defective and that perfect salvation comes through old practices. Yet salvation does not lie in the past, in earthly things, or in Judaizing perfections. Rather, for Christians, "our commonwealth is in heaven"...with "the Lord Jesus Christ" who is savior (3:20).

In speaking of heaven, the Lord Jesus, and resurrection, Paul seems to be drawing on materials from stanzas III and IV of the hymn. After Jesus gave up his former status ("form of God...equal to God"), God "above exalted" him. God raised him, seated him in heaven as "Lord," and gave him dominion over all, both living and dead. Jesus' latter status is better than his former status; perfection lies in the future, not in the past. And so Paul begins to tell the Judaizers that their pursuit of perfection (3:12) and their confidence (3:3-4) is misplaced. According to the pattern of Jesus, perfection and confidence are heavenly realities, not earthly things; they are attainable only at the resurrection, not in present law observances. Salvation and holiness lie in the future, in Jesus the Savior, not in present observances and pseudo-salvific acts.

Paul speaks of Jesus' saving work as "the re-shaping of our humble body to conform to his glorious body" (3:21a). This means our future resurrection. In this phrase Paul echoes the proclamation of Jesus as Lord of the living and dead, where the hymn reads "every knee in heaven, on the earth and under the earth shall bow" (2:10). As Lord of the living and the dead, Jesus is expected both to raise the dead and judge them (see John 5:28-29; 2 Tim 4:1). But Paul sees this Christological confession as a direct corrective of the Judaizers' doctrines. They "set their minds on earthly things" (3:19c); they "glory" in their present, fleshly body; they consider perfection a matter of circumcision and dietary observances. According to the Christ hymn, this is clearly incorrect: what we have on earth is only a "humble," not a glorious body—for it will die. Perfection and "glory" are not found on earth, in "confidence in the flesh" (3:3-4). Rather, perfection is the gift of Christ only in the future and glory is likewise only in the future, when Christ will "re-shape our humble bodies to conform to his glorious body."

Paul notes that Christ does this "by the power which enables him to subject all things to himself" (3:21b). This seems to allude to stanzas III & IV of the hymn, where "God exalted him. . .gave him a name." The "power which enables him" is the same God who "above-exalted him" and made him Lord. And Christ's power is sweeping and universal: he can subject "all things" to himself, Jews and Gentiles alike. This echoes the second half of the hymn where "all knees bow" to Jesus and "all tongues" confess him. The universal scope of Jesus' Lordship is important in the argument with the Judaizers, for it means that *all* people should see in Jesus their savior and *all* await their perfection in Jesus' resurrection. The Judaizers are clearly wrong for their failure to see Jesus as the universal and absolute Savior.

And so in 3:20-21 Paul seems to continue his use of the hymn. As 3:3-17 drew mainly on stanzas I & II, 3:18-21 draw on stanzas III & IV. In 3:3-17, Paul was exposing the basic pattern of Christian holiness and so the allusions to stanzas I & II were appropriate, as he stressed voluntary change from one status to another as the key to Christian holiness. In 3:20-21, Paul finishes his attack on the Judaizers' doctrine by showing that it is totally at variance with the pattern of Christian faith. According to the hymn, especially stanzas III & IV, there is a future, new status which God gives, which is "above" the former status. That new status is a heavenly one; it is radically future; it means resurrection of the humble body. So, if one sees perfection in earthly things and places confidence in the flesh, one is clearly at variance with God's plans in Jesus. The hymn, then, continues to be used as correction of the Judaizers' position.

Again, it is not just the pattern of the hymn that Paul picks us, but also a host of key words from the hymn as well. For example:

1. Jesus "*is* (hyparchōn) in the form of God" (2:6),
   and "our commonwealth *is* (hyparchei) in heaven" (3:20).

2. As Jesus was "in the *shape* (schēmati) of mortal man" (2:8),
   so Paul states that in the resurrection, Christ will "*re-shape*
   (metaschēmatisei) our humble bodies" (3:21).

3. As Jesus "*humbled* (etapeinōsen) himself" (2:8),
   so Jesus will exalt "our *humble* (tapeinōseōs) body" (3:21).

4. As Jesus was "in the *form* (morphē) of God" (2:6),
   so Jesus will "*conform* (summorphon) our humble body to his
   glorious body" (3:21), by his resurrection.

5. As Jesus had "a name above *all* (pan) names" (2:9),
   and as "*all* (pan) knees bow" to him, and "*all* (pasa) tongues
   confess him," so Jesus has power "to subject *all* (panta)
   things to himself" (3:21).

In summary, part of the argument against the Judaizers is to show in 3:4-15 that whatever former perfection or value was found in Judaism is now made void in Christ's cross. Voluntary emptying of oneself of Judaism is true likeness to Jesus; it is true salvation. But the second half of the argument proves that perfection and confidence lie not in the past, but in the future, not on earth, but in heaven. That is, they lie in Jesus, the risen Lord, who will himself make us perfect when he conforms us to his risen body, not his Jewish, earthly body. As stanzas I and II functioned in 3:4-15 to undercut "past" Jewish value, so stanzas III and IV function in 3:17-21 to affirm the unique and surpassing value of the future. The hymn, then, serves a necessary and useful purpose in Paul's correction of the Judaizing issue. The hymn, moreover, is basic Christian preaching: no frills, no secret meanings, no "mature" doctrine which only the initiated can learn. Paul appeals to known, basic tradition.

C. In 4:10-13, we find one last echo of the hymn. Paul, in prison and somber in the prospect of death, finds in the pattern of Jesus a model to interpret his personal experience and make it meaningful in Christian terms. He says: "I know how to be humbled. I know how to abound. In any and all circumstances I have learned the secret of facing plenty and hunger, abundance and want' (4:12). Paul's "knowing" and "learning" are synonymous with "having this mind which was in Christ Jesus" (2:5). He knows because he has learned to imitate the pattern of Jesus' career which is contained in the hymn. And the pattern is just as Paul describes it: emptiness/abundance, death/resurrection. Just as Jesus "humbled" himself (2:8), so Paul knows how to be "humbled" (4:12). Paul knows, moreover, of abundance and plenty. Just as Jesus was "above exalted" and had a name "above" all names (in Gk *hyper*, 2:9-11), so Paul knows that in Christ he too has a share in Christ's "above-ness" or abundance (4:12).

Paul, moreover, says that "I can do 'all things' in him who strengthens me" (4:13). Just as Jesus was raised above "all things" and "all tongues" confess him and he is Lord of "all things," so Paul shares in the sweeping dominion of Christ over "all things." For Paul's power lies, not in the past or in his Jewishness, but in Christ, who has "power which enables him to subject 'all things' to himself" (3:21). And so, Paul himself learns from the pattern of the crucified and risen Christ, from Jesus who emptied himself and who was above exalted.

PART THREE

POST-PAULINE CHRISTOLOGICAL PORTRAITS

POST-PAULINE
CHRISTOLOGICAL PORTRAITS

It is generally agreed among contemporary scholars that Paul did not author both Ephesians and Colossians. One of the differences between these two letters and Paul's authentic letters is the way the Christology is presented. In Paul's letters there tends to be a single, focussed portrait of Jesus, which serves as a fund of images and arguments for the agenda of the letter. In Ephesians and Colossians, we find a more complex portrait of Jesus which is not concentrated in a single image or located in a strategic place in the letter. The Christological portrait in Ephesians and Colossians is more diffused throughout each letter and consists of a rich variety of images.

Despite the complexity of Christological portraits just mentioned, there is in each letter a centrality given to the image of Jesus as "Head" of the body, which is the church. My interest in these two letters rests in how differently Ephesians and Colossians understand this common image of Jesus and how they use it to support diverse arguments. One common portrait of Jesus, then, is understood in diverse ways and functions differently in diverse situations.

The procedure for investigating the Christology of Ephesians and Colossians is a blend of all the procedures used in this book. 1. Like Paul's letters, we must first assess the situation of the author and his audience. And so we must undertake an investigation of the situation and occasion of each letter, asking what in each church needs support and what requires correction. When this is clear we can ask the specific question of the Christology of each letter.

2. As in the case of the gospels, many different images of Jesus occur in these two letters; and the Christology of each is diffused throughout each letter. A variety of arguments is made in each letter and a distinctive Jesus image or portrait is used in support of each argument. And so some survey of Christological images in the letters is appropriate. Each letter, moreover, speaks in a special way about Jesus as "Head" of the body, which is the church. And each letter speaks in an explicit way about "the Church," and not just about "this church." In the author's exposition of "the Church," questions arise about who belongs to the Church, how church people ethically live, how they understand themselves, and so forth. These are the very topics which functioned as catchbasins for Jesus' opinions in part one of this book. And these topics are again useful here, because the Christology of each letter is explicitly correlated with the understanding of church. If Jesus is the "Head" of the body, which is the church, then it matters how that body is described and what that church means. The two terms of the description of Jesus as Head of the body are important. Whatever the author means by "Head" cannot be understood except in relationship to what is meant by body.

3. In many ways, the Christologies of Ephesians and Colossians are quite different, as we shall see. But amid this diversity of Christological images, a certain centrality is given in each letter to the portrait of Jesus as "Head" of the body. After exposing this common image, I will compare and contrast how it is understood by each author and how it functions in the argument of each letter.

The interesting point in studying Ephesians and Colossians lies in the fact that diversity in New Testament Christology resides not only in the plurality of images and portraits, but also in the diverse ways a common image may be understood and used. This can be reduced to the observation which undergirds this whole book, that diverse Christian groups had diverse experiences which led them to find a Jesus word appropriate to their individual situations. Diversity resides in the experiences as well as the portraits of Jesus in the New Testament churches.

Chapter Eight

CHRISTOLOGY IN EPHESIANS AND COLOSSIANS: JESUS AS HEAD OF THE CHURCH

I.
Ephesians

When we turn to the letter to the Ephesians, we do not find a narrative of Jesus' career. The letter is rich in materials about Jesus, but no complete or continuous story is told about Jesus' earthly career which might serve as the foundation "myth" for the Ephesian community. Rather, the letter addresses the problems distinctive to this Christian group and uses *ad hoc* bits and snatches of Jesus material in addressing those problems. Immediately we note, then, a shift from story to exhortation, from continuous narrative to discrete pieces of information, and a shift in emphasis from the earthly Jesus to the heavenly Lord.

Gospels	*Ephesians*
1. story	1. exhortation
2. continuous narrative	2. discrete pieces of information
3. earthly Jesus	3. enthroned Lord

We must expect that the content and function of the Jesus materials in Ephesians will be different from that of the gospels.

As we have been continually arguing, it is imperative for anyone who would understand and appreciate the Jesus mateials in Ephesians to strive to know the audience to whom this document was addressed, their situation and experience. For, as we continually notice, the Christology of a given document is adapted to the situation of the audience and is pastorally tailored to meet their specific needs. So we begin our inquiry into the Christology of Ephesians by asking a series of questions about the audience and its situation. What was the *Membership* of Ephesians? What is its sense of *Group Self-understanding*? What is their place in salvation history, their *Eschatology*?

MEMBERSHIP

We may confidently say that the Christian group at Ephesus was composed basically of Gentile converts. The letter consciously addressed them as "former Gentiles."

> 1. In contrasting their present status as Christians with their former status, the author reminds them: "Remember that at one time *you Gentiles* in the flesh..." (2:11).
> 2. It is emphatically stressed that prior to hearing the gospel, the audience was a total stranger to God's covenant plans: "You were at that time alienated from the commonwealth of Israel, and strangers to the covenants of promise" (2:12).
> 3. In exhorting them to a new and Christian way of living, the author contrasts their old behavior with what is expected of a Christian: "You must no longer live as the Gentiles do" (4:17); and again, "For once you were in darkness, but now you are light in the Lord" (5:8).
> 4. In dealing with this audience, Paul (or someone writing in his name) appeals to a divinely given mission to evan-

gelize the Gentiles: "To me this grace was given, to preach to the Gentiles the unsearchable riches of Christ" (3:8).

5. In fact, the author boasts knowledge of "the mystery hidden from ages," viz., "how the Gentiles are fellow heirs" with Jews of the promise of membership in God's covenant (3:6).

The members of the church at Ephesus, then, were recent Gentile converts.

But being a "Gentile" convert could have negative connotations, like being a former slave, or a former displaced person or a former minority-group member. One often gets the impression from some New Testament documents that Gentiles were an afterthought in God's plans. The Jews were called first; but because they rejected the call, the Gentiles were God's second choice (see Mt 22:1-10; Rom 11:17-19; Acts 13:46). The author of Ephesians also shares the view that Gentiles are unclean sinners; and they are acknowledged as having been wilful "aliens" to God's covenant (2:12). Gentiles are "darkened in their understanding, alienated from the life of God because of the ignorance that is in them, due to their hardness of heart" (4:18). Gentiles were "in darkness" (5:8). Former Gentile life was characterized negatively when the author says: "Put off your old nature which belongs to your former manner of life and is corrupt through deceitful lusts" (4:22).

Former Gentile status and life, therefore, are viewed quite negatively in Ephesians. But this stands in sharp contrast to the announcement of the great blessings, the new status and the wonderful dignity which come with belonging to God's covenant people. Membership in the Christian group is decribed in Ephesians in glowing terms.

1. Although Gentiles, they are *not* afterthoughts in God's plan, but belong in that great plan from the beginning. Hence the author starts the letter with a blessing or thanksgiving to God for that great gift of inclusion: "Blessed be the God and Father of our Lord Jesus Christ,

who has blessed us... even as he chose us in him before the foundation of the world" (1:3-4). God indeed "predestined" us: "He (pre)destined us in love to be his children" (1:5).

2. God's plan for the Gentiles is called by a special name, "the mystery"; and the mystery, which is ancient and goes back to creation, is only now being revealed (3:3-5). Nevertheless, the Gentiles are *not* God's second choice, an afterthought.

3. Gentiles were formerly enemies of God and subjects of the devil (2:1-3); they were objects of God's wrath. But "God, who is rich in mercy," elected and chose such Gentiles for inclusion in God's covenant. Membership means no less than being "raised up with Christ and made to sit with him in the heavenly places" (2:6).

4. Gentiles who were "once afar off" have now been "brought near" to God's holy presence (2:13 & 17).

5. Gentiles now have "the riches of a glorious inheritance" (1:18) and the gift of the Holy Spirit, "guarantee of our inheritance" (1:14).

Despite the negative allusions to former Gentile status, Ephesians also states how positively the Gentiles are now viewed.

The following chart lists the major ways in which former and present status is contrasted. Hence Gentile converts are reminded of the great blessing it is to belong to the new group:

Gentile Status	*Christian Status*
1. Afar off	1. Brought near
2. Children of wrath	2. Children of God
3. Sinners	3. Saints
4. Aliens	4. Citizens
5. Strangers	5. Family & members of God's household
6. In darkness	6. In light
7. Having no hope	7. Having hope
8. Old nature	8. New nature

9. Dispossessed . . . .   9. Inheritors of inheritance
10. Not called . . . .   10. Called

Conversion to Christianity, then, was interpreted as a great status reversal.

GROUP SELF-UNDERSTANDING

Gentiles who became Christians obviously gained a new identity. The author of Ephesians spends considerable time at the beginning of the document rehearsing for the new converts the scope of that new identity.

> 1. The converts are first told that they are "chosen" (1:4) and "called" (4:1, 4), terms which allude to covenant membership in God's "chosen people."
> 2. The converts are told that they now have a new citizenship. No longer are they "strangers" (2:12, 19) or "sojourners" (2:19), but now are "fellow citizens with the saints." Now they belong to the "commonwealth of Israel" (2:12).
> 3. Converts become "members of the household of God" (2:19) and gain numerous "brothers and sisters" in Christ, as well as a "Father," who is God.
> 4. They should think of themselves as members of a body, of which Christ is the head (1:22-23; 4:15; 5:23).
> 5. They are stones which form part of a new temple building (2:20-22), a place where God's holy presence dwells.
> 6. Being brought near from afar (2:12-13, 17), the converts find themselves near to God; they "have access to the Father" (2:18).

It is important to remember that all of these descriptions of the new place where converts dwell are allusions to Old Testament descriptions of the covenant people. And so, Christian converts are told to think of themselves as true Israelites, as the authentic members of the covenant. They are the genuine objects of the "promise in Christ" (3:6); they are no longer strangers to "the covenants of the promise" (2:12).

It is curious to note how the converts are told to think of themselves in new *spatial terms*. They have a new place on the map, a new location in the world, and a new building to belong to. This is not surprising when we recall that converts crossed many lines and boundaries when they became Christians. They joined a new *household*, entered a new *building*, became part of a new *commonwealth* and members of a new *body*. The full importance of this spatial imagery will be discussed later in comparison with the spatial imagery of Colossians.

ESCHATOLOGY

We now ask where should the converts situate themselves in the plan of salvation history? What is their place in God's plan? The answer is emphatically repeated again and again that by conversion they *already* belong in God's kingdom and *even now* begin to take possession of God's covenant blessings. The chart which demonstrated the changes in status for converts gives one a clear sense of the "nowness" of God's blessings for the converts. In fact, the author uses striking temporal terms to stress the "alreadyness" of God's favor: "*once* afar off. . . you have *now* been brought close" (2:13) and "*once* dead through trespasses and sins. . . you are (now) made alive" (2:1) and "*once* you were in darkness, but *now* you are light in the Lord" (5:8).

At one point, the author goes so far as to speak of a quasi-heavenly enthronement even now for the converts: "God raised us up with him and made us sit with him in the heavenly places" (2:6). This is probably a metaphorical way of saying what 2:18 states more flatly, "through him we have access in one Spirit to the Father." But it does underscore the sense of a present and real blessing which converts have. In one sense, eschatology is "realized" for the converts.

There is a future dimension to the picture as well. The converts are warned that they must live a life worthy of their calling, for sinners will be judged and exclude from God's presence: "Be sure of this, that no fornicator or impure person, or one who is covetous has any inheritance in the kingdom of Christ and of God" (5:5). Converts are told to put on armor and gird themselves to defend their gift of grace, which implies that the final battle for their permanent membership in God's kingdom is yet to come (6:11-18). And it is implied that while converts already have great blessings, an inheritance, and a share in God's covenant, they still have an inheritance which is reserved for them in heaven, the full completion of which is only begun by God now on earth. The Spirit which we have is a "guarantee of that inheritance" (1:14), not proof of present, full possession of God's blessing. The main thrust of the letter, nevertheless, stresses the "alreadyness" and "nowness" of the converts' place in God's plan.

EXPERIENCE

We already know how the group of Christians at Ephesus would describe itself. But are there any special experiences that have happened to the group? Any crisis? Any trauma? The most important fact about them should be self-evident by now. They are mostly Gentile converts. As such, they have crossed significant lines and boundaries to be "in Christ." This entails social and personal dislocation, which prompted a need for a full explanation of the converts' new identity and location. We have seen how plentifully this was supplied in the letter's account of the new status of the group. We noted also how the author dealt with the negative aspect of being a former pagan and a non-Jew. How carefully it was stressed that Gentiles were not afterthoughts in God's plan but were "chosen" and "called" even before the foundation of the world.

The occasion for the letter, then, would seem to be the need for a basic socialization of the converts as Christians. The identity of the new converts needed to be established; their place in the new Christian scheme of things needed to be clarified; and their value as full citizens and full members of the covenant needed to be articulated. The letter, then, focuses on the community rather than on Jesus' career. Whatever was said of Jesus was told in function of confirming the basic socialization of the new convert "in Christ."

CHRISTOLOGY

We note immediately that we are told nothing about Jesus' earthly career, only about his death (1:7; 2:13-16; 5:25-26), resurrection (1:20), and enthronement (1:20-22; 2:6; 4:8-10). Already we know that a special selection of the Jesus story has been made for this letter. We know, moreover, that many of the statements about Jesus in this letter are unique to it (1:10; 2:14; 5:21-30). I am suggesting two things: a) a careful selection was made of traditional materials about Jesus, a selection governed by the pastoral needs of the situation and b) other aspects of Jesus' career were freshly developed by the author himself, development which is again shaped by the needs of this group.

A. *New Adam Christology Figure.* Jesus is proclaimed as the figure who "creates in himself one new man in place of two, so making peace" (2:15). This probably implies that for the author Jesus is the New Adam. The original Adam was created as "one," but soon became "two." The original Adam was fragmented with his sins, and so there crept into the world polarizations of humanity. The story of the tower of Babel is a good example of this; for it shows how originally there was one language understood by all, and how that oneness was fractured by sin (i.e. building the tower) and led to diversity and animosity. We know from other places in the New Testament that baptism was described as a healing of those sinful divisions. One baptismal formula merely calls baptism a "new creation" (2 Cor 5:17), implying that unity is restored which was the hallmark of the first creation. Another formula explicitly mentions how in the new creation the old divisions are healed:

> For as many of you as are baptized into Christ have put on Christ. There is neither Jew nor Gentile, there is

neither slave nor free, there is neither male nor female (Gal 3:28).

According to the baptismal formula used at Corinth, baptism results in reunification: "For by one Spirit we were all baptized into one body — Jews and Greeks, slaves and free" (1 Cor 12:13).

In Ephesians, when Jesus is said to make "one new man" in place of two (2:15-16), this should be seen in conjunction with the statement in 1:10 that in God's plan "all creation would be unified in him, things in heaven and on earth." Jesus is the New Adam, unifying in his own person all the diversities of creation. First this means that the author of Ephesians is trying to show how Gentile converts should no longer be looked down on by those of Jewish ancestry. Jews may call them "the uncircumcision," that is, outsiders; but true Jewish Christians do not exclude them. The "two" (Jew and Gentile) are joined together in the "one new man," which is the church, the body of Christ. The Christological statement in 2:15-16, then, functions to confirm the basic unity of the Christian group.

Second, in uniting diversity in himself, Jesus is also reconciling heaven and earth (1:10). In Jesus there is "peace" between God and humankind (2:14). Not only is there peace and unity between humans (2:17), but there is also an end of hostility between God and creation (2:1-5).

B. *New Covenant Christology.* Jesus is acclaimed as the end of the old covenant and the beginning of the new. Jesus "abolished in his flesh the law of commandments and ordinances" (2:15), that is, the old covenant of Moses. What replaces this covenant of Mosaic law is the "covenant of the promises" (2:12), which was made to Abraham (Gen 15) and David (2 Sam 7). The interim covenant of law with Moses is ended and the former covenant of promises, which was only promised to Abraham and David, is now actualized in Jesus.

Inasmuch as non-Christian Jews would be said to belong to the Mosaic covenant, it is important to note that Gentile

Christian converts are not incorporated into the Mosaic covenant. They are not circumcized or required to keep any of the distinguishing Jewish customs, because they are not entering the old covenant. They take their place, rather, in the original and better covenant of the promises. That covenant is realized in Jesus, who ended the interim covenant and established the new covenant. Thus Gentiles are not an afterthought in God's plans, a second choice; for they were included in God's original covenant plans right from the beginning (1:3-4). Abraham was to be "the Father of many nations" (Rom 4:17/Gen 17:5). As Paul noted, God foresaw that he would justify the Gentiles and so God preached the gospel to Abraham: "In you shall all the nations (i.e. Gentiles) be blessed" (Gal 3:8/Gen 12:3).

C. *New Temple Christology*. Jesus performed a demolition role, for he has "broken down the dividing wall of hostility" (2:14). In the Jerusalem temple, the Gentiles were allowed to stand on the extremity of the precincts, separated from the Jewish insiders by a wall. Jesus is said to have broken down that "wall" and so to give Gentiles equal access to God along with Christian Jews. There is no Jew or Gentile in Christ, no second-class citizenship.

Not only does Jesus demolish, he builds. Jesus is "the cornerstone in whom the whole structure is joined together and grows into a holy temple in the Lord" (2:20-21). The apostles and prophets are the "foundations" of this new building (2:20); Christ is the cornerstone, which joins Jew and Gentile together; Christians are the stones which collectively are gathered and built into a unified structure. Again it is emphasized how Jesus joins divided things together and makes a new and holy unity of them.

D. *Headship Christology*. Jesus is said to be enthroned in heaven. God "raised him from the dead and made him sit in the heavenly places" (1:20). God, moreover, "has put all things under his feet and made him the head over his body" (1:22). This Christological statement is important first of all because it stresses the "alreadyness" of Christian history. Jesus has conquered and been enthroned in heaven, and this sheds light on what is said about the present status of converts:

Jesus (1:20)	*Christians* (2:6)
"God raised him from the dead...	"God raised us up with him...
and made him sit at his right hand...	and made us sit with him...
in the heavenly places"	in the heavenly places."

We converts conform to Jesus: in his death we die, in his resurrection we are raised. His story is our story. Inasmuch as Jesus is already at God's right hand, we too now share in some way in that presence and power.

Second, 1:20-22 insists that Jesus is "head of the body." This means that all the diverse members are joined into one body. This need not mean that all members have the same social role, for some function as "apostles, prophets, evangelists, teachers and pastors" (4:11). But all of these diverse functions are the functions of one unified body; they serve only "to equip the saints for the work of ministry, for the building up of the body of Christ" (4:12). Through diverse limbs, ligaments, and linkages, the "whole body, joined and knit together by every joint with which it was supplied, makes bodily growth and upbuilds itself in love" (4:16). Thus, "in Christ," the diverse Christians are unified into one body, whose only "head" is Jesus himself. This image reinforces what we saw earlier about Jesus' unifying Jew and Gentile into "one new person" by his breaking down of the wall and by his being the cornerstone joining together Jew and Gentile.

This Head image in 1:20-22 has a third function in that it serves as a model for the individual convert. Just as the social body is structured as head and members with clear purpose and power located in the head, so the individual body (the individual Christian) is to be completely structured in a comparable way. S/he is to be "rooted and grounded" in Christ, ordered and structured in one's practical life so that Christ's gospel will be the central organ, that is, it will "dwell in your hearts" (3:17). With so clear a power and guide, the body will have purpose and power to live a life worthy of its calling.

A fourth aspect of 1:20-22 needs to be addressed. Jesus is given *all* power. He alone is Lord and has absolute authority over God's covenant people. Not only is he "at God's right hand," but he is "far above all rule and authority and power and dominion." God "put all things under his feet." This is a sensitive issue for modern readers of this document; for while we find no particular difficulty in acclaiming Jesus' absolute sovereignty over us as our Lord, we are less keen on seeing the structural implications of this confession in our actual live. We take a second breath when church authority figures are said to share exclusively in authority for the church, or when husbands are said to have authority over their wives. These are surely cultural differences between our world and that of the church at Ephesus. But without trying to impose Ephesus' cultural values on us, let us see how clearly the author of Ephesians used the authority of Jesus as "head" functionally as a model for authority structures in his own group.

In socializing new converts to the Christian group, the author talked about abolishing division and dividing walls (2:14-16). If one concluded that "in Christ" all would be socially and politically identical, one concluded wrongly. "In Christ" there are clear roles. The "apostles and prophets" function as foundation stones of the new church-as-temple (2:19). Christ himself gave specific gifts to the church; he established that "some should be apostles, some prophets, some evangelists, some pastors and teachers" (4:11). These figures clearly have Christ's authority over the church. In the baptismal catechesis, the convert might hear that "in Christ" there is no male or female (Gal 3:28), but Ephesians does not see a total revolution of social roles in Christian families. And so he can say: "Wives be subject to your husbands, as to the Lord. For the husband is the head of the wife as Christ is head of the church" (5:22-23). This authority, of course, is specified not in terms of power but in terms of loyalty and commitment. Jesus, who is "head," loves the church and gave himself up for her (5:25). So the husband, who is "head," should be head as one who loves his wife and nourishes and cherishes her (5:28-29). But make no mistake, for the image of Jesus as "head" serves a clear social function in the letter. It serves to legitimate both the authority of the heads of individual Christian households as well as the leadership of the group itself.

E. *Pentecostal Christology*. Jesus is mentioned in connection with Spirit and Father in another key Christological passage:

> There is one body and one Spirit, just as you were called
> to the one hope that belongs to your call,
> one Lord, one faith, one baptism
> one God and Father of us all,
> who is above all and though all and in all (4:4-6).

This passage proclaims *unity*: a) *unity* among Spirit, Lord and Father, b) *unity* of faith, hope and love, and c) *unity* of call and baptism, viz., unity of members of the church. This, of course, is what the author commands as he begins this section of the letter: "I beg you. . . be eager to maintain the unity of the Spirit in the bond of peace" (4:1-3).

But the passage has a special function, for it continues with a stress on how Jesus is the cause of *diversity* in the church by giving diverse gifts to the unified body which is the church (4:8-11). So 4:4-6 and 8-11 tell two complementary stories: a) there is radical unity in God and in heaven in regard to the church and there is fundamental *unity* on earth among the members of the body of Christ; b) there is also *diversity* in the church body, a diversity created by its "head" and Lord. Hence, although baptism makes of converts "one new body" and abolishes divisions such as slave-free, Jew-Gentile, the body of Christ still has differentiation within it in terms of legitimate roles and functions. Jesus is author of both unity and differentiation in the same body.

II.
Colossians

As we turn to the Letter to the Colossians, we are immediately faced with a problem. When Ephesians and Colossians are compared, one notices a host of similarities between the two letters, similarities so close that most New Testament scholars ask the obvious question: "Did the author of one letter borrow from the other letter? Which is the primary document?" This question can lead to a problem, in that, if the two letters are similar in thought and content, one might be tempted to say that they reflect the same situation and experience. Nothing could be further from the truth. Despite their enormous similarities, Colossians reflects a different historical situation and a set of problems different from Ephesians. As we use our familiar categories to investigate the letter to the Colossians, we will be able to compare and contrast the two letters.

MEMBERSHIP

The letter is written to Gentile converts in the Christian covenant community. Their entrance into the group is called "a circumcision made without hands" (2:11). Inasmuch as circumcision was the formal entrance ritual for proselytes into Judaism, the author is appealing to this known entrance ritual as a symbol of what Christian initiation means. Like Eph 3:4-6, the author speaks of the great mystery of God, "how great among the Gentiles are the riches of the glory of this mystery" (1:27). Gentiles they are, but without the negative stigma which Ephesians noted was attached to former Gentile identity.

Their entrance into the Christian covenant community is marked by rituals such as baptism.

> 1. The author alludes to their dying and rising, the metaphor Paul used in Rom 6, "You who were dead in trespasses, God made alive together with him (Jesus)"

(2:13). And again in 3:1-3, allusion is made to the passage from death to resurrection: "If you have been raised with Christ, seek the things that are above...For you have died and your life is hid in Christ."

2. The author alludes to a new creation, a typical metaphor for baptism: "Do not lie to one another, seeing that you have put off the old nature and have put on the new nature which is being renewed in knowledge after the image of its creator" (3:9-10).

3. In what must be an allusion to the baptismal reunification formula (see Gal 3:28; 1 Cor 12:13), the author stresses the unity and equality of the new converts: "Here there cannot be Greek and Jew, circumcised and uncircumcised, barbarian, Sythian, slave, free man, but Christ is all and in all" (3:11)

While Ephesians and Colossians are both addressing Gentile converts, important differences need to be noted. The emphasis in Col is less urgently on the new and equal status of Jew and Gentile converts; unity of all, while important, is less urgent in Col. The focus, then, does not lie precisely in the newness and uncertain status of converts at all, as it did in Eph.

ESCHATOLOGY

Like most New Testament writings, there is a strong sense of the "alreadyness" of God's blessings on converts to the covenant-in-Christ. Already we give thanks to God for "he has delivered us from the dominion of darkness and transferred us to the kingdom of his beloved son" (1:3). Already converts have put off the old nature and "put on the new nature, which is being renewed in knowledge after the image of its creator" (3:9-10). Already they have "redemption, the forgiveness of sins" (1:14).

This sense of "alreadyness" is linked with converts' baptismal participation in Jesus' death and resurrection. "You were buried with him (Jesus) in baptism, in which you were also raised with him through faith" (2:12; see 3:1-3). The reality and importance of being in the covenant-in-Jesus is underscored by these strong affirmations of the alreadyness of salvation in Jesus.

Of course, there are balancing comments which indicate that, while God's blessings are already available in Jesus, there is a future in Christian life where God's saving work remains to be completed. Christians "have a hope laid up for you in heaven" (1:5). That "hope" consists in "glory," the full realization of God's plans for us. "When Christ who is our life appears, then you also will appear with him in glory" (3:4). This future time is a moment of scrutiny, when the wicked will be dismissed (3:6) and those who are "spotless and blameless and irreproachable" will stand before God (1:22).

This profile of the Colossians' sense of "already" and "not yet" is typical of New Testament writings. But what is distinctive here is the sense that there are false conclusions being drawn from this material in the church at Colossae. One could re-read the first paragraph above on the "already" quality of Christian existence and take from it the imperative that one is "to seek the things that are above where Christ is" (3:1). "Set your mind on the things that are above not on things that are on earth" (3:2). From this one could get the impression that things on earth are inferior, but what is in heaven alone is important. Having died with Christ and put on a new nature, one should strive to think, live, and worship as though one were *already in heaven*. While there is some truth in this, it can lead one to depreciate our material and earthly lives. They could be seen as unnecessary encumbrances to be shed. All that is connected with our earthly lives may also be radically devalued, such as sacraments, church structure and order, daily ethical lives, etc. There is strong evidence in the letter that such was the case. Heaven was seen by some to eclipse earth.

ETHICS

Colossian Christians are marvelously exhorted in the letter. 1. Their "faith, love and hope" are underscored (1:4-

5). 2. They are given an extensive list of virtues and vices which are the logical extension of their rising to life from death (3:1-3), their putting off the "old nature" and putting on the "new nature" (3:9-10), and their seeking heavenly rather than earthly things (3:5).

Virtues	*Vices*
Compassion	Fornication
Kindness	Impurity
Lowliness	Passion
Meekness	Evil desire
Patience	Covetousness
Forebearance	(3:5)
Love (3:12-14)	

3. In keeping with this sense of behavior appropriate to new converts, we find a code of household duties which urges proper ethical activity on wives/husbands, children/parents and slaves/masters (3:18-4:1). This is typical and standard moral exhortation, which is echoed regularly in other New Testament letters. There is little distinctive here.

But the author of Colossians has several other concerns, which are important to note. He prays that the group have correct knowledge, that it be stable in the gospel and that it hold to the tradition and eschew false knowledge. One might say that the prime action to which the Colossians are exhorted is their holding to the tradition of the gospel — a matter of correct information and firm allegiance. The author prays for the church that it "be filled with the knowledge of God's will in all spiritual wisdom and understanding" (1:9). He urges them to "continue in the faith, stable and steadfast, not shifting from the hope of the gospel which you heard" (1:23). He says that he strives for the group, that they "have all the riches of assured understanding and the knowledge of God's mystery" (2:2). Thus he exhorts them to grasp the whole truth and to hold on to it. Conversely, he exhorts them to avoid being a prey to "philosophy and empty deceit, according to human tradition" (2:8). He urges them to avoid certain specific practices, such as questions of food, festivals and purity (2:16-17, 20-22). "These," he remarks, "have an appearance of wisdom in promoting rigor of devotion and self abasement and severity" (2:23). Such things are *not* part of the correct and true tradition; they are in competition with the gospel and so are to be avoided.

GROUP SELF-UNDERSTANDING

Part of the self-understanding of any group is its sense of leadership and where it invests authority. If two contradictory doctrines are being urged at Colossae, then there would seem to be a conflict in the leadership of the group. Someone is urging the doctrine which the author censures. The letter goes on to identify by name just who is orthodox and is to have teaching authority for the group:

1. Paul, the alleged author of the letter, rehearses his divinely-given role and authority, thus underscoring the weight of his advice in the letter. Paul is "an apostle of Christ Jesus by the will of God" (1:1)—no mean figure. In urging them to hold to the traditional gospel, "Paul" supports the validity of that gospel in indicating how he became its "minister" (1:23). He is minister also of the church: "of which I became a minister according to the divine office which was given to me for you" (1:25). His authority is not oppressive, for he prays for their enrichment (1:9-12); he strives for their enlightenment (2:1-3). He claims divine authority to be the official teacher of the group.

2. Epaphras is singled out as a legitimate and trustworthy leader. He initially taught the church at Colossae the gospel, and he is confirmed as being an orthodox teacher and squarely in the correct tradition: "He is a faithful minister of Christ on our behalf and has made known to us your love in the Spirit" (1:7; 3:13). Through his link with the orthodox Paul, Epaphras is confirmed. He sends greetings to Colossae, urging the group to be orthodox and hold to the gospel: "Epaphras greets you...

(praying) that you may stand mature and fully assured in all the will of God" (4:13).

3. An official ambassador is named, Tychicus, who is presumably carrying the letter and will explain it (4:7-8). With him is Onesimus (4:9).

4. A local leader is identified, Archippus, who is urged to do his job, possibly to guide the group more and more in the orthodox tradition (4:17).

Obviously there are other teachers in the group who are urging contrary doctrine. They are not named, but only alluded to as people who introduce "human tradition" (2:8) and who urge new practices "according to human precepts and doctrines" (2:22). The author has tried to identify, even by name, the legitimate teachers of the group. He has consistently linked these named figures to "Paul," and praised their loyalty to the tradition. Paul and his followers are said to enjoy "divine" authorization, whereas the false teachers are said to have mere "human" teaching. These touchstones serve to distinguish the orthodox teachers from the false teachers whose troublesome doctrines are dealt with at some length in ch 2.

EXPERIENCE

When we ask what was the experience of this church and what special problems were troubling it, we turn immediately to chapter 2. There is a genuine crisis in the group which might be said to center around the group's worship. When one reads Isa 6, one gets a vision of God's throne in heaven surrounded by worshiping angels who sing and chant praise to God day and night. In Ezek 1, the prophet sees in heaven God's "chariot" throne surrounded by myriads of angels and especially the four great classes of angels with the likeness of four living creatures: men, oxen, lions, eagles (Ezek 1:10). This same image is found in Rev 4 where the reader is given a vision of God's throne in heaven surrounded by "the four living creatures" who "day and night never cease to sing 'Holy, holy, holy is the Lord God Almighty, who was and is and is to come!' " (4:8). All earthly worship is but a poor image of the true worship in heaven; Moses made only a paltry replica on earth of the tent of God's house which is genuinely in heaven (Ex 25:40; see Heb 8:5; 10:1). Whatever worship took place in the house church in Colossae, it would seem that one could only be satisfied with the genuine worship of God which was celebrated in heaven. Heavenly worship is complete and genuine; earthly worship is but a shadow of it. And so it seems natural and good to desire to join the heavenly worship. We have evidence in the letter that some sought to join this heavenly worship and came to despise all earthly worship (2:18).

What would it mean for a Christian in the covenant group in Colossae to join the heavenly worship? How would one do this?

> 1. The author criticizes "visions," on which some take their stand (2:18), implying that through such mystical and visionary transports, the worshipper travelled to heaven, there to worship around God's throne with the heavenly angels.
>
> 2. Rigorous asceticism seems to be joined to this. By despising the flesh and all things earthly and by radical abstinence from all things material, one could dispose oneself for life in the heavenly realm. This comes in for criticism by the author of Colossians, who discredits this radical asceticism. The false teachers seem to be urging the community to abstain from all things earthly and material: "Do not handle! Do not taste! Do not touch!" (2:21).
>
> 3. This asceticism was supposed to lead to "self-abasement and severity to the body" (2:23; see 2:18). It is hoped that the soul, once purified of earthly entrammelments, would rise to heaven.
>
> 4. The purpose of all such asceticism and severity is the promotion of "would-be worship" (2:23).
>
> 5. As the false teachers promoted asceticism, visions,

and heavenly worship, they depreciated all earthly cere-
monies and customs, such as "food and drink...festival or
new moon or sabbath" (2:16).

The author of the letter obviously disagrees with this. He
criticizes people who hold such ideas as being "puffed up
without reasoning" (2:18). He labels all such practice as
"human precepts and doctrine" (2:22), which contrasts its
humanness with the *divine* character of his call and his
message. He brands this as "philosophy and empty deceit,
according to human tradition" (2:8). He keeps on insisting,
as we saw above, on fidelity to the tradition and loyalty to
the gospel. But there is ambiguity here, for the "traditional"
way of describing initiation into the group was to speak of it
as a "circumcision made without hands" (2:11) which
implies that a heavenly, non-material ritual is better than the
earthly circumcision of the flesh. He speaks of the "alreadyness" of Christians as raised from the dead (2:12); he urges
Christians to seek the things that are above (3:1). Perhaps he
does not see how his own traditional words might be misunderstood and used against him in the promotion of a pro-
heavenly, anti-earthly stance.

Something else is implied in this crisis. If by asceticism
and self-abnegation one could rise to heaven, then one does
not need earthly structures or earthly leaders. If by "visions"
one could be transported to the real realm of God, then this
would tend to relativize the importance of teachers and
preachers on earth. The author senses that in the pro-
heavenly, anti-earthly stance of these unorthodox people,
there is a fundamental challenge to the whole world as he
knows it. May I draw out the radical implications of this
maverick stance and show how pervasive its effect would be.
If heavenly is preferred and earthly is depreciated, then:

1. *Earthly worship* is inferior, even useless.
2. Church *leadership* is unnecessary, even harmful.
3. The *material cross of Christ* and his *physical body* lose
   value; they certainly are not needed any longer.

4. *Sacraments* lose value; asceticism is the way to God's presence.
5. The *church* of earthly, physical people with material needs and earthly joys and pleasures is not a commanding value anymore.
6. The *individual* can go it on his/her own, by asceticism and by visions; s/he does not need other Christians.
7. The *gospel tradition,* guaranteed by human witnesses, loses its priority as the norm of faith.

The radical implications of this pro-heavenly, anti-earthly stance are deeply troublesome for they imply a judgment on Jesus' humanity and a devaluing of his earthly life, teaching, and death. If through visions and asceticism one could ascend to heaven and God, then is Jesus even needed at all?

In summary, then, the author of Colossians assesses the situation in that church as a moment of crisis in which most immediately he passes judgment on rigorous ascetical practices which are proposed as a way of facilitating a visionary ascent to heaven for the purpose of participation in the angelic worship of God (2:16-23). The author also senses the implications of this practice as equally dangerous. If heavenly worship is the primary value, this value tends to depreciate all earthly and human values: leadership, sacraments, creation, covenant, even the humanity of Jesus. It is in this context that we must examine the Christology of the letter.

CHRISTOLOGY

The letter has both traditional and unique things to say about Jesus. Granted the wealth of what could be said about Jesus, we should pay special attention to what is actually said and to the function of these chosen remarks in view of the situation of the church. I am presupposing that the sheer exercise of authority and power by the author would not solve the crisis at Colossae, for the author's authority is challenged by certain false teachers. The prime means for dealing with this conflictual situation would seem to be an appeal to the basic Jesus story, which is used functionally to address the particular needs and experience of this church in crisis. The scope of the Jesus story and the particular details which are brought forth seem to be governed precisely by the situation there and they function vis-à-vis that situation.

Traditional comments about Jesus' death and resurrection appear. And these function in an explanation of baptism as a ritual which reverses one's status. As Jesus died and rose, so Gentiles die with Jesus in baptism and rise to new life with him (2:12-13; 3:1). These remarks about Jesus' death and resurrection also function in the exhortatory part of the letter as a warrant for a new mode of living. If one is dead to the old, sinful pagan life, then one should "put to death what is earthly in you: fornication, impurity, etc." (3:5). If one has been "raised with Christ" (3:1), then one should "put on compassion, kindness, lowliness, etc." (3:12).

The letter, however, tells a new story of Jesus as Lord, which seems to be related to the crisis in the church. The impression was given from the author's polemic in ch 2 that certain people devalued all things earthly, fleshly, and material. But the key Jesus story in the letter is an account of Jesus' close relationship with creation.

   1. Jesus is called "the image of the invisible God, the first-born of all creation" (1:15). Since the invisible God cannot be seen or sensed, we mortals can only know God through God's effect in creation and through a mediator. Jesus is the visible or sensible expression and imprint of God. In knowing Jesus — earthly, historical figure — we know God. Being in contact with Jesus means being in contact with God. For Jesus is not just another "image" of God, as was Adam (Gen 1:27), but is the unique ("first born") image (1:15).
   2. Jesus' humanity, flesh, and materiality are not embarrassing to the author, nor are these things to be fled from, as the heavenly worshipers think. The author speaks positively of Jesus' "blood" (1:20), which has saving or

unifying effects on us. Likewise Jesus' "body of flesh" is salvific (1:22). In fact the author goes so far as to say of Jesus' humanity that "in him the fullness of deity dwells bodily" (2:9).

3. The blood, flesh, and body of Jesus, moreover, are heralded as the unique means of our contact with God. By his blood, Jesus "reconciled" all things to God, "whether in heaven or earth, making peace by the blood of his cross" (1:20). By his body of flesh, Jesus has reconciled sinful and material humanity to the holy and invisible God (1:22). The body of Christ contains God's peace, life and blessings for us, and so when we are "in Christ," "you have come to fullness of life in him" (2:10).

4. Great emphasis is put on being "in Christ" in this letter. This, of course, means being "in the body of Christ," which is the church. Christ is the "head of the body, the church" (1:18), but the church is unabashedly acknowledged as the "body of Christ" (1:24; 2:19; 3:15). If one is "in Christ" (1:2; 2:7, 10-15), one is "in the body." And this "body" has "joints and ligaments" which knit it together and nourish it (2:19), which is probably an allusion to the authoritative roles of teachers in the group. The value of Jesus' humanity is replicated in the positive value put on the body of Christ. In it one is linked with Jesus, the head; in it one is linked with joints and ligaments; in it one finds "the fullness of life," reconciliation with God and peace. Clearly the author sees great value in the corporeal and corporate body of Christ.

5. Jesus is intimately linked with creation. "In Him all things were created...all things were created through Him and for Him" (1:16). Jesus, of course, is acknowledged as holy, as especially close to God, and as "God's unique image." He is solidly and unmistakably on God's side. So when Jesus is heralded as the source of material creation and as its goal, this contingent and material world is given enormous value. Creation is seen as primarily good, as an act of grace and favor. There is no dualism here which envisions God vs. world, heaven vs.

earth, and spirit vs. matter. Inasmuch as "the fullness (of God) was pleased to dwell in Jesus" (1:19), and "the whole fulness of deity dwells bodily in him" (2:9), Jesus is seen as linking the heavenly God and the material world.

6. As we saw above, Jesus' humanity reconciles us to God and makes peace. This reconciliation in Christ is made explicit in the letter: "He is before all things and him all things hold together" (1:17). Jesus, then, gathers "all," unifies "all," as well as he creates "all." This emphasis on "all" in Christ should not be taken for granted, for it is a theme repeatedly and consciously developed:

1:15 the first-born of *all* creation
1:16 *all* things were created in him...
         all things were created through him & in him
1:17 in him *all* things hold together
1:20 ...to reconcile *all* things through him
2:10 (Christ) who is the head of *all* rule & authority
3:11 Christ is *all* in *all*

It would be very difficult from this perspective to eschew earthly and material things as defective, valueless, or as inhibiting one from contact with God.

III.
Jesus as Head: Comparison and Contrast

In many ways the Christology of Ephesians resembles that of Colossians. In both, Jesus is acclaimed as "Head" of the body, which is the church. In both, there is concern to depict Jesus in spatial terms: 1) as the cornerstone, 2) as the point of unification of things heavenly and earthly, 3) as one new man in place of two, and 4) as the one in whom all things are created and reconciled. But as we look more closely, we note that these images have different purposes and function differently in their respective letters.

Jesus is indeed "Head" of the body. In Ephesians this image functioned in a variety of ways. It undergirded the hierarchical perception of legitimate authority in that church. Christ is "Head," but there are other legitimate leaders such as apostles and prophets. Since the "authority" of the head is to fill the body, love, and cherish it, this image can serve as a model for the use of authority in the body by other "heads" (see 4:15-16; 5:21-30). And the image of Christ's one body ("he created in himself one new person in place of two," 2:15) served to underscore the unity and equality of Jew and Gentile in the church. The head-body image focussed on the internal composition and operation of the church.

In Colossians, however, this image served a different function, viz., to undergird the value of life in the church, in the material and earthly body of Christ. The body is the appropriate space in which one should live; earth-denying, ascetical tendencies, and flight to heaven are thereby moderated.

In both letters, this image of head and body served to draw a map for Christians, indicating where they belong and where they find meaning. But the maps serve different functions because of the different situations of each church. In Ephesians, the image functions to support Gentile inclusion as full covenant members and to socialize them in their new Christian life. In Colossians, the image functions to correct anti-earth tendencies by celebrating how Christ is a member of creation and a sacramental mediation with God.

Likewise, in Ephesians, Jesus is the cornerstone of a new temple. He creates a holy space where God's spirit dwells and Christians are near to God and worship God in truth. This new temple gives Gentiles and Jews equal access to God; it is an earthly temple, built on the apostles and prophets, the converts being the very stones of this new temple. Alternately, in Colossians, there is a re-emphasis on the body of Jesus as the locus of blessings which one associates with a temple: redemption, forgiveness of sin. The fullness of the deity dwells bodily in this "temple" who is Jesus. So contact with Jesus, his flesh and blood, is contact with God.

Even this image of Jesus as Temple and Cornerstone functions differently in the two letters. In Ephesians, the new temple image stressed equality of Jew and Gentile and equal access to God (2:14-15, 17). In Colossians, the correct worship of God is found in Christ's body, the church, through sacraments and in contact with Christ's blood and flesh. This sharply contrasts with the anti-earthly, pro-heavenly orientation of some who would worship God with the angels in heaven. Thus the distinctive Christological stories and images in Ephesians and Colossians, while similar, function differently because they are addressing different situations in different churches.

Chapter Nine

SUMMARY, REFLECTIONS, AND CONCLUSIONS

See p. 7

It is appropriate at this time to review the project of this book and to reflect on the approach taken. In doing this, we hope to become more aware of the implications of this approach and to see where they have taken us.

1. *The Project*

In recovering the diverse portraits of Jesus in the New Testament we have learned that there are at least two basic ways in which those portraits are formed and how they function. A. In the Gospels in particular, the Christology very closely reflects the experiences of the individual churches. The portraits of Jesus were shaped so as to reflect and to speak to the experience of each respective Christian group. This experiental or reflective Christology functions in a basic apologetic way: the portrait of Jesus is shaped so as to interpret, legitimate, and consolidate certain values and experiences of the individual Christian churches. The experience tended to be either alienation (sectarian self-development, as in the case of early Matthew and John) or missionary inclusiveness (as in the case of Mark, Luke, and the final editor of Matthew). B. In other places, especially the letters of Paul, the Christology was formulated to correct and so shape the experience of specific Christian groups. These didactic portraits of Jesus functioned basically as polemical or exhortatory arguments: the portrait of Jesus was formulated there to affirm certain values and structures and to correct suspect values and behavior. In short, Christological portraits in the New Testament are no mere historical reminiscences, nor are they neutral as regards the way Christians live and see themselves. Rather, the portraits are themselves affected by events and in turn affect the experience of the individual Christian groups.

2. *Variety and Diversity*

We have, in fact, confirmed the modern assertion that there is deep diversity in New Testament portraits of Jesus, even contradictory portraits — and that within the same document (e.g., early, late Matthew). Jesus may be described in one situation as Prophet and Judge (early Matthean group) but in a later stage of the development of that same group, as Healer and Savior. One community can stress Jesus' humility, how he "humbled himself...emptied himself," while in another community, Jesus is presented as the exalted Head and supreme authority of the Church. But variety and diversity are not capricious, nor are they simply a matter of semantics. Rather, as we have seen, they are rooted both in the diverse experience of the individual groups which made up the emerging Christian covenant community of the first century and in the pastoral preaching of the churches' leaders.

In evaluating this diversity, we have had to reflect on appropriate models for understanding and evaluating this diversity. The *evolutionary model* of development does not seem appropriate: it is not necessarily true that Christology progressively became more profound, sophisticated, or consistent with the passing of time. A straight-line direction of evolving Christology is not accurate or appropriate for describing New Testament Christological portraits. Despite what the Beatles said, New Testament Christology was not "getting better all the time, a little better, all the time." Nor is the *degeneration model* of development accurate. The best was not early, and then degenerated in the series of successive ages, on the order of golden age, silver age, bronze age, etc. What is closest to the historical Jesus is not automatically to be preferred to the viewpoint of the later evangelists. Nor is what is genuinely Pauline *ipso facto* preferable to what is from the later Pauline school. The Church does not necessarily distort the kerygma about Jesus.

This study has indicated that the most accurate and appropriate model for describing the diversity of New Testament Christology is the *pastoral preaching model*. As was noted in the Document on Revelation from Vatican II, the sacred authors "explicated" Jesus' words and the traditions about him in view of the situations of their respective churches. Their preaching was radically historicized; it was pastorally adapted to the experience and the needs of the specific, historical churches. Neither evolution nor degeneration capture the dynamic relationship of preacher to community. From this perspective we can begin to see the value of the redaction-critical method in contemporary New Testament studies, for it allows us to recover the worth of the later apostolic writers.

3. *Dynamic Character of the Scriptures*

In studying the portraits of Jesus from this perspective, we are perhaps urged to revise our understanding of the character of the New Testament documents. In times past, we operated with a model of the Gospels in which we claimed that Jesus' very disciples, Matthew and John, wrote down Jesus' very words; it was claimed the Mark and Luke wrote down the reminiscences of Peter or Paul. The immediacy of the evangelists to Jesus assured us of their historical literalness. The emphasis in this model was on the accuracy of the evangelists' writings and on the traditional character of the portrait of Jesus. In this model, the Gospels are rather static documents, preserving precise, accurate information which is timeless and applicable to all churches and every person.

More recently a different model of the New Testament

has emerged, which sees the Gospels as the preaching of the apostles and other apostolic people to different Christian churches. This model does *not* argue that there was no historical interest in recalling Jesus' words or that there was no sense of a tradition which was handed on (see 1 Cor 11:23; 15:3). Rather the new model sees the Gospels primarily as preaching to the churches, preaching which is ongoing, and creative. In this model, the Gospels are dynamic documents, adapting the traditional preaching in fresh and ever-changing ways to ever-changing churches. If the older model focussed primarily on Jesus himself, this new model focuses on the community; the older model emphasized accuracy, the new model adaptation; the older model stressed timelessness, the new model pastoral change. The key to the new perception is the description of the Gospels as preaching.

4. *Timeless Value*

We used to say of the New Testament that it is the *norma normans non normata*. It was "the standard by which all theology and preaching are criticized, but it is not subject to criticism itself." This implied that the New Testament was seen as eternal, non-historical truth which transcends time and space. As we study the New Testament in this modern age, we understand it primarily in terms of the historical situation in which it was written; and so we have had to adjust our understanding of it as a document which is validly subject to the canons of literary and historical criticism. We have seen in this book that the New Testament most basically reflects apostolic preaching to particular Christian groups; it contains diverse portraits of Jesus; it addressed a spectrum of situations. Its radical historicality means particularity, not universality. Minimally, then, the New Testament presents a range of images and portraits of Jesus, the very diversity of which is limited only by the number of communities which are reflected. The New Testament, then, is a minimum, a beginning. Inasmuch as it does not exhaust the range of experience of Christian groups, it is limited. The New Testament does not reflect all cultures, each historical experience, and every need of the churches through time and history. And so we can say that the New Testament is a limited historical document. The task of the Church in time and history is to preach Jesus to every age, every culture, and every situation. The stuff of preaching, while based and grounded in the New Testament, is not confined to it. The task of preaching is to find the pastorally appropriate portrait of Jesus, whether that is in the New Testament or elsewhere. Following the process of this study, we should be more moderate in speaking of the timeless value of the New Testament. It is still a standard for Christian preachers and churches, but in many senses it is subject to legitimate historical study and criticism.

5. *Experience*

We have use this term extensively. It is a convenient term which covers a lot, but also obscures a lot. We can speak of common human experience which all people have: all are born and die; most marry and raise families; many go through regular cycles of infancy, youth, maturity, and old age. But there is also experience which is particular: each of us can say that we belong to *this* church, with *this* minister, in *this* city, and at *this* time. Our particular experience may be positive or negative; there may be much to praise and much to blame in the particularity of this experience. Paul found much at Corinth that he could praise (1 Cor 11:1), but also much that needed pastoral correction (1 Cor 11:17). And we can speak not only of historical experience, but also of general cultural experience: we belong to the Atomic Age, not the Graeco-Roman world; we live in an industrial, not agricultural context; we are urban dwellers, not peasants. Here also there is cause for praise and blame, just as Paul could criticize the pagan cultural milieu from which his converts came. "Experience," then may seek to find legitimate resonance in the New Testament traditions about Jesus and so be confirmed, or it may require confrontation as a sick and sinful context which requires a healing word. As it was in New Testament times, so it is today.

It is a hallmark of our age that we "begin with experience." How often preachers today tell us to "get in touch with our experience." This is reflected in the phrase which has entered our language, "I hear where you are coming from." The valuing of individual experience was given official sanction for us in the Vatican II Document on Religious Liberty, where in the affirmation of the duty to follow one's conscience, we were led to understand and to evaluate positively the individual religious experience and confession of people who are not like ourselves. As we noted above, "experience" may be praiseworthy or worthy of blame. Nevertheless, experience is the starting point of any reform or conversion.

At this point, I remind the reader of the model of B.J.F. Lonergan which was presented in the opening chapter. Lonergan maintains that all knowledge begins in experience; we are an empirical people who learn through our senses. This experience is then processed by our minds and interpreted and understood there. It issues in an act of judgment in which insight is formulated. Hence the sequence of the human mind is: experience—understanding—judgment. This model, I suggest, helps us to interpret the survey of New Testament Christological portraits of this book. The New Testament writings themselves begin with the experience of the community addressed; and that experience both shapes and is reflected in the understanding process whereby preachers seek to speak to their audience. This understanding issues in the insight or formulation which is the actual document, the very preaching of this author to this church.

Yet when the experience changes, when Gentiles begin to stream into the once-Jewish church, or when problems develop in the churches, then we should expect that a new period of understanding will take place to process and digest this new experience. And that new understanding will issue in a new formulation of Jesus vis-a-vis the new experience, the new crisis, or the new situation. New experiences always call for new understandings, and issue in new insights. If not, the preaching of Jesus is not adequate to the needs of the audience.

6. *The Social Dimension of Faith*

We know that confessions of Jesus and portraits of him do not exist "out there" as timeless Platonic ideas. We have seen that they originate in experience, and are shaped by events and in turn address those events. They are historical. This means that Christological portraits *de facto* have and should have a social dimension. They address our genuine lives, shaping how the church should be structured, how Christian lives should be lived, and what values or actions should be promoted. This is important today, as we now search for ways to preach certain values such as justice. For example, we hear of the "faith that does justice," a code slogan for the need to preach Jesus in ways that show the intrinsic connection of Christian faith and the critical social problems of this world. This study has indicated that a distinctive portrait of Jesus was developed in churches which Mark, Luke, and Paul addressed, which portrait supported the "justice" of including the Gentiles in God's kingdom as full, first-class members. Jesus was portrayed as an inclusive figure, welcoming outsiders into the group. He showed preferential concern for the poor, the unclean, and the outsiders — he was God's "physician" who was sent to the sick. Jesus was portrayed as standing against his culture in this regard. Such images of Jesus dramatize the point that Christological portraits have a strong social dimension. The Gospels are by nature social statements, for they do not present non-historical ideas, but speak a particular word so as to shape and structure how people realistically see themselves in God's covenant.

7. *A Total Christology?*

What we have presented in this book is not a total Christology by any means. We began by noting that we were recovering the value of the evangelists' redaction. Former ages placed almost exclusive priority on the Quest for the Historical Jesus, seeing that as the only valuable material for faith; other ages stressed the Church's tradition of defining Jesus in conciliar statements as the most valuable data for theology and preaching. Both historical and traditional aspects of Jesus are important. But they need to be supplemented by the approach taken here, for a total Christology needs to value the contribution of the early apostolic preachers as well. As we said in the introduction of the book, source and form criticism need to be supplemented by redaction criticism of the New Testament.

Since the preaching of Jesus is a dynamic, on-going task of speaking a word that can be heard by diverse people in different times and places, the task of Christology is never finished. It will continue indefinitely. As long as there is new "experience," there must be fresh understanding and judgment. There can never be a "total" Christology, a timeless Christology, but only a preaching about Jesus that is shaped by and responsive to the experience of hearers of the word.

8. *A Principle Emerges*

One positive value of this study is the discovery of a principle in the very New Testament documents. The preaching of Jesus did in fact speak to the experience of hearers; it did in fact reflect the situation of the hearers; it was in fact flexible and adaptable. If that was the principle operative in the New Testament writings, then it is a valid principle today for the preaching of Jesus. There is a warrant in the New Testament itself for the practice of pastoral adaptation of the gospel about Jesus to the new situations of the churches. That, after all, was what the remark in the Vatican II Document on Revelation was all about: "They explicated things in view of the situations of their churches" (# 19). What was true then is true now also. *Aggiornamento* is not just a slogan about the structures of the Church; it touches its preaching as well.

9. *Hot and Cold Knowledge*

Abstract, philosophical knowledge is described as "cold" knowledge; it may be true, but it does not "speak to us," touch our emotions or relate to our every-day lives. Yet there is "hot" knowledge which does just that: it engages our experience. According to this book, New Testament Christological portraits were "hot" knowledge: they were preaching about Jesus; they intended to persuade, to shape, and to

Only mentioned as book ends.
Fails to tell how NT provides any
hold on US

engage the social lives of hearers. Preaching is a "hot" medium. Then as now, the task of the Church is to preach a word about Jesus which is "hot," viz., reflective of the experience of hearers and challenging to them. Revelance remains a pastoral issue.

10. *Dangers and New Tasks*

Dangers abound with any position and stance. Those which attend this approach should be noted. With an emphasis on experience, there is the danger of subjectivism and relativism. With an emphasis on pastoral adaptation, there is the danger of making light of the claims of the Scripture or disregarding the claims of the Christian tradition. With an emphasis on historical particularity, there is the danger of reductionism and the loss of a sense of transcendence. To paraphrase Genesis, there is the danger that we will make God in our own image and likeness. These are the dangers attendant upon what is particular and historical. To note them is the first step in avoiding them.

Alongside those dangers lie many new tasks. First we should be aware of those dangers and assess them. Also we should be aware that our Church is engaged in *aggiornamento,* a process that will conceivably continue as long as there are Christians. This leads us to see our Church, its rites and its theology in a more historical way. And this means that we are also adjusting our understanding of the nature of the New Testament writings as "historical" documents. In the New Testament, there are diverse Christologies; in a single document there may be many stages of development which present many and differing Christologies. This little book is fully a product of this *aggiornamento.* Aware of the dangers, we take up the tasks.

11. *Some Conclusions*

1. The New Testament has taught us a principle that the preaching of Jesus must be pastorally adapted to the experience of those who hear it.

2. Pastoral adaptation both reflects that experience as well as shapes it. What is praiseworthy is confirmed; what is worthy of blame is addressed.

3. The task will never end. The liturgical year requires that our preaching of Jesus be adapted to its cycle. Pastoral concerns require that we adapt our preaching to address the social, historical, and cultural context of those to whom the Word is preached.

4. Permission is given for this task, first in the New Testament itself, and then in the Church's own self-awareness in the Vatican II Document on Revelation (# 19).

5. The precise use of any Scriptural passage today is itself a pastoral decision, for it entails a pastoral judgment as to what is appropriate for this community at this time. Not all passages are equally appropriate.

6. Our Christological portraits and stories of Jesus are in fact systematic codes which contain values and express structures and authorize behavior. Christology is necessarily social — it confirms and addresses experience.

12. *Gaudium et Spes*

The project of this book is best summarized in the following citation from the Vatican II Pastoral Constitution on the Church in the Modern World:

> "For, from the the beginning of her history, she has learned to express the message of Christ with the help of the ideas and terminology of various peoples, and has tried to clarify it with the wisdom of philosophers, too. Her purpose has been to adapt the gospel to the grasp of all as well as to the needs of the learned, insofar as such was appropriate. *Indeed, this accomodating preaching of the revealed Word ought to remain the law of all evangelization.* For thus each nation develops the ability to express Christ's message in its own way" *(Gaudium et Spes* # 44, emphasis added).

But the message does have some definite content

SELECTED BIBLIOGRAPHY

I. Chapter One: Introduction

Bousset, Wilhelm, *Kyrios Christos* (New York: Abingdon, 1970); for critique of Bousset, see Larry Hurtado, "New Testament Christology: A Critique of Bousset's Influence," *Theological Studies* 40 (1979) 306-317.

Brown, Raymond E., " 'Who do men say that I am?' Modern Scholarship on Gospel Christology," *Horizons* 1 (1974) 35-50; also in his *Biblical Reflections on the Crises Facing the Church* (New York: Paulist, 1975) 20-40.

Bultmann, Rudolph, *The History of the Synoptic Tradition* (New York: Harper and Row, 1963).

Doty, William G., "The Discipline and Literature of New Testament Form Criticism," *Anglican Theological Review* 51 (1969) 257-319.

Duling, Dennis C., *Jesus Christ Through History* (New York: Harcourt Brace Jovanovich, 1979).

Perrin, Norman, *Rediscovering the Teaching of Jesus* (New York: Harper and Row: 1976).

——————, "Recent Trends in Research in the Christology of the New Testament," *A Modern Pilgrimage in New Testament Christology* (Philadelphia: Fortress, (1974) 41-56.

Reumann, John, " 'Lives of Jesus' During the Great Quest for the Historical Jesus," *Indian Journal of Theology* 23 (1974) 33-59.

Vermes, Geza, *Jesus the Jew* (New York: Macmillan,1974).

II. Chapter Two: Mark

Achtemeier, Paul J., "The Origin and Function of the Pre-Markan Miracle Catenae," *Journal of Biblical Literature* 91 (1972) 198-221.

Kingsbury, Jack Dean, *The Christology of Mark's Gospel* (Philadelphia: Fortress, 1983).

——————, *Jesus Christ in Matthew, Mark, and Luke* (Philadelphia: Fortress, 1981) 28-60.

Robinson, James M., *The Problem of History in Mark* (London: SCM, 1957).

Senior, Donald, "The Struggle to be Universal: Mission as Vantage Point for New Testament Investigation," *Catholic Biblical Quarterly* 46 (1984) 63-81.

III. Chapter Three: Matthew

Duling, Dennis, "The Therapeutic Son of David," *New Testament Studies* 24 (1978) 392-410.

Harrington, Daniel, "Matthean Studies since Joachim Rhode," *Heythrop Journal* 16 (1975) 375-388.

Hill, David, "Son and Servant: An Essay on Matthean Christology," *Journal for the Study of the New Testament* 6 (1980) 2-16.

Jacobson, Arland, "The Literary Unity of Q," *Journal of Biblical Literature* 101 (1982) 365-389.

Kingsbury, Jack D., "Observations on the 'Miracle Chapters' of Matthew 8-9," *Catholic Biblical Quarterly* 40 (1978) 559-573.

—————, *Jesus Christ in Matthew, Mark, and Luke,* 1-27, 61-93.

IV. Chapter Four: Luke-Acts

Dupont, Jacques, "The Poor and Poverty in the Gospels and Acts," *Gospel Poverty: Essays in Biblical Theology* (Chicago: Franciscan Herald Press, 1976) 25-52.

Fitzmyer, Joseph A., *The Gospel According to Luke I-XI* (Garden City: Doubleday and Co., 1981) 143-258.

Franklin, Eric, *Christ the Lord* (Philadelphia: Westminster, 1975) 1-8, 48-69.

Hill, David, "The Rejection of Jesus at Nazareth," *Novum Testamentum* 13 (1971) 161-180.

O'Toole, Robert, "The Activity of the Risen Jesus in Luke-Acts," *Biblica* 62 (1981) 473-498.

Talbert, Charles H., "The Redaction Critical Quest for Luke the Theologian," *Perspective* 11 (1970) 171-222.

V. Chapter Five: John

Brown, Raymond E., *The Community of the Beloved Disciple* (New York: Paulist, 1979).

Interpretation 31 (Oct. 1977) 339-393.

Martyn, J. Louis, "Glimpses into the History of the Johannine Community," *The Gospel of John in Christian History* (New York; Paulist, 1979) 90-121.

Meeks, Wayne A., "The Man from Heaven in Johannine Sectarianism," *Journal of Biblical Literature* 91 (1972).

Neyrey, Jerome H., "The Jacob Traditions and the Interpretation of John 4:10-26," *Catholic Biblical Quarterly* 41 (1979) 419-437.

VI. Chapter Six: 1 Corinthians

Barton, Stephen, "Paul and the Cross: A Sociological Approach," *Theology* 85 (1982) 13-19.

Dahl, Nils A. "Paul and the Church at Corinth," *Studies in Paul* (Minneapolis: Augsburg, 1977) 40-61.

Theissen, Gerd, "The Strong and the Weak in Corinth: A Sociological Analysis of a Theological Quarrel," *The Social Setting of Pauline Christianity* (Philadelphia: Fortress, 1982) 121-144.

VII. Chapter Seven: Philippians

Howard, George, "Phil 2:6-11 and the Human Christ," *Catholic Biblical Quarterly* 40 (1978) 368-387.

Martin, Ralph, *Carmen Christi: Philippians ii, 5-11 in Recent Interpretation and in the Setting of Early Christian Worship* (Cambridge: University Press, 1967).

Murphy-O'Connor, Jerome, "Christian Anthropology in Phil. II, 6-11," *Revue Biblique* 83 (1976) 25-50.

Talbert, Charles H., "The Problem of Pre-Existence in Philippians 2:6-11," *Journal of Biblical Literature* 86 (1967) 141-153.

VIII. Chapter Eight: Ephesians and Colossians

Francis, Fred O., "Humility and Angelic Worship in Col 2:18," *Conflict at Colossae* (Missoula: Scholars Press, 1973) 163-196.

_____, "The Christological Argument of Colossians," *God's Christ and His People* (eds. Wayne Meeks and Jacob Jervell; Oslo: Universitiesforlaget, 1977) 192-208.

Meeks, Wayne A., "In One Body: The Unity of Humankind in Colossians and Ephesians," *God's Christ and His People, 209-221.*

Smith, D., "The Two Made One. Some Observations on Eph 2:14-18," *Ohio Journal of Religious Studies* 1 (1973) 34-54.

Vawter, Bruce, "The Colossians Hymn and the Principle of Redaction," *Catholic Biblical Quarterly* 33 (1971) 62-81.

IX. Chapter Nine: Summary, Reflections and Conclusions

Brown, Raymond E., *Jesus God and Man* (Milwaukee: Bruce, 1967).

_____, *The Critical Meaning of the Bible* (New York: Paulist, 1981).

Fitzmyer, Joseph A., *A Christological Catechism* (New York: Paulist, 1981).

Select Questions on Christology (Washington: United States Catholic Conference, 1980).

Senior, Donald, *Jesus* (Cincinnati: Pflaum, 1975).

INDEX OF SCRIPTURAL PASSAGES

OLD TESTAMENT

Genesis

1:26-30	223-225
1:26-27	221, 225
	264
2:2-3	162
2:17	222-225
2:20	224
3:3	222-225
3:5	222-223,
	225
3:17-19	223-224
3:19	222, 224-
	225
12:3	251
15	91, 159, 250
17:5	251
28:12	154
28:16-17	154
38:8	36

Exodus

3:2-16	36, 39
3:14-15	160
4:22	55
12:46	146, 154
20	91, 159
20:12-17	86-87
20:12	36
25:40	261

Leviticus

19:18	87
21:18-20	84

Deuteronomy

6:4	148, 165
14:1	55

18:19	114, 132
20:12	36
24:1-3	36
25:5	36

Joshua

14:7	223

1 Samuel

10:1	55
16:13	55

2 Samuel

3:18	223
7:14	55, 91, 250

1 Kings

17:8-16	57
17:17-24	57, 131
19	159

2 Kings

2:6-8	57
2:12-14	57
4:1-7	57
4:18-37	57
4:32-37	131
5:1ff	57

Job

5:13	212

Psalms

2:1-2	112, 150
2:7	55
8:2	85
22:1	39

22:7	39
22:18	39, 146
35:19	173
78:2	85
82:6	55
86:2	223
89:3	223
89:27	55
94:11	212
105:6	223
105:26	223
110:1	39, 41, 85
118:22-23	86

Wisdom of Solomon

1:13-14	222, 225
2:23	222, 225

Isaiah

5:1-2	39, 46
6	159-160,
	260
6:9-10	36, 85
7:14	85, 100
9:1-2	82, 85
29:13	36, 39, 85
29:14	205, 212
29:18	58
35:5	58
40:3	39, 85
42:1-4	85, 101
51:12	160
52:6	160
53:4	85, 101
56:7	36, 39
58:6	111
61:1-2	111, 124

NEW TESTAMENT

INDEX OF TOPICS

"Spirit" — no entry

"Jewish scriptures"
160

mediator
100, 114, 264

up-down
224

"conformed"
230-235
252